THE UNITED STATES
AND THE EUROPEAN PILLAR

The United States and the European Pillar

The Strained Alliance

William C. Cromwell
Professor of International Relations
The American University, Washington, DC

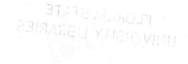
St. Martin's Press   New York

First published in the United States of America in 1992

Printed in Great Britain

ISBN 0–312–06831–X

Library of Congress Cataloging-in-Publication Data
Cromwell, William C.
The United States and the European pillar : the strained alliance
/ William C. Cromwell.
p. cm.
Includes bibliographical references and index.
ISBN 0–312–06831–X
1. Europe—Foreign relations—United States.   2. United States–
–Foreign relations—Europe.   3. Europe—Foreign relations—1945–
I. Title.
D1065.U5C73   1992
327.4073'09'045—dc20   91–28402
                                                             CIP

For Ellen

Contents

Foreword
BY JOSEF JOFFE[1]

Though a source of unending crisis and frustration, the Atlantic Alliance represents a most distinguished chapter in the annals of American foreign policy. America's lasting entanglement in the affairs of Europe marks the maturing of a great power and the final break with a tradition born in the rejection of the Old Continent. Acquired almost in a fit of absentmindedness, America's new role and responsibility did not come easily, but the returns of that investment have muffled the doubters and vindicated those who – like Truman, Acheson and Vandenberg – pushed and cajoled the nation into shouldering the burden of leadership.

Having left Europe to its own devices in 1919, the United States had another war on its hands a mere twenty years later – only a far bloodier and more perilous one than World War I. By contrast, the commitment undertaken in the late 1940s has paid off beyond the most optimistic of calculations. Though the defeat of Germany merely brought a more fearful challenger to the door, World War III was not to be the fate of Europe and America. Instead, there was peace – the longest peace in the history of the European state system. And there was more: the expansion and consolidation of democracy in a part of the world that had given rise to the twin totalitarianism of Communism and National Socialism. Finally, America's lasting intrusion pacified a half-continent which had been the fountainhead of almost permanent war for centuries.

Gauls and Germans overcame their 'arch enemy', the nations of Western Europe linked hands in the grand enterprise of integration, and rivalry gave way to community because the United States had transformed the rules of the ancient self-help system. Stronger than France, Britain and Germany, the United States pulled the sting of rivalry, insuring each and all against the risks of cooperation. Protecting the Europeans not only against the Soviet Union but also against each other, the United States laid the indispensable foundation of community among those who, in the past, had only known discord and strife.

Partition and heavily armed confrontation was the price of peace. But that story began to develop a brighter side exactly forty years

ix

after the birth of the Alliance in 1949. Worn down by ideological as
well as economic failure and unable to convert great military strength
into lasting, much less legitimate, influence, the Soviet Union let
go of its East European empire in 1989. One year later, President
Gorbachev virtually declared his country's surrender in the cold war
by consenting to the unification of Germany under Western auspices.
At last, Europe now has the chance to grow together again in peace
and freedom – precisely the great purpose of American foreign policy
in the past forty years.

Yet here too success will breed its own problems. If the cold
war is truly over, then the Atlantic Alliance will not survive in
its traditional shape. Indeed, no alliance has ever lived past victory; logically, the idea of alliance requires the idea of a foe and a
threat. If the Soviet Union completes its withdrawal from Eastern
Europe while eschewing a new form of dictatorship, then the threat
will wane along with the urgency of alliance and the necessity of
America's enduring entanglement. In that case, the great question
of the next 40 years will be: Can Europe's ultra-stable order – in
the last analysis a gift of the United States – persist on its own? Or
will the rules of the self-help system reassert themselves, souring
the magnificent record of European integration? Will the United
States retract too, or might it even be pushed into withdrawal by
Europeans tired of the burden of the US military presence? What
about the future of free trade, whose foundations were also laid
after World War II when the United States opened its markets to
both Western Europe and Japan? With the military bond fraying,
neither the US nor the EC might muster the will (previously conditioned by security dependence) to resist protectionist pressures
at home.

In revolutionary times, history is not necessarily the best guide for
the future, but without an understanding of the past, any attempt to
peer beyond the horizon of current affairs would be as enlightening
as reading tea leaves. In this book, William Cromwell offers some
indispensable tools for analysis and perspective. By elucidating the
evolution of the Euro–American relationship, the author lays bare its
functions and structures, its conflicting interests and abiding dilem-
mas. And the moral of the story is hardly without relevance for the
future. The history of the Alliance has been the history of its crises.
But it has also been the record of a most successful experiment in
interstate relations. Otherwise, we could not explain the amazing
longevity of this compact.

The Alliance has delivered an enduring object lesson on the adjustment of conflict and the benefits of cooperation, and that lesson transcends the peculiar stringencies of the cold war. It is not at all clear whether the need for cooperation has lost its hold on the nations of the Atlantic realm. Though the 'twin-hegemony' (as Charles de Gaulle has called it) is waning, the world is neither pacified nor democratic. Indeed, the end of the cold war has brought new (and predictable) instabilities, and beyond the Atlantic realm, the threat of war is hardly receding. And so, John F. Kennedy's vision of the 'Altantic partnership', which is the *leitmotiv* of this book, might yet evolve from a vital myth into a practical reality.

Josef Joffe
Harvard University

Preface

This book was conceived in one set of circumstances, concluded in quite another, and written largely during the transition between the two. In 1988, notwithstanding the recent signing of the US–Soviet INF Treaty banning intermediate-range nuclear missiles, which broke the superpower impasse on arms control, and despite encouraging signs that Moscow's 'new thinking' portended major improvement in East–West relations, the prevailing attitude in the West was one of caution and 'wait and see' regarding constructive change in Soviet domestic, foreign and security policies. The Reagan administration era in the US was ending, with mixed assessments as to the significance of its defence and arms control policies in promoting a more positive Soviet orientation toward the West. The European Community was plodding forward with its '1992' internal market programme, and reached a landmark decision on future financing linked to more rigorous control of agricultural expenditures. Atlantic political relations were in somewhat of a holding pattern – having been buffeted by frequent US–West European differences over global issues in the 1970s and 1980s, yet cushioned by the felt need to preserve Alliance solidarity in the context of the still prevalent (albeit softening) intellectual paradigm of East–West confrontation. Except in West Germany, the general view was that NATO should proceed cautiously with respect to further European arms control measures, until the results and implications of the INF Treaty had been fully digested, and the Alliance remained preoccupied with issues of defence burden sharing and the modernisation of its short-range nuclear forces.

By the end of 1990, of course, all of this had changed. The policies of Soviet President Mikhail Gorbachev, for which he was awarded the Nobel Peace Prize, had catalysed a largely peaceful democratic transformation in Eastern Europe, initiated military withdrawals from the region, eventually facilitated agreement on the unification of Germany, helped to codify East–West parity in key weapons systems through the Conventional Armed Forces in Europe Treaty, and contributed to a sea-change shift from confrontational to cooperative approaches to European security symbolised by the Paris summit agreements of the 34-nation Conference on Security and Cooperation in Europe. The EC had achieved major progress toward completing the internal market programme, agreed to the establishment of a central bank in 1994, launched intergovernmental conferences to advance the goals of economic, monetary and political union, initiated outreach programmes to assist the new East European democracies and the Soviet reform process, and had established itself as a major anchoring framework for the unified Germany. In contrast to earlier concerns that the changes in Eastern and Central Europe might enfeeble and divert the momentum for unity in the West, by the end of 1990 precisely the opposite seemed to have occurred. The Atlantic Alliance had steered a transition from a predominantly military coalition to one of political stabilisation in a continent engulfed by change, the Warsaw Pact had virtually disintegrated, and the Conference on Security and Cooperation in Europe had acquired new albeit modest roles emblematic of the emerging pan-European security environment.

The book's main feature is the presentation and analysis of principal developments in Atlantic political relations since 1948 from the perspectives of, first, US policy toward a unifying Western Europe and, second, Western Europe acting, or attempting to act, as a collective body toward the United States. The book challenges the traditional American assumption, embodied in the concept of Atlantic partnership, that a more closely knit Western Europe would view its interests on global issues in essentially similar terms as the United States. The early post-war formative period of Atlantic and European security organisation is briefly reviewed, the clash between American and Gaullist concepts on the nature of Atlantic relations is examined, the Atlantic crisis of 1973/74 is analysed as a turning point in US attitudes toward European unity, the evolution of a European pillar in foreign policy and defence is surveyed, and case studies are provided to illustrate differing US and West European assessments and responses toward major global issues in the 1970s and 1980s. US and European responses to the dramatic European upheavals in 1989/90 are considered in the context of efforts to define and operationalise a post-cold war European political and security architecture. The book's twin-pillar approach is intended to provide a useful framework for studying post-war Atlantic relations and a basis for considering their evolution as Western Europe progresses toward further unity in the 1990s. Indeed, the likely continued (if uneven) internal consolidation of the EC and the expansion of its functional scope, combined with the ending of the cold war and hence the diminished importance of Alliance defence issues, will enhance the importance of US–EC relations as a major framework for Atlantic diplomacy.

The book does not apply a rigorous definition of what is meant by a European pillar, mainly because the usage of the term, and indeed its very meaning, are fraught with ambiguity. As defined by Webster's New Universal Unabridged Dictionary, 2nd edn, a pillar is a column 'used to support a superstructure; also, such a column standing alone'. Given the somewhat open-ended teleology of the European unity movement from the beginning, it is not surprising that the term 'European pillar' – which can denote a collective European core as part of an Atlantic 'superstructure', or a free-standing European entity, or something in between – has long been a staple of the discourse on US–European relations. While its initial usage was often in reference to the EC as an economic pillar, implicitly siding toward the 'independent' meaning of the word, since the 1970s it has been used most often to describe or advocate movement toward a European defence pillar of the Atlantic Alliance, thus siding toward the word's 'superstructure' meaning. Hence, because of the European dependency implied by this latter application, the EC has generally eschewed references to itself as a pillar, preferring instead the image of transatlantic equality conveyed by the term EC–US partnership.

The semantical ambiguity has both aided and confused discussion about the future of US–European relations, while glossing over underlying differences within Europe as to the scope of its role and identity as a collective actor. The multiple possible meanings of 'European pillar' have provided a loose and ill-defined reference point for virtually all forms of West European cooperation – including those in defence which have accepted (with varying nuances) the Alliance superstructure but advocate (again, with varying nuances) stronger European cohesion within it, and those others (mainly the European Community, including European Political Cooperation) which have promoted an independent European identity and an equal cooperative relationship with the United States. Such deliberate equivocation was convenient so long as the cold war rendered the Atlantic Alliance indispensable to European security, enabling postponement of serious attention to the construction of a distinctively European pillar in security and defence. For much the same reason, the European identity in defence has been closely tied to NATO, and the European pillar in foreign policy and security has been constrained by ultimate national-level decision making authority (preserving locales for US influence), and by the effort to limit differences with Washington while promoting independent European positions. Indeed, the evolution of common European positions in foreign policy (and more incipiently in security) has represented somewhat of a mid-point between a European pillar conceived as part of the Atlantic Alliance on the one hand, and as an independent entity on the other.

As 1990 drew to a close, the Atlantic Alliance resembled less a super-structure than one of several European security groups (along with the European Community/European Political Cooperation, the Western European Union, and the Conference on Security and Cooperation in Europe) demarcated by somewhat interwoven boundaries of pur-pose. Despite the end of the cold war, and partly because of it, EC governments were moving to refine and extend their collective regime in foreign policy and security – including a possible role in defence linked to the WEU – pointing in the long term toward greater internal coherence and capability for common action along a widening range of issues. This combination of circumstances – a lessened role for the Atlantic Alliance and steady momentum toward developing a European pillar (however conceived) – portended a continued evolution toward a more equal US–West European political relationship in the 1990s requiring major adjustments in attitude and mutual sensitivity on both sides of the Atlantic.

I would like to express my appreciation to F. Gunther Eyck, Vladimir Lehovich, Christopher W. Murray, Ernest D. Plock, Jean de Ruyt and Stanley R. Sloan who read portions of the manuscript and shared valuable comments. A huge debt of gratitude goes to Luzia M. Lehmann who shared the travail of the project from start to finish and whose qualities of sound judgement, conscientiousness, reliability and exactitude were of the highest order. Thanks also go to Todd L. Quinn who provided research assistance. The EC Office of Press and Public Affairs and the NATO Information Office in Washington, DC, were particularly helpful in furnishing documentation.

Special acknowledgement is due to Dean Louis W. Goodman of the School of International Service for his consistent support of the project throughout, and to the School's indefatigable Faculty Services Office which was responsible for manuscript preparation. In particular, I want to thank Leslie C. Higley and Anita G. Lundry for their good spirited diligence at the word-processor, despite many competing demands for their time. I also want to express appreciation to Belinda Holdsworth, my editor, for her unfailing support and cooperation in bringing the book to completion. Finally, I want to acknowledge the permission granted by the Foreign Policy Research Institute to adapt previously published materials by the author for use in the book.

W. C. C.
Washington, DC
January 1991

1 The Formative Period of Atlantic Relations and the European Pillar, 1948–55

Support for West European unity has been a consistent theme of US foreign policy since the early post-World War II period. Initially shaped by the emerging cold war, American policy advocated unity as a means to end Europe's fratricidal national rivalries, to promote economic and trade cooperation to advance recovery and political stability, to buttress Western Europe's capability to resist domestic communist radicalism and external pressures from the Soviet Union, and to stabilise and anchor West Germany within a Western economic and political order. The aim was to consolidate a West European entity as a component of a wider Atlantic community representing the western pole of the emerging bipolar European and global cold war configuration.

Key elements of US policy were geared explicitly toward achieving these goals. In keeping with the Truman administration's strong support for 'progressively closer integration' in Western Europe, the Foreign Assistance Act of 1948, which launched the European Recovery Programme (Marshall Plan), was expressly predicated upon institutionalised cooperation among recipient countries. The establishment of the Organisation for European Economic Cooperation (OEEC) as a vehicle for coordinating recovery programmes also reflected strong US pressure to use Marshall aid to promote trade liberalisation and economic cooperation within a European institutional framework. In the security field, the US commitment to European defence through the North Atlantic Treaty in 1949 had been based on a prior demonstration of collective European self-help willingness through the five-member (Belgium, Britain, France, Luxembourg, Netherlands) Brussels Treaty defence pact of 1948. Indeed, the European negotiations leading to the Brussels Treaty had been conducted in close consultation with Truman administration officials who had

1

encouraged such a step as a European self-help measure preliminary to a formal US defence commitment. Thus by the late 1940s, key elements of US policy had become linked to the goal of promoting West European unity. In 1951, Congress declared ambitiously that 'political federation' as well as economic unification were objectives of US policy toward Europe.

Yet from the outset there was a fundamental difference in the American approaches to European unity. In the economic sphere the US encouraged, indeed insisted upon, European-centred institutions and processes intended to facilitate rapid and self-sustaining recovery and growth by the end of the planned four-year span of the Marshall aid programme. As presidential advisor Charles Bohlen stated flatly: 'An essential element in this long-term recovery program is its aim to terminate as rapidly as possible Europe's dependence upon the United States for assistance . . . The program aims at assuring Europe's complete and lasting independence'.[1] Republican Senator Arthur Vandenberg, echoing a similar view, assured his budget-minded colleagues that the aid programme 'means to take western Europe completely off the American dole at the end of the adventure'.[2] The emphasis on European recovery initiatives and multilateral cooperation within the OEEC was intended to stimulate this development. While providing a vehicle for European coordination of recovery planning, the OEEC was also intended to promote the lowering of national trade barriers and lay the basis for a more unified West European economy. Only such an approach, it was believed, would enable the European countries to end their dependence on American aid and establish indigenous momentum for recovery and growth. US assistance was viewed as supplying a necessary transitional stimulus for a process of collective European decision-making and institutional development. While the OEEC itself eventually played only a limited part in the adoption of European economic liberalisation measures by the early 1950s,[3] its role as a forum for joint discussion of economic planning issues contributed significantly to the later development of habits and patterns of multi-lateral consultation in the European Community.

The proposal by French Foreign Minister Robert Schuman in 1950 for a common West European market in coal and steel products, lead-ing to the establishment of the European Coal and Steel Community (ECSC) in 1952, was warmly greeted by the Truman administration. Unlike the OEEC, the Schuman Plan was of indigenous European origins, though in line with US efforts to promote economic unity in

Europe. In 1951 Secretary of State Acheson remarked privately that failure to adopt the plan would constitute a 'major political defeat for the US'.[4] Jean Monnet, the plan's originator, was effective in inspiring support in Congress for what he described as 'the first European government as such that has ever been set up or has ever existed . . . the beginning of a United States of Europe'.[5] In 1954, the Eisenhower administration approved a $100 million loan to the ECSC as a sign of support for the first supranational European organisation, and in a vain attempt to encourage ratification of the European Defence Community Treaty as a companion to it in the security field.

In contrast to the prevailing pattern of Europeanisation in the economic sphere, the adoption of the North Atlantic Treaty in 1949 signalled the beginning of an Atlanticist predominance in matters of defence and security. The Brussels Treaty of 1948, motivated partly by West European efforts to obtain a firm US commitment to continental security, was quickly superseded in importance by Atlantic-level defence planning and organisation. The view of some State Department officials that the Brussels Treaty group should become a significant European pillar of the Alliance did not attract wide support.[6] From the formation of the Brussels Treaty to 1951, the United States never exerted pressure for a West European solution to its defence needs, unlike its approach in the economic sphere. This was the case for a number of obvious reasons, most conspicuously Western Europe's military weakness *vis-à-vis* Soviet power on the Continent. Moreover, a coordinated European-centred defence effort would have required a far greater degree of political cohesion than either existed or was foreseeable at the time. The achievement of significant progress in the less sensitive field of economic cooperation had already presented sufficiently formidable difficulties. It would have been unrealistic to expect parallel progress toward the creation of a European defence nucleus and to have insisted upon such progress as a condition for either an American security commitment or for active military assistance. In addition, it would have been beyond the capabilities of the European countries to achieve rapid economic recovery while at the same time diverting substantial resources into a European system of defence. Indeed, the European countries were able to avoid serious conflict between the goals of economic recovery and those of security precisely because, until the Korean War, the former was accorded priority on both sides of the Atlantic. Finally, though in 1948/49 prevailing estimates did not anticipate Soviet military aggression, it was clear that the general West European sense of insecurity and vulnerability could be overcome only through a firm demonstration of American willingness to defend Europe in the event of military attack and to assist in the gradual strengthening of Europe's capacity to resist direct and indirect aggression.

Following the outbreak of the Korean War in June 1950, which many US officials believed might portend a more aggressive Soviet policy in Europe, the Truman administration initiated a programme of rapid military expansion and called upon its European allies to do likewise. American forces in Europe were increased with a view toward stimulating a parallel upward spiral of defence preparations among the European allies. Though American policy thinking had already come to regard a German military contribution as essential to the achievement of a credible defence posture in Europe, the Korean War enabled the administration for the first time to advance concrete proposals calling for German participation in allied defence plans. A French initiative (the Pleven Plan), calling for the integration of small German combat teams into a European army after the creation of a European political authority, at first was not favourably received in Washington and was regarded, not without justification, as a scheme for delaying German rearmament by linking it to the formidable task of building an effective European political organisation. In the American view, the urgency of the situation required prompt recruitment and training of German combat forces which would then be integrated into the command structure of the North Atlantic Treaty Organization (NATO). A European defence and political organisation was seen as a time-consuming and militarily unnecessary diversion. Nevertheless, by 1951 stubborn French insistence upon both a European and an Atlantic level of control for West German rearmament led the Truman administration to endorse the European army idea.

Acceptance of the concept of a European military authority as a basis for the rearming of Germany immediately posed the question of the relationship between European and Atlantic levels of defence organisation. However, the Marshall Plan approach, involving the expected demonstration of European self-help and the creation of European institutions as a condition for US assistance, was deemed to have only partial relevance to the defence field. To be sure, in announcing substantial increases in US forces to be stationed in Western Europe, President Truman added: 'A basic element in the implementation of this decision is the degree to which our friends match our actions in this regard'.[7] However, the important distinction between the two approaches lay in the different conception of the relationship of the United States to the activities it was encouraging in Europe. The European Recovery Programme entailed a European-centred planning and programming effort involving a European organisation which it was hoped would provide the nucleus for further progress toward European unity. The role of the United States was conceived as that of an external catalyst to stimulate economic transformations within Europe, gradually decreasing Europe's economic dependence on the United States. Though US defence assistance was also predicated ostensibly upon parallel and commensurate European efforts, these were conceived from the outset within an Atlantic framework of mutual security and joint military preparations, rather than as an American programme to assist in the building of an independent and self-reliant European defence force.

Nevertheless, during the debate in Congress over increasing US forces in Europe, and the parallel debate in the Alliance over creating a European army, some US officials contemplated an eventual devolution of defence responsibilities upon Europe. To an extent, of course, this view was motivated by efforts to assuage congressional apprehensions about a major long-term American military presence abroad. Thus, notwithstanding the early Atlantic emphasis in Alliance defence organisation and planning, Truman administration officials often asserted that the main purpose of American assistance was to provide immediate defence support as a prod to Europe's own rearmament measures. The tone of administration statements occasionally suggested that the scale of the American effort might decrease as that of the Europeans grew larger. Indeed, during testimony before the Senate Foreign Relations Committee in February 1951, General Eisenhower, NATO's first supreme commander, speculated that US troops might be withdrawn from Europe within ten to thirty years after adequate European defence forces were in place. As to the possibility of a complete withdrawal of US forces, Eisenhower affirmed: 'I don't know whether you would get to zero, but that would be the objective in any planning in which I took part'.[8] Secretary of Defence Marshall expressed a similar view.

To be sure, from the outset US support for the European army plan was conditional upon it being 'clearly a part of and under [the] NATO umbrella',[9] as Acheson put it. Yet for the longer term, he apparently viewed the plan as providing a permanent nucleus of European defence whether or not American forces remained on the

Continent. Indeed, Acheson stated privately that in the long run it was probably neither practical nor in the best interests of the US or Europe for substantial numbers of US forces to remain on the Continent. This view underscored all the more the need for a European political and military authority to eventually assume primary responsibility for European defence. While acknowledging the need for US and British forces on the Continent 'for some time to come', Acheson suggested that the European army should be organised so that it 'would not have to be changed in any fundamental way whenever the time came that the overseas contingents might be withdrawn'.[10] A European army would have to be ready to take over in the event of 'the possible withdrawal of British and American troops' and 'upon any dissolution of the NATO Supreme Command'.[11]

Despite such long-range speculations, discussions with European leaders convinced the administration that the European army idea was viable only in the context of its firm association with the Atlantic Alliance. France, in particular, was unwilling to accept the rearmament of West Germany except in the framework of its military integration at both European and Atlantic levels. Eisenhower remarked in 1951 that 'The French have an almost hysterical fear that we and the British will one day pull out of Western Europe and leave them to face a superior German armed force'.[12] In effect, the French sought to avoid the very scenario that Acheson seemed to anticipate – that the creation of a solid European defence structure could be a prelude to an eventual American withdrawal, thus posing for France the danger of growing German predominance on the Continent. The smaller European countries also insisted upon a firm European defence link to the Atlantic Alliance, seeing in such association a counterbalance to possible French and/or West German hegemonic ambitions. Increasingly sensitive to such considerations, Acheson asserted that it was 'a dangerous tendency' to view European integration and a European army as final solutions for all problems, including that of security toward Germany, and that it was necessary for the United States to be permanently involved in the defence of the Atlantic area.[13] Noting the West German insistence that it be treated as a political equal in defence arrangements, and the French demand that German rearmament be accompanied by appropriate safeguards, Acheson and Truman concluded that satisfactory progress toward increased European integration 'can be secured only within the broader framework of the North Atlantic community'.[14]

An explicit premise of US policy by the early 1950s was that growing unity in Western Europe would be fully compatible with and essential to the strengthening of US–European ties in an Atlantic security framework. Yet the two did not represent equal value commitments. Enhancing Atlantic solidarity was the primary aim, and West European unity was to be encouraged to the extent that it contributed to that goal. Accordingly, Acheson advised US embassies in Europe that the US could support purely European actions in defence and other areas in so far as they promoted common US–European interests and strengthened the North Atlantic community.[15] The relative prioritisation of the two aims was typically expressed by 'within the framework' terminology, as in Acheson's explanation of US policy as 'helping to bring about real unity to the European Community within the framework of the Atlantic Community'.[16] US Special Representative in Europe William Draper put it still more directly: 'European unity . . . is an attainable objective *provided* – and to my mind this proviso is crucial – *provided* the movement toward unity in Europe continues to take place as part of the growing unity of the Atlantic community'.[17] European governments, eager for strong Atlantic ties as a counterweight to both the Soviet Union and Germany, readily accepted the concept of a European army and NATO 'not as two separate bodies . . . [but rather] two closely related organizations, one working . . . within the framework of, and reinforcing the other'.[18] It soon became standard practice to include in NATO and bilateral US–European communiqués a reference to European unity and the European Defence Community (EDC) within a constantly developing Atlantic community.

Thus during 1951, US policy came to support the European army plan as the most practicable means of achieving German rearmament within a framework that would meet European concerns about the revival of German military power, while at the same time encouraging defence and political unity in Western Europe. General Eisenhower, who was initially cool toward the European army project, became persuaded by this argument in the spring of 1951 after which the administration formally supported the proposal to create a European Defence Community, a modified version of France's Pleven Plan. In 1952, the Truman administration began to exert active diplomatic efforts to secure adoption of the EDC Treaty. Though originally American support for the EDC derived primarily from the need to find an acceptable formula for West German rearmament, the EDC gradually became an end in itself as both symbol and substance of the progress desired toward the goal of European integration. Following the signature of the treaty in May 1952, American officials spoke optimistically of the prospects for a united Western Europe. The proposal under consideration to create a European political community with limited supranational powers was welcomed as an important adjunct to the EDC. Fully aware of British aversions to Continental unification schemes, the administration supported the British decision to remain outside EDC out of concern that British participation might damage the prospects for achieving real unity, as had occurred through the earlier OEEC and Council of Europe experiences. The proposed political and military communities were regarded as powerful and essential supplements to the partial economic integration begun under the European Coal and Steel Community and the limited economic cooperation achieved within the OEEC. Once again, Congress reinforced the administration's policy by affirming in the Mutual Security Act of 1951 its intention to encourage 'the economic unification and political integration of Europe'. In the Mutual Security Act of 1952, providing for US military assistance to Europe, Congress was even more emphatic, for the first time signalling its readiness to use military aid as pressure to bring about further progress: 'In order to provide further encouragement to such efforts, the Congress believes it essential that this Act should be so administered as to support concrete measures for political federation, military integration and economic unification in Europe'.[19]

The EDC Treaty represented a step in the direction of harmonising the Atlantic and European elements of American policy that remains unique in the history of US–European relations. The European defence forces called for by the treaty were to consist of national divisions drawn from member countries, including twelve to be furnished by West Germany, organised into international army corps under the direction of a European commission, council of ministers and parliament, closely paralleling the institutional structure of the ECSC. Thus the risks of rearming Germany would be addressed by integrating West German units into a European political and military governance framework. Member states were not to maintain separate national forces except in specified cases, such as to meet defence responsibilities in non-European areas. To further reassure France, the US and Britain pledged that any threat to the integrity or unity of the community 'from whatever quarter' (including action by Germany) would be regarded as a threat to their own security, and further resolved to station their forces in

Europe, including West Germany, as appropriate to NATO defence needs.

Of crucial significance was the treaty's relationship to the political status of West Germany, still under post-war occupation control by the US, Britain and France. The growing importance of the Federal Republic as an engine of European economic recovery and its obvious centrality to any viable European defence scheme had persuaded the three Western powers to accede to German demands that its contribution to European defence be accompanied by reduced occupation controls and acceptance of the Federal Republic's sovereignty and role as an equal partner in the West. This was accomplished through the so-called Bonn accords, signed along with the EDC Treaty, providing for the normalisation of West Germany's political status to become effective upon ratification of the EDC Treaty. Thus the relationship between the Federal Republic's defence contribution via the EDC and its acquisition of sovereignty was made contractually explicit.

The EDC Treaty, which also projected the creation of a European political community, represented an ambitious move toward the ECSC model of European-level institutional responsibility. The plan for a political community, as proposed by an *ad hoc* assembly to EDC signatory states in 1953, provided for uniting the ECSC and the future EDC under a European executive council, two-chamber parliament, and court of justice, with a council of national ministers serving as a link to member governments. The plan anticipated the gradual development of a common European foreign policy and evolution toward a unified economic market within an overall federal or confederal structure.[20]

Yet the Eurocentric symmetry of these combined undertakings was more apparent than real. While the defence forces called for by the EDC Treaty were to be organised and managed by European bodies, they were not to operate autonomously but rather as a military adjunct of the Atlantic Alliance. Agreements on the relationship between NATO and the EDC provided that the command and employment of EDC forces were to be the responsibility of the Supreme Allied Commander Europe, an American general, and that the European force 'will receive its strategic direction and political guidance exclusively from the North Atlantic Treaty Organization'.[21] For the United States, the EDC had become the indispensable key to bolstering the Alliance's defence posture under American leadership, overcoming Europe's national rivalries through strengthened regional association, advancing the goal of European unity, and firmly anchoring the Federal Republic of Germany in a West European and Atlantic political/security order.

However, developments in Europe boded ill for the EDC Treaty. France in particular, always a reluctant recruit to the idea of rearming Germany, developed deep misgivings about the project during 1952–54 as the outlook for ratification turned increasingly bleak. While professing to favour the treaty, successive French governments declined to risk parliamentary repudiation by proposing it for ratification. Protracted delays in seeking parliamentary approval were accompanied by efforts to secure preconditions and amendments to the treaty to meet one or another domestic factional concern. Britain's refusal to join the EDC, only partly mitigated by its pledge to maintain 'appropriate' forces on the Continent, increased France's sense of isolation and vulnerability as it faced the prospect of a rearmed Germany.

Moreover, external developments worked against the treaty. During the prolonged discussion of German rearmament and the EDC, the Soviet Union made known its apparent willingness to accept a unified and non-aligned Germany as an alternative to a rearmed West Germany linked to NATO via the EDC. While the US and the government of Konrad Adenauer in Bonn viewed the idea as a trap, designed to revive protracted Four Power discussions on Germany's future as a scheme for delaying rearmament, France believed it necessary to exhaust all possibilities for an agreement on Germany before adopting the EDC plan. In addition, the Korean War truce and the death of Stalin in 1953, coupled with signs of a more moderate Soviet leadership thereafter, pointed to a decline in the Soviet threat to Europe and new possibilities for an abatement of East–West tensions. In other words, by 1953/54 the East–West climate had noticeably improved and the short-lived sense of danger in Europe that had followed the outbreak of the Korean War was replaced by more relaxed assessments of Soviet intentions. Thus much of the military rationale for rearming Germany – to bolster the Alliance's forward defence posture in Europe – no longer appeared so persuasive. Finally, it became increasingly clear that budgetary constraints, combined with the reduced Soviet threat, meant that NATO would fall short in its ambitious programme for expanding conventional forces, as agreed at Lisbon in 1952. To compensate for its inferiority in conventional forces, the Alliance came to rely increasingly on tactical and strategic nuclear weapons for deterrence and defence, which undermined the rationale for expanding conventional forces through German rearmament.

The Eisenhower administration, zealously dedicated to the EDC as the focal point of its European policy, grew frustrated with delays in ratifying the treaty. Shortly after assuming office early in 1953, at which time no government had ratified the treaty, Secretary of State Dulles remarked publicly that 'certainly it would be necessary to give a little re-thinking' to American policy toward Europe if its movement toward unity should fail. Privately he was more blunt. During an extensive tour of European capitals in February, Dulles reportedly threatened a cut in US aid if the EDC Treaty were not promptly ratified.[22] In July, Dulles pointedly told French Foreign Minister Bidault that 'it was impossible to exaggerate the importance which we attach to European integration'[23] and the tragic effects if it were to fail. Congress strengthened the administration's position through legislation barring US military assistance to countries that had not ratified the treaty.[24] In December, by which time France was the chief holdout on ratification, Dulles warned the North Atlantic Council in Paris that rejection of the EDC 'would compel an agonizing reappraisal of basic United States policy', later explaining that this would include a reassessment of the disposition of US forces, implying a withdrawal of American troops, and re-examination of the Alliance's forward strategy for the defence of Europe.[25] Unmoved by American remonstrations, the French National Assembly repudiated the treaty in August 1954, an action which also ended discussions on the political community, which in any case had been moribund since earlier in the year.

Dulles' fervent advocacy of the EDC, and what were widely viewed in France as bullying tactics to secure its ratification, were probably contributory though not decisive factors in the rejection of the treaty. Nonetheless, American pressure for ratification hardened rather than softened French resistance to EDC, reinforcing the other factors that steered it toward defeat. Indeed as early as May 1952, the month the treaty was signed, the US Ambassador in France reported a tendency to regard the EDC not as a French initiative supported by the US 'but as something forced upon France by US pressure', and cautioned against any American action that could be construed as threats or pressure.[26] Moreover, while Dulles' public statements emphasised EDC as a major step toward Franco-German reconciliation and European unity, the treaty's purpose of rearming Germany became the main focus of attention and apprehension. As State Department official Leon Fuller put it in an analysis prepared for the Policy Planning Staff at the time: 'EDC failed, in the last analysis, because in the showdown it represented to many Europeans, particularly French, a US project to force *premature* federation along *military* lines involving a high risk of ultimate *German* predominance in a European union, and with a too apparent concern for realization of EDC as a device for mobilizing German armed forces'.[27]

The collapse of EDC led to a flurry of diplomatic activity to salvage the situation. Dulles repeated his earlier warning that the French action imposed 'on the United States the obligation to reappraise its foreign policies', particularly in relation to Europe. France was made to understand that its rejection of EDC would not be allowed to prevent the rearming of West Germany. As a result of Western ministerial meetings in London and Paris during September and October, agreement was reached on a British-inspired proposal to broaden the five-member Brussels Treaty to include West Germany and Italy and to re-christen the new group the Western European Union (WEU). WEU was to replace EDC as the European-level framework for German rearmament. However while WEU was provided with a ministerial council and assembly, gone were the earlier plans embedded in EDC and the anticipated European political community to build toward a supranational European political and defence pillar. Lacking provision for a European military affairs management authority, matters of defence policy moved increasingly under the NATO umbrella. West German defence forces, as provided by the EDC Treaty, were now to be assigned directly subordinate to the NATO supreme command. The role of WEU was primarily to monitor compliance with agreed restrictions on West German rearmament, including limitations on the size of its armed forces, a prohibition on the manufacture of atomic, biological and chemical weapons, and restrictions on the manufacture of designated offensive military equipment. Upon ratification of the London and Paris agreements, the earlier concluded Bonn accords were to go into effect, providing for the ending of West Germany's occupation status and its acquisition of sovereignty. Of decisive importance to the eventual French acceptance of the plan was a British commitment to maintain its ground and tactical air forces on the Continent and not to withdraw them against the wishes of the majority of WEU powers, a pledge nevertheless qualified by the option retained by Britain of unilateral force redeployments if necessary to meet an acute overseas contingency.

The adoption of the Western European Union had the effect of reinforcing the Atlantic emphasis in Western defence arrangements and encouraging a shift away from further attempts to create a European military and political nucleus. The European defence forces core of EDC and the proposed European political community had no real counterpart in the Western European Union. The aborted efforts to achieve military and political unity in Western Europe through the defence and political communities thrust the main work of organising Western defence more firmly into the North Atlantic Treaty Organisation. Defence planning carried out through an American dominated NATO supreme command structure, and the increased weight of US forces on the Continent, consolidated a predominantly Atlantic framework for European security. This pattern was further underscored by the adoption at the December 1954 meeting of the NATO Council of military plans which called for reliance upon the use of tactical nuclear weapons in the event of even a Soviet conventional aggression in Europe. Since these weapons and their delivery systems initially were controlled and operated exclusively by American forces, the pre-eminent role of the United States in European defence was given added emphasis. Hence, by 1955, the European Coal and Steel Community represented the only effective organ to carry forward the goal of unity in a specifically European institutional setting.

During the first post-war decade, except for the ECSC, most of the significant steps toward West European unity had been advanced and promoted by the United States. For the most part, the European role was one of responding to and participating in the shaping of American initiatives. After 1955, the American interest in West European unity did not abate but the American role as an advocate and catalyst of change was visibly altered. Henceforth, the United States encouraged West European efforts toward unity, but more as an approving spectator than as an active innovator and participant in what became primarily European-centred initiatives and decision-making. There were a number of reasons for this. On the one hand, the EDC experience persuaded American policy-makers that US pressure for a particular form of European unity could have counterproductive effects. Furthermore, important American objectives had been achieved through the London and Paris agreements and the establishment of the Western European Union. The German occupation statute was terminated, allied controls were mostly abolished and the Federal Republic acquired sovereignty and became a member of WEU and NATO. Provisions for German rearmament and German arms control were secured within the framework of West European and Atlantic institutions. Moreover, the climate of Franco-German relations began to improve, leading eventually to the return of the Saar to Germany, thereby resolving amicably the last major issue of bilateral friction since the war.

In addition, the United States observed with approval the efforts of the Europeans themselves to extend the practice of economic integration begun by the European Coal and Steel Community to other sectors of the economy. The European conferences at Messina (1955), Venice (1956) and Rome (1957) brought to reality through creation of the European Economic Community the idea of establishing a customs union among the Six (Belgium, Federal Republic of Germany, France, Italy, Luxembourg, Netherlands) supplemented by commitments to harmonise or align other areas of their economies. The goal of West European unity, including the full participation of the Federal Republic, was being accomplished through the politically less resistant route of functional economic integration. It was recognised on both sides of the Atlantic that the efforts to achieve unity through direct political and military fusion had been premature and would have to await an expanded climate of mutual confidence that economic interdependence would help to foster. It had also become apparent, through the behaviour of Britain and the Scandinavian countries in the Council of Europe and the OEEC, and the British refusal to join the ECSC or the EDC, that meaningful unity in Western Europe could only be achieved by limiting membership to those countries which were prepared to go beyond intergovernmental consultation and accept some supranational authority in the management of their relationships. Hence, the United States could view with satisfaction the resumption of progress toward European unity now initiated by the Europeans themselves, having sought to promote precisely this kind of activity since the early days of the European Recovery Programme.

Thus the failure of EDC and the subsequent renewed European impulse toward unity marked an important transitional phase in US–European relations. The era of American inspired and promoted ideas for European recovery and unity had ended and was replaced by new European-centred initiatives and progress which were to transform the structural context of European and Atlantic relationships during the next decade. Nevertheless, it is clear that the outcome of the EDC affair helped to perpetuate and reinforce the asymmetry between Europeanism in the economic sphere and

Atlanticism in the security field, a divergence rooted in the largely separate paths followed in the two areas since the 1947/48 period. While the Atlantic Alliance helped to foster a climate of security which facilitated progress toward European economic unity, at the same time it indirectly discouraged a wider scope of future European-level collaboration beyond the economic domain. By firmly implanting Western Europe's defence preparations and its political attitudes and decision-making culture on security matters within an Atlantic frame of reference, there existed little rationale or incentive for attempting distinctively European approaches.

2 What Kind of European Pillar?

THE KENNEDY ADMINISTRATION AND ATLANTIC PARTNERSHIP

In the early 1960s, the development of the European Economic Community (EC)[1] prompted the Kennedy administration to revive the European pillar idea in the form of a proposal for an Atlantic partnership with the emergent EC. Advanced as both a conceptual and programmatic model for US–European relations, Kennedy's 'grand design' envisaged the two sides of the Atlantic working together as separate and increasingly equal entities, yet unified and mutually reinforced by common or similar interests and purposes. As described by presidential advisor McGeorge Bundy in December 1961, 'the most productive way of conceiving the political future of the Atlantic Community is to think in terms of a partnership between the United States on the one hand and a great European power on the other'.[2] President Kennedy later elaborated the theme in a major address in Philadelphia on 4 July 1962, proclaiming the need for closer interdependence between the United States and a unifying Europe:

> We believe that a united Europe will be capable of playing a greater role in the common defense, of responding more generously to the needs of poorer nations . . . We see in such a Europe a partner with whom we could deal on a basis of full equality in all the great and burdensome tasks of building and defending a community of free nations.[3]

Programmatically, Atlantic partnership was envisaged as a process of trade liberalisation, later advanced by the Kennedy round of tariff negotiations, intended to reduce the discriminatory effects of the EC's common external tariff on US export access to Europe, thereby alleviating American balance of trade and payments problems. On the political level, the partnership idea encouraged the expectation that an increasingly stable, prosperous and unified Western Europe

16

should turn outward and shoulder a greater share of free world responsibilities in such areas as Alliance defence support, development assistance, and global diplomacy. Explicit in all of this was the assumption that West European unity, including eventually political unity as well, was in the US interest, and that the evolving Atlantic partnership would reinforce and energise the economic, political and security strength of the West in the context of East–West bipolarity and the cold war. The assumed political benefits of European unity and Atlantic partnership were to compensate for any harmful consequences to US trade interests resulting from the EC's customs union and agricultural policy.

It was recognised, of course, that the Atlantic partnership was an evolutionary design that would require further progress toward European unity to produce an economically and politically consolidated European pillar. Under-Secretary of State George Ball, a key administration spokesman for Atlantic partnership, acknowledged that 'until Western Europe attains a substantial degree of political unity, it is unlikely to make a contribution to world leadership commensurate with its resources'.[4] Still more pointedly, Ball told a European audience: 'We regard a united Europe as a condition to the development of an effective partnership'.[5] While American policy-makers acknowledged that US and West European outlooks on global issues might not always be the same, it was expected that the ultimately common interests assumed to be at stake and sustained consultation would yield roughly common conclusions as to appropriate courses of action.

Atlantic partnership, however, when applied to the defence field, had a profoundly different conceptual and practical meaning. In defence matters, partnership had always in fact meant an integrated Atlanticist approach characterised not by separate US and West European organisations and decisional bodies, as in the economic sphere, but by a unified strategy and command organisation represented by NATO. Thus the perpetuation of American hegemony in Europe through transatlantic defence arrangements contrasted with US readiness to adjust to an independent European entity as a basis for a separate but equal partnership in economic relations. As Kennedy aide Arthur Schlesinger, Jr observed:

Those concerned with the economic and political aspects of the relationship were thinking more and more in terms of a dual Atlantic partnership resting on two distinct entities, the United

States and the European Economic Community. Those concerned with the military aspects were thinking more and more in terms of a single Atlantic community based on NATO and the indivisibility of the nuclear deterrent. The divergence was, in the language of the American civil rights movement, between "separate but equal" and "integration".[6]

In one sense, of course, the asymmetry between the two notions of partnership was simply a reflection of the existing structure of trans-atlantic relations and of the expected evolution of the European pillar. European security dependence on NATO was the reality, accepted everywhere but in France, and Alliance debates centred on the terms of joint defence arrangements, not on the principle itself. On the other hand, an independent European Community was the reality in the economic sphere, yet further progress toward political and defence unity was problematic and remote. In any case, as will be discussed below, most EC governments, again excepting France, favoured fur-ther defence evolution of the European pillar within the framework of the Alliance, thus in effect choosing not to emulate the model of an economically independent EC in the defence field. Yet it is also clear that the United States did nothing to encourage such an EC model evolution, then or later, seeing in Alliance defence arrangements a means for preserving its influence iin Europe, countering Gaullist tendencies toward European separatism and, later, circumscribing the role of European organisations in defence and security matters.

American attitudes toward the European role in NATO defence arrangements stemmed from the US–Soviet strategic confrontation and the predominance of US nuclear forces within the Alliance. As discussed previously, since 1954 NATO doctrine had professed to rely primarily on tactical and strategic nuclear weapons as instruments of deterrence and, if need be, defence. By the late 1950s, however, the development of the Soviet nuclear arsenal, and hence an emerging US vulnerability to a Soviet strike, cast doubt on the deterrence credibility of a strategy which, if executed, could result in nuclear destruction inflicted on the United States.

In these new circumstances of mutual superpower vulnerability, and thus the declining credibility of a strategy based on nuclear reliance, the Kennedy administration moved to shore-up deterrence by placing renewed emphasis on conventional forces, an approach that had been largely discarded since the failure of NATO to meet the ambitious conventional military buildup plan approved at Lisbon in 1952. The new strategy, dubbed 'flexible response', envisaged a range of NATO conventional and nuclear options which could be selected according to the level of any Warsaw Pact attack, while preserving the option of nuclear escalation as a deterrent to a major Warsaw Pact aggression with conventional forces. Administration spokesmen acknowledged in effect that US–Soviet mutual vulnerability had rendered less credible the first use of nuclear weapons by either side, particularly in response to a conventional attack, thus requiring a buttressing of deterrence at the sub-nuclear level. Deterrence against conventional aggression would be enhanced, it was argued, if NATO possessed strong conventional forces of its own whose use would be more believable, and hence more efficacious as a deterrent to a Warsaw Pact conventional assault. If deterrence nonetheless failed, the Alliance would be spared the choice between defeat and early resort to nuclear weapons. Tactical nuclear weapons remained central to the new strategy as a deterrent to Warsaw Pact first nuclear use, but beyond that their role was ambiguous. US defence planners, concerned with the risks of nuclear escalation, wanted to reduce reliance on nuclear weapons by expanding NATO conventional forces to a level sufficient to defeat even a large-scale Warsaw Pact conventional aggression. If such an attack could not be contained, tactical nuclear weapons would be employed, thus anticipating a mixed conventional–tactical nuclear weapons battlefield environment in Europe.

Europeans, on the other hand, wishing to reduce the risk of precisely this scenario, emphasised the role of tactical nuclear weapons not as war-fighting instruments but as a link in the chain of escalation to US strategic forces. Only the threat of such an escalation, which many believed was undercut by talk of flexible response, would achieve the critical security objective of deterring all forms of possible Warsaw Pact military action against Western Europe. Faced with the dilemma arising from the declining credibility of nuclear deterrence and the absence of an acceptable alternative to it, the Europeans sought both to straddle and to deny it. The 'straddle' entailed a simultaneous acceptance of the conventional and nuclear components of the Alliance's defence and deterrence strategy, while manifesting scepticism in the viability of the former and a rather naïve yet uneasy confidence in the latter. The 'denial' entailed the acceptance of American commitments at face value, denying the erosion of active nuclear deterrence through US–Soviet parity, and reaffirming the essential role of a substantial American military presence in

Europe as an assurance of the continued reliability of the nuclear component as the *ultima ratio* of deterrence.

However persuasive the strategic logic of flexible response, the new doctrine introduced for the first time a differential between the US and NATO–Europe regarding the possible risks, costs and levels of involvement in the event of a European war. The earlier strategy of primary reliance on nuclear forces had presumed the virtually simultaneous military engagement of the US and European members of the Alliance if deterrence failed. Should flexible response be implemented, however, Western Europe might suffer critical and unrecoverable losses as a result of a major conventional or even limited tactical nuclear war in Europe, which might or might not engage US strategic forces. Indeed, the United States and the Soviet Union could be immunised from such a war through the continued functioning of US–Soviet mutual strategic deterrence which both might deem it in their interest to respect. The circumstances of US–Soviet mutual deterrence and the simple facts of geography gave the US options for responding to a war on the continent that were inherently unavailable to Europeans. Talk by American defence planners about 'pauses' and 'firebreaks' between conventional and nuclear ripostes and warfighting scenarios on European soil only served to sharpen European anxieties. Europeans resented a strategy that could preserve the US and the Soviet Union as privileged sanctuaries, each remaining out of harm's way through bilateral strategic deterrence, while Europe could become once again a battlefield. US assurances as to the continued indivisibility of the security of the Alliance as a whole clashed with a strategy that seemed to underscore critical differences in US–European exposure to the risk of war. European misgivings about flexible response, voiced most outspokenly by France, postponed NATO's formal adoption of the strategy until 1967, following the French withdrawal from the NATO military command structure the previous year.

Such European concerns were magnified by awareness that the important Alliance defence decisions would be made in Washington. In 1962, the NATO Council adopted the so-called Athens guidelines whereby the nuclear powers would consult their allies 'time and circumstances permitting', prior to launching nuclear weapons deployed on their territories. The guidelines sought to reconcile the political need for allied consultation on the use of nuclear weapons with the strategic need for a deterrence posture based on a capability for swift response not necessarily subject to allied agreement. Yet the conditional nature of the consultations served to underscore all the more European dependence on the United States for critical defence decisions. At the strategic level, guided by the planning of Secretary of Defence Robert McNamara, the Kennedy administration emphasised the need for centralised control over all aspects of the Alliance's deterrence forces.

A corollary of the administration's position was its hostility to independent nuclear forces which, as McNamara asserted, were 'dangerous, expensive, prone to obsolescence, and lacking in credibility as a deterrent'.[7] Moreover, independent deterrents posed the risk that an ally could trigger a nuclear exchange on the assumption, or with the intention, that it would engage US strategic forces. The British nuclear force was accepted, though without enthusiasm, having been developed with American assistance during the Eisenhower administration. Also, US and British targeting plans were coordinated, thus creating a presumption, albeit not binding, that British nuclear forces would not be used independently. Nevertheless, despite exemption of the British nuclear force from direct criticism by US officials, it remained an awkward exception to the Kennedy administration's opposition to the proliferation of national deterrents. In a revealing explanation of the administration's thinking on the issue, McGeorge Bundy wrote privately in 1962:

If we had it to do over again today, we should not encourage the British in this nuclear effort, and it is our guess that over a period of time all merely national deterrents in the hands of powers of the second rank will become uneconomic and ineffective . . . the difference between our position toward Great Britain and our position toward France is simply that a commitment was made to Great Britain at a time when thinking on these matters was very different from what it is now.[8]

This of course was by no means the whole story as far as France was concerned. US nuclear assistance to Britain was provided under legislation enacted in 1958 which authorised US transfer of information and materials for the production of nuclear devices to allies that had already achieved 'substantial progress' in developing their own nuclear weapons. At the time, only Britain qualified under the substantial progress proviso. In April 1962, however, two years after France's first atomic test, a divided Kennedy administration decided against aiding France in the construction of its own nuclear force.

By this time of course, as will be discussed later, France's President Charles de Gaulle had already made known his dissatisfaction with NATO, had begun to withdraw French units from the NATO command, and was seeking to create a European political union with an independent foreign and defence policy. Against the advice of the Pentagon and the US Ambassador in Paris, who believed that nuclear assistance would encourage a more positive French attitude toward NATO, Kennedy decided, as recalled by special counsel Theodore Sorensen, that 'such aid would not win General de Gaulle to our purposes but only strengthen him in his'.[9]

Clearly, US aid for the British nuclear deterrent, however rationalised by historical antecedents, was inconsistent with the administration's convictions about unified (that is, US) management of Alliance nuclear affairs and its effort to discourage the proliferation of national nuclear forces. However, the pull of the special nuclear relationship with Britain proved strong. In 1960, the Eisenhower administration had begun development of the Skybolt air-to-ground missile and agreed with British Prime Minister Harold Macmillan to make it available to Britain if it went into production. The Macmillan government, having cancelled its own plans to build a land-based medium range missile, came to rely on the availability of Skybolt to extend the usefulness of Britain's ageing and vulnerable bomber force. In late 1962, however, the Kennedy administration abruptly cancelled the project, citing development problems and cost overruns, yet at the same time revealing insensitivity to the political importance to Britain of maintaining an independent deterrent.

An incipient crisis in US–British relations was averted when Kennedy and Macmillan met at Nassau in December and agreed on an alternative to the ill-fated Skybolt. Feeling an obligation to the British over the Skybolt affair, Kennedy agreed to provide Polaris submarine-launched missiles to Britain, to be fitted with British warheads, thus enabling the perpetuation and modernisation of its deterrent force. However, the effort to reconcile the Polaris transfer decision with the administration's desire to discourage national nuclear forces, having just done the opposite, was bound to be unconvincing.

The attempt to do so, nonetheless, produced an agreement to develop a multilateral NATO nuclear force to include the British Polaris submarines and at least an equal contingent of US forces. In the meantime, the agreement looked toward creating a NATO nuclear force consisting of elements of already existing US and British strategic and tactical nuclear forces. Thus the prospective creation of a multilateral NATO nuclear force, assigned and targeted according to NATO plans, implied that its British (and American) components would not operate independently but as part of an Alliance deterrent with control arrangements to be worked out. Yet the furore in Britain over Skybolt had magnified the political requirement that Macmillan return from Nassau with an independent British deterrent intact. The ambiguous compromise of these conflicting values lay in Macmillan's agreement that British forces would be used for the 'defense of the Western Alliance in all circumstances . . . except where Her Majesty's Government may decide that supreme national interests are at stake'.[10] Arguably, of course, Britain's supreme national interests would automatically be at stake in any circumstance involving the possible use of nuclear weapons.

Sensitivity to the implications of the new nuclear partnership for Britain's application to join the EC resulted in agreement to offer the Polaris deal to France on the same terms as Britain. However, given de Gaulle's long-evident disenchantment with NATO, and the fact that France lacked the warheads and submarines to make use of Polaris in any case, rejection of the offer was virtually a foregone conclusion. Moreover, the form of the offer to de Gaulle was incredibly maladroit, the outcome of a US–British negotiation without French knowledge or participation and presented to de Gaulle after it had already been published in the press. Finally, de Gaulle suspected that the plan for a multilateral NATO nuclear force, together with the idea of assigning existing forces to NATO, was intended in part to bring the developing French nuclear force under the umbrella of NATO. De Gaulle's rebuff of the Polaris offer came in his famous press conference of 14 January 1963, in which he also announced French rejection of Britain's bid to join the EC. While the relationship between the Nassau agreement and the French veto on British membership in the EC has been much debated, it is clear that Nassau resolved any doubts de Gaulle may have held about Britain's readiness to join the kind of independent Europe he was seeking. In de Gaulle's view, Nassau confirmed and extended the US–British military partnership at the core of the Alliance, providing further evidence of Britain's preference for an Atlantic Europe and hence the perpetuation of American dominance. If Britain (and others) joined the EC, de Gaulle warned that 'in the end there would appear a colossal Atlantic Community under American dependence and leadership which would soon completely swallow up the European community'.[11]

The Nassau agreement put into sharper focus the issue of nuclear sharing in the Alliance, a subject unresolved since 1960 when the outgoing Eisenhower administration suggested the creation of a sea-borne multilateral nuclear force (MLF). The idea stemmed from a number of military and political factors that had begun to surface in the late 1950s. The military rationale for such a force, though never a dominant consideration, was to counter Soviet medium-range missiles deployed in the 1950s and targeted on Western Europe. On the political side, a multilateral force, in which the United States would be closely involved, was seen as providing reassurance to the European allies of the steadfastness of the American nuclear commitment, hence assuaging doubts that had arisen as a result of the emerging US vulnerability to Soviet nuclear attack. The idea also sought to accommodate growing European desires for a larger role in the management of the nuclear affairs of the Alliance. Relatedly, the MLF concept was viewed by American planners as a device for discouraging the proliferation of national nuclear deterrents. Whereas West Germany was barred by earlier agreements from producing nuclear weapons, and did not wish to do so, there was concern nonetheless that the nuclear status of Britain and France might eventually prove contagious in the Federal Republic. Thus West German participation in a multilateral force would give it a role in nuclear management and enhance its status in the Alliance, while avoiding the further proliferation of national nuclear programmes.

Nevertheless, nuclear sharing had not been a priority issue in the US or Europe prior to the Nassau accord. Rather than developing further the Eisenhower initiative for an MLF, the new administration focused on expanding Alliance conventional force capabilities in the context of the emerging flexible response strategy, while at the same time enlarging the US strategic and tactical nuclear arsenal. Thus in his address to the Canadian Parliament at Ottawa in May 1961, Kennedy had stressed the importance of strengthening conventional forces 'as a matter of the highest priority', and asked the NATO allies to 'assign an equally high priority to this same essential task'.[12] He spoke of 'the possibility' of eventually establishing a NATO multilateral missile force, if desired and found feasible by the allies, 'once NATO's non-nuclear goals have been achieved'. Given traditional European resistance to conventional force increases, sharpened by new anxieties that flexible response could weaken deterrence, there was small likelihood that this would happen. While the initiative served a useful Alliance political purpose, by indicating American readiness to share nuclear control in a joint allied force, there was little expectation that anything would come of it. As Sorensen recalled, the Ottawa address 'deliberately left the initiative with our allies to come forward with a feasible plan and first to fulfill their conventional force quotas. Inasmuch as he doubted that they would do either, Kennedy had at that time paid little further attention to the matter'.[13] Indeed, given the administration's strong emphasis on centralised control of deterrent forces, its interest in nuclear sharing with allies could only be lukewarm at best.

The administration's promotion of the twin-pillar Atlantic partnership concept led to a shift of emphasis in its handling of the nuclear sharing issue. The need was to reconcile any NATO nuclear sharing plan with parallel US encouragement of progress toward West European unity. However, as in the Nassau agreement's attempt to reconcile nuclear integration with nuclear independence, the underlying incompatibility between European and Atlantic solutions to the problem of nuclear control was all too apparent. Though not without some ambiguity, the Kennedy administration clearly insisted on the latter. The shift in emphasis entailed public speculation about a European deterrent force as an approach to nuclear sharing, though never with pointed support, and invariably linked to the requirement that such a force be closely linked to US strategic planning and control. Thus McGeorge Bundy, repeating the administration's opposition to independent deterrent forces, told an audience in Copenhagen that if it were needed and wanted, the United States would not veto 'a genuinely multilateral European deterrent, integrated with ours in NATO'.[14] Yet the administration did not 'wish to press for a European answer when in our own honest judgment the instrument of NATO itself may serve as well or better'. Writing in *Foreign Affairs*, Bundy emphasised the costs and burdens of membership in the nuclear club, which led the United States to believe that 'countries which do not apply are wise'.[15] President Kennedy and Secretary of State Rusk aptly summarised the administration's overall attitude toward nuclear sharing in an instruction to Charles Bohlen, the newly assigned US Ambassador to France:

> We recognize that a Europe reviving in strength and confidence may wish to play a greater role in the nuclear field . . . We are not, of course, ourselves pushing for change in this field. Nevertheless, if it should turn out that a NATO or European force – genuinely unified, multilateral, and effectively linked with our own – is what

is needed and wanted, we would be prepared seriously to consider this possibility.[16]

It seems clear from both the tone and substance of such statements that prior to the Nassau accord the Kennedy administration, for political reasons, wished to remain on record as being willing to support an appropriate form of European nuclear participation, closely tied to the US, while at the same time seeking to discourage it as a feasible and worthwhile undertaking.

The low priority initially accorded the nuclear sharing issue by the Kennedy administration abruptly changed, albeit only briefly, during the winter of 1962/63. Rusk's comment at a news conference on 11 December that 'we have not ourselves put forward a precise plan'[17] for a multilateral nuclear force was quickly overtaken by the Nassau accord two weeks later. Having adopted the MLF formula as a means for legitimising Polaris aid to Britain, the administration turned its energies toward building a consensus for it in Europe. A second spark that revived the MLF was the Franco-German Treaty, signed in January, 1963 which appeared to portend the beginning of a close French–German political and military partnership in line with de Gaulle's ambition to build an independent Europe. As will be discussed below, the Kennedy administration began to promote adoption of MLF, with a major role to be assigned to West Germany, as a means for countering the Gaullist challenge and anchoring the Federal Republic more firmly in the Atlantic Alliance.

DE GAULLE'S COUNTER-DESIGN

As the Kennedy administration began to promote its Atlantic partnership idea, diplomatic movement was already underway in Europe among the six founding members of the EC to develop their own cooperation in the political field. In 1959, EC foreign ministers took the first concrete step by agreeing to meet quarterly to consult on matters of international policy including the political implications of the EC. The exercise was fraught with difficulty from the outset. French President Charles de Gaulle, inveterately hostile to supranational agencies such as the EC Commission, insisted that Europe could only be built on the pillars of the states which were 'the only entities that have the right to order and the authority to act'.[18] While conceding that certain 'more or less extranational' organs possessed technical value, 'they do not have, they cannot have authority and, consequently, political effectiveness'. In a September 1960 directive to Prime Minister Michel Debré, de Gaulle wrote: 'The Europe of [state-to-state] cooperation will be launched as of now. The Europe of [supranational] integration cannot but yield forthwith . . . If we succeed in giving birth to the Europe of cooperation, the communities will be put in their place ipso facto'.[19] In calling for regular coopera-tion, not integration, among the EC states, de Gaulle set forth what was to be his guiding principle for the political organisation of Europe, while at the same time signalling his resistance to supranational authority within the existing European Community. Both facets of de Gaulle's 'Europe of states' approach complicated the ensuing discussions on political unity. France's partners, most notably the Belgians, desired a stronger supranational parallelism between the EC and a possible structure for political cooperation; at the same time, they opposed what they suspected was de Gaulle's desire to undermine supranational authority in the EC and to use provisions for intergovernmental political cooperation for this purpose.

The question of the relationship between a developing European political entity and the Atlantic Alliance in defence matters posed further problems. Even before his return to power in 1958, de Gaulle had confided to C. L. Sulzberger of *The New York Times* his view that 'NATO is no longer an alliance. It is a subordination', and that he would quit NATO if he were running France.[20] In de Gaulle's perspective, Europe had abdicated responsibility for its own defence to an American dominated NATO command structure which was incompatible with the need to construct a distinctively European grouping capable of joint action as one of the major world powers.

Moreover, de Gaulle was piqued by US willingness to aid the construction of the British nuclear force, an assistance denied to France, which further crystallised French feelings of subordination within an Anglo-American dominated NATO, while sharpening de Gaulle's determination to make France a nuclear power through its own means. The French nuclear force became the centrepiece of de Gaulle's strategy – initially a basis for his claim to equality within the Alliance, and subsequently a means for reducing France's security dependence on the Alliance. Government statements implied that the French nuclear force would provide the nucleus for a West European defence system when the requisite political unity had been achieved. While this represented an obvious effort to encourage a realignment of European defence thinking away from reliance on Washington, de Gaulle never went beyond a professed willingness 'to study how the French deterrent might be used in the framework of a politically organized Europe'.[21]

De Gaulle's animus toward NATO as an integrated military organisation did not extend to a rejection of the Atlantic Alliance *per se* based on the mutual defence obligations accepted through the North Atlantic Treaty. While his long-range goal was to promote the dissolution of both military blocs in Europe and achieve a gradual pan-European *rapprochement* through *détente*, he recognised that as long as the cold war endured a Western alliance was necessary as a factor of security and equilibrium in the bipolar setting. But the Alliance in its existing form, with France regarding itself as a subordinate member, would not do. Thus de Gaulle's interim policy, pending changes in East–West relations that would create prospects for *détente*, was to seek reform of the Alliance that would enhance France's position within it.

De Gaulle's initial overture in this direction, contained in a proposal to President Eisenhower and British Prime Minister Macmillan in September 1958, was to establish a tripartite organisation of the Alliance's world powers (the US, Britain and France) which would have major responsibility for drawing up strategic plans and taking joint decisions on world problems, explicitly including the possible use of nuclear weapons.[22] Thus de Gaulle proposed a global broadening of the scope of the Alliance under triumvirate leadership and, audaciously, what amounted to a French veto over the possible use of US or British nuclear weapons at a time when France was not yet a nuclear power. Ominously, de Gaulle ended by hinting that France's continued participation in NATO would be dependent on it being accorded an equal role in the elaboration and execution of the Alliance's global strategy. It strains credulity to believe that de Gaulle thought that his tripartite proposal, particularly regarding joint consensus on the use of nuclear weapons, had a reasonable chance of acceptance. It is more plausible to interpret the proposal, as de Gaulle himself later acknowledged,[23] as a *démarche* that he believed would be rebuffed, with such rejection then being used as justification for the progressive French military disengagement from NATO which he had probably determined to accomplish in any case. However, this could be done – with fewer political repercussions potentially injurious to France – under the pretext of a US refusal to accept de Gaulle's proposed reforms, packaged in the form of US–British–French equality of status in an expanded Alliance concept.

Eisenhower's response to de Gaulle's initiative was to endorse it partly in form while denying most of its substance. On the one hand, de Gaulle was told that the US global structure of regional defence pacts, only two of which included France, precluded an extension of Atlantic Alliance responsibilities into other areas. Also, the administration was sensitive to the discriminatory implications inherent in formalising a two-tiered Alliance. Thus Dulles told de Gaulle in December that the US was prepared to initiate tripartite consultations on world problems but would not go beyond an exchange of views. Several such meetings took place in 1959 involving diplomatic and military officials of the three countries. What de Gaulle demanded, however, was the formalisation at the highest political level of joint tripartite leadership of the West as a visible symbol of the acceptance of French equality as a great power.

De Gaulle continued to press his reform ideas on the Eisenhower and Kennedy administrations in the early 1960s. Faced with refusal of his proposal, de Gaulle took aim at NATO asserting that defence 'must have a national character', a concept he began to implement by withdrawing the French Mediterranean fleet from the NATO command structure in 1959. In 1961, insisting that it was intolerable for a great state to leave its destiny in the hands of another, however friendly it may be, de Gaulle proclaimed 'the right and the duty of the European continental powers to have their own national defense'.[24] He skilfully exploited the tendency of his European partners to view NATO and the Atlantic Alliance as one and the same, which of course he did not. Given this distinction, de Gaulle's frequent assurances that his proposed reforms would strengthen the Alliance obscured for a time the deeper underlying differences toward NATO that prevailed.

Thus de Gaulle opposed 'integration' at both the European and Atlantic levels, seeing in such provisions the relegation of France to a role as 'a back-seat nation', while granting unacceptable powers to EC institutions in the one case, and entailing European subordination to an American-dominated NATO in the other. As these views conflicted with those espoused by France's European partners, the EC ministerial consultations on foreign policy questions initiated in 1960 could not begin auspiciously. Indeed, they were characterised by a continued and deepening mistrust, particularly by the Dutch and the Belgians, of de Gaulle's motives and purposes with regard to the EC and NATO. Moreover, following the British application for membership in thhe EC in July 1961, the question was posed of Britain's relationship to the discussions on the political organisation of Europe.

As Belgian and Dutch suspicions of de Gaulle's intentions grew, they became more insistent on the inclusion of Britain in any plan for political unity as a counterbalance to possible French pressures for a European dealignment from NATO and to offset de Gaulle's own hegemonic tendencies.

Despite such differences, however, in July 1961 the EC heads of government agreed to meet regularly and 'to concert their policies and to reach common positions in order to further the political union of Europe, thereby strengthening the Atlantic Alliance'.[25] This formulation, linking political unity to a strengthened Alliance, and a reference in the communiqué to a united Europe allied to the US, represented the lowest common denominator of agreement among the Six on Atlantic ties, while glossing over the fundamentally different attitudes that existed toward NATO itself. A previously appointed study group, the so-called Fouchet Committee named after its chairman, French Ambassador Christian Fouchet, was instructed to prepare a draft treaty for the establishment of a union of the European peoples.

The first French proposal for such a treaty,[26] the so-called Fouchet Plan, was presented to the committee in October bearing the distinctive markings of de Gaulle's approach to European political construction. A central aim of the proposed union, according to the French draft, was to bring about the adoption of a common foreign and defence policy, the latter 'in cooperation with the other free nations', though neither NATO nor the Atlantic Alliance was mentioned. The treaty was to establish 'a union of States' based on intergovernmental cooperation without such supranational features as an independent executive and majority voting among governments as embodied in the EC. Decisions, which would be binding, were to be made unanimously at regular meetings of a council at the level of heads of government or foreign ministers, though absence or abstention by one or two members would not prevent a decision from being taken. A political commission was to be created, composed of senior foreign ministry officials, tasked with assisting in the preparatory work of the council and carrying out its decisions. The European Parliament, already existing for the EC, would be empowered only to deliberate and address questions and recommendations to the council on matters pertaining to the political union. A controversial revision clause provided that the treaty would be reviewed three years after coming into force with the object of introducing 'a unified foreign policy and the gradual establishment of an organization centralizing, within the Union, the European Communities'.

This latter aspect provoked suspicion that de Gaulle intended to use the intergovernmental mechanisms of the political union as a device for suppressing or circumventing the supranational provisions of the EC.

Reactions to the Fouchet Plan varied from general support expressed by West Germany, Italy and Luxembourg to specific criticisms voiced by the Dutch and later the Belgians. The latter countries were particularly concerned that the treaty lacked guarantees for the institutional integrity of the EC, that the political union contained no provision for evolution toward supranational decision-making, and that the aim of creating a common European defence policy was not explicitly linked to the Atlantic Alliance. Moreover, given the recent British application to the EC, the Belgians and Dutch desired British involvement in the political union talks as a counter to de Gaulle's suspected ambitions.[27]

In January 1962 a second French draft plan, reportedly prepared by de Gaulle himself, was placed before the Fouchet Committee which extended the intergovernmental scope of the union while not taking into account the expressed objections to the first draft. In particular, economics were included within the authority of the union, which gave further credence to suspicions that de Gaulle sought to undermine supranationality in the EC by making its actions subject to review by the council acting through the political union. Moreover, whereas the second draft retained the goal of achieving a unified foreign and defence policy, gone was the reference to cooperation with other free nations, thus suggesting that de Gaulle aimed at creating an independent European political and defence entity. The proposal was rejected by France's partners, who proceeded to produce their own draft.

The ensuing negotiations between January and April, facilitated by Italian mediation, yielded a narrowing of differences in some areas. Agreement appeared possible on a reference to NATO in the treaty's preamble, and the EC's competence in economic affairs and its supranational features were to be respected. Disagreement persisted on the review clause, with some EC members pressing France to accept eventual majority voting in decisions taken by the council of the union. Despite some progress, however, the Belgians and Dutch continued to hold deep misgivings about the course of the negotiations, being mistrustful of de Gaulle's aims while resenting the West German tendency to align with France in seeking compromises on key issues. Belgian Foreign Minister Spaak confided to US Ambassador MacArthur that he had 'no confidence' in de Gaulle's foreign policy and suspected that he sought to create a third force between the United States and the Soviet bloc 'based on a coalition of European national states dominated and controlled by a Paris–Bonn axis' from which Britain might be excluded.[28]

The immediate issue that doomed the talks, however, was the question of Britain's relationship to the negotiations. On 10 April Britain's Edward Heath, then Lord Privy Seal, formally proposed that his government join in the discussions. While Heath expressed support for de Gaulle's insistence on an intergovernmental rather than supranational approach to political union, he underscored his own strong view that any European defence policy should be directly related to the Atlantic Alliance. The effect of Heath's initiative was to fortify the long-held Dutch and Belgian desire for British involvement in the political union talks before reaching definitive agreement on the text of a treaty. Given the well-known British aversion to supranational institutions, the Belgians and Dutch were prepared to accept de Gaulle's intergovernmental approach to political union, at least in the beginning, as the price for bringing Britain into the negotiations. Yet France remained adamantly opposed to British participation pending successful conclusion of the negotiations on Britain's EC membership, which had not by then progressed very far. The irreducible conflict between these two positions led to the suspension of the political union negotiations on 17 April. Subsequent efforts through the summer to revive the talks failed.

While there is no available evidence that the Kennedy administration sought directly to influence the course or outcome of the Fouchet negotiations, it nevertheless tried to do so indirectly through the parallel promotion of its Atlantic partnership idea as an alternative to the Gaullist concept of an independent Europe. With regard to the trade liberalisation aspect of partnership, the administration linked the US ability to maintain its overseas troop commitments to a strong balance of trade and payments position, which in turn required a lowering of tariffs between the US and the EC, the latter representing the largest single market for US exports. As Kennedy told the National Association of Manufacturers in December 1961: 'Unless our balance of trade, and our surplus, is sufficient . . . then we have no remedy but to start pulling back . . . I don't want the United States pulling troops home because we are unable to meet our problems another way'.[29] Thus the administration used the implicit threat of troop reductions in Europe as leverage to encourage lower EC barriers to American exports.

On the political side, the administration's move to encourage a European pillar as part of a wider Atlantic partnership appears to have been influenced not so much by the EC, which already was an economic pillar, as by the launching of the Fouchet negotiations, amid early signs that de Gaulle's plan for political union had been generally well received in Europe. From the beginning, the State Department was kept informed of the course of the negotiations through detailed reports from US diplomatic missions based on European sources privy to the talks, sometimes in strictest confidence and with the understanding that US knowledge would not be divulged. McGeorge Bundy's seminal speech on 6 December 1961, proposing a partnership between the United States and a politically unified Western Europe, closely paralleled the deliberations of the Fouchet Committee on the first French draft plan. Of course, public statements by US officials advocating partnership and European unity were at a level of gener-alisation that did not address the specific issues under discussion in the Fouchet talks. This was because the administration did not wish to be seen as overtly attempting to influence the negotiations; also, until the presentation of the second French proposal in January, it appeared that European agreement on a modified version of the first French plan might be possible, including a suitable reference to the Atlantic Alliance linked to the aim of developing a common European defence policy.

As previously mentioned, however, the second French plan for pol-itical union submitted in January 1962 was widely regarded as a step backward in the negotiations by revealing de Gaulle's apparent deter-mination to insist upon a strictly intergovernmental union embracing economic affairs and committed to developing an independent foreign and defence policy. While the United States remained an informed spectator of the negotiations after January, there is little doubt that the Kennedy administration inclined toward the Belgian and Dutch position in the talks and may have discreetly encouraged their resist-ance to the French. Based on several conversations with Spaak, US Ambassador MacArthur reported that 'it seems quite clear that on fundamentals of European political and economic integration our views and Spaak's are [the] same'.[30] For example, the administration appears to have shared the Dutch and Belgian view that British participation was worth the cost of an only intergovernmental political union. Indeed, this attitude was already implied by the administra-tion's support for Britain's membership in the EC, which had been motivated in major part by the expectation that British influence would encourage an Atlantic-oriented Europe while serving as a check on de Gaulle's apparent ambitions. Obviously the administration concurred with the position, advanced most strongly by the Belgians and Dutch, that a common European defence policy must be explicitly linked to the Atlantic Alliance. Indeed, the Dutch sought inclusion of the phraseology 'within the framework of the Alliance', which of course was anathema to de Gaulle.

Thus the administration continued to stress the importance of the Atlantic connection as the Fouchet negotiations progressed, lending support to those governments advocating explicit linkage between the goal of a common European defence policy and the Atlantic Alliance. President Kennedy's State of the Union address in January 1962 drew attention to the emergence of the new Europe 'being matched by the emergence of new ties across the Atlantic', observing that the Atlantic community grows 'like a coral reef, from the accumulating activity of all',[31] a metaphor that must have irritated de Gaulle. Under-Secretary Ball sharply criticised the European 'third force' perspective, often attributed to de Gaulle, disparaging the view that a powerful continental entity 'will be tempted to try a new kind of balance-of-power politics, to play the East against the West, to sell its weight and authority to the highest bidder, to serve its own parochial objective'.[32] Symbolic of the administration's emphasis on Atlantic relations, in March the Department of State announced the creation of a new post of Deputy Assistant Secretary of State for Atlantic Affairs to coordinate US economic, political and security relations with Western Europe.

Following the suspension of the Fouchet negotiations in April, the administration continued to follow efforts in Europe over the next several months to revive the talks and conclude a treaty. While maintaining its formal non-interference stance on the political union issue, the administration continued pressing the Atlantic partnership theme with its obvious implications for the kind of united Europe it was seeking. In May, Kennedy publicly reiterated the US commitment to Western Europe's defence while cautioning that it was 'not automatic' but dependent on 'a common, united defense, in which every member of the Western community plays a full and responsible role'.[33] Extolling Atlantic unity as 'the true course of history', Kennedy warned that 'a coherent policy cannot call for both our military presence and our diplomatic absence'. The latter remark may have been a public rejoinder to de Gaulle's reported comment to US Ambassador Gavin, during a private discussion about the organisation of Europe, that the 'US should not be mixed up in Western European difficulties and should keep itself apart only bringing its weight to bear in case of necessity. It would suffice for Western Europe to know that if war were to start it could rely on [the] US'.[34] Gavin, who on previous occasions had argued for a more conciliatory US policy toward de Gaulle with respect to nuclear assistance, reported that he 'was almost startled by [the] cold harshness of his unqualified statement that [the] US should stay out of [the] affairs of Europe'. Reacting to de Gaulle's remarks, Kennedy asked Gavin to 'spell out [to de Gaulle] our inability to accept the notion that we should stay out of all of Europe's affairs while remaining ready to defend her if war should come'. On the issue of European political unity, Kennedy observed: 'If Europe were ever to be organized so as to leave us outside . . . it would become most difficult for us to sustain our present guarantee against Soviet aggression. We shall not hesitate to make this point to the Germans if they show signs of accepting any idea of a Bonn–Paris axis'.[35]

Kennedy's address at Independence Hall in Philadelphia on 4 July 1962, calling for 'a concrete Atlantic partnership'[36] with a united Europe, closely followed overwhelming passage of the administration's Trade Expansion Act by the House of Representatives, with favourable action by the Senate virtually assured. The legislation was the economic core of the Atlantic partnership, which was expected to establish a pattern of trade liberalisation between the US and the EC to be achieved through a substantial lowering of the EC's tariffs against American exports. Thus with the Trade Expansion Act firmly on track, and with the European political union issue as yet unresolved, Kennedy used the opportunity of his address at Philadelphia to declare that the US would be ready for a 'Declaration of Interdependence' with a 'United Europe' and to discuss 'ways and means of forming a concrete Atlantic partnership'. It was an attempt to nudge the EC down the path of Atlantic trade liberalisation while at the same time encouraging resolution of the political union issue in favour of a Europe closely allied with the United States.

The close cooperation between France and Germany evident during the Fouchet negotiations accelerated after the efforts to continue the talks ended in failure. Since the late 1950s, Franco-German relations had warmed considerably, facilitated by their joint participation in the European Coal and Steel Community, the return of the Saar to Germany, and a close personal rapport between de Gaulle and West German Chancellor Konrad Adenauer. Adenauer valued de

Gaulle's strong support in opposing Soviet pressures against Berlin during the 1958–61 crisis period, in contrast to what he viewed as British and American wavering. Moreover, Adenauer had acquiesced to de Gaulle's leadership in shaping the political union plan, being less concerned about the intergovernmental versus supranational debate, and apparently taking at face value de Gaulle's assurances regarding the Alliance and the EC. Finally, both leaders keenly desired a formal symbol of the achievement of Franco-German reconciliation anchored in a programme of joint cooperation for the future. Consequently, following the collapse of the political union negotiations, bilateral diplomacy quickened between Bonn and Paris, culminating in the signing of the Franco-German Treaty of Friendship and Cooperation on 22 January 1963.

The Franco-German Treaty, in some ways resembling the Fouchet Plan writ small, envisaged regular consultations between the two governments to promote cooperation in foreign policy, defence, youth and education activities, and scientific research. The treaty pledged consultations before taking decisions on important foreign policy questions and efforts to adopt common positions as far as possible. On defence, the aim was to arrive at common strategic and tactical concepts. To allay suspicions that an exclusive Franco-German axis was in the making, the treaty pledged that the other EC governments would be kept informed of the progress in Franco-German cooperation.

Nevertheless, the Franco-German Treaty yielded little practical substance in the short term while, ironically, setting the stage for a widening of Franco-German differences on key issues. The signing of the treaty, scarcely more than a week after de Gaulle's peremptory veto of British membership in the EC, unavoidably associated Adenauer with French policy, particularly when Adenauer declined requests to intercede with de Gaulle on Britain's behalf. De Gaulle's action, whatever the remaining problems connected with the British–EC membership negotiations, was influenced if not determined by the US–British accord at Nassau in December providing for US assistance in the development of Britain's nuclear missile submarine force. As already noted, de Gaulle rejected a similar American offer of aid to France, while interpreting the Nassau agreement as evidence that Britain had accepted strategic dependence on the United States and thus was insufficiently 'European' to join a grouping that in de Gaulle's view must aspire to independence in all areas. Thus by excluding Britain from the EC, and concluding the cooperation treaty with West Germany, de Gaulle further clarified his opposition to an 'Atlantic' Europe while signalling his continued determination to forge a European pillar of continental states initially around the core of Franco-German solidarity. Yet in doing so, de Gaulle had dramatically magnified the differences between his own views and those that generally prevailed elsewhere in Europe, including West Germany, hence contributing to France's isolation and further undermining any basis for a European consensus organised around French leadership.

THE DENOUEMENT

The apparent coupling of de Gaulle's moves in January 1963 away from Britain (and the US) and towards Germany provoked countervailing pressures that frustrated his plans. In West Germany, where there existed broad-based support for British membership in the EC and a strong commitment to NATO, mounting concern was expressed that the aging German chancellor had embraced de Gaulle's concept of Europe with potentially damaging consequences for German interests *vis-à-vis* Europe and the US.[37] Indeed Adenauer's authority within his own Christian Democratic Union was slipping, anticipating his replacement as chancellor later in the year by Ludwig Erhard, who favoured strong Atlantic ties. In a brusque repudiation of the Gaullist design, and indirectly a rebuff to Adenauer himself, the German Bundestag ratified the Franco-German Treaty in May 1963 with a preamble that reaffirmed basic objectives of West German policy: 'close cooperation between Europe and the United States; joint defense within the framework of the North Atlantic Treaty Organization and the integration of the armed forces of the States belonging to the Alliance; the unification of Europe along the path . . . of the European Communities, including in the process the United Kingdom and other States that are willing to join'.[38] For de Gaulle, the Bundestag preamble represented a nullification, not a ratification, of the aims of the Franco-German Treaty and a lasting setback to his effort to enlist West German support for his European and Atlantic policies. While the consultations envisaged by the treaty went forward, they were deprived of substantive meaning by sharp divergences of outlook between France and Germany on key European and Atlantic issues.

A potent impetus to the West German shift away from France in 1963 was the activation of US policy on the MLF in the aftermath of the Nassau accord, the veto on British EC membership, and the Franco-German Treaty, the latter two being viewed as frontal challenges to the American concept of Atlantic partnership. In the new situation, West Germany became the pivotal country – a kind of arbiter of the rivalry between the Gaullist and Kennedy designs for US–European relations. In this context the MLF, having received only half-hearted US support before, was catapulted into the forefront of the administration's strategy to solidify West Germany's commitment to the Atlantic Alliance and to head off the possibility of Franco-German nuclear collaboration under Gaullist leadership, which some feared was foreshadowed by the new treaty. In mid-January, Kennedy planned a trip to Europe for the spring, to include a major appearance in West Germany, as part of a campaign to reassure the allies that the American defence commitment remained firm and that NATO was the essential expression of that commitment – for both the United States and Western Europe. The administration 'put a lot of pressure' on Bonn, as Ball later recalled, to get the West German Parliament to attach an interpretive statement to the Franco-German Treaty reaffirming the primacy of its Atlantic ties.[39] Kennedy told the National Security Council that he appreciated the MLF as a means to 'increase our influence in Europe and provide a way to guide NATO . . . [and to] weaken de Gaulle's control of the [EC] Six'.[40] US diplomatic missions were sent to Europe to explain MLF, which gradually assumed the form of a proposed fleet of twenty-five surface ships equipped with Polaris missiles to be operated by multinational crews and jointly financed and controlled by those allies who chose to participate. Positive control of the force, that is, a decision to launch the missiles, would require unanimous concurrence by participating governments while negative (veto) control could be exercised by any one participant. As the promotional campaign got underway, the administration dropped its earlier insistence on a European proposal and prior progress toward meeting conventional force goals as preconditions for creating an MLF.

Some administration spokesmen hinted that greater European control over such a force could evolve with the achievement of increased political unity. As Deputy Assistant Secretary of State Schaetzel argued: 'The multilateral force would also inevitably make easier the eventual development of a European nuclear force, should this be the desire and within the grasp of the Europeans'.[41] Then Vice-President Lyndon Johnson described MLF 'as a first step toward a greater European voice in nuclear matters. Evolution of this missile fleet toward European control, as Europe marches toward unity, is by no means excluded'.[42] Such a prospect was appealing to US proponents of Atlantic partnership, particularly in the State Department, inasmuch as it looked toward partly revising the structural incongruity between 'Atlantic' and 'twin pillar' patterns in the organisation of US–European relations.

Nevertheless, despite the futuristic nature of such projections, it is hard to see how the strong US insistence on unified control of deterrent forces could have accommodated a genuinely autonomous European nuclear force, if such was indeed envisaged. Moreover, without a radical and unlikely change in French policy, such a force could only be organised without the participation of France, which other European governments almost certainly would have deemed unacceptably divisive with respect to their own sought-for political cohesion. An Alliance nuclear force whose effect would be to deepen divisions within Europe itself could not provide a promising long-term basis for US–European defence collaboration.

In addition, the possibility of an eventual European nuclear force, indeed the MLF proposal itself, inevitably raised troubling questions about West Germany's role in nuclear defence while underscoring latent contradictions within both concepts. Given the nuclear positions of Britain and France – one not needing and the other rejecting on principle a collective deterrent – a major political purpose of a multilateral force was to accord nuclear status to West Germany, yet in a form that would preclude positive control of the force by West Germany as well as by any other participant. If West Germany found MLF attractive because of the enhanced nuclear role it would acquire, other European governments, to the extent that they were interested at all, saw it as a means for closely limiting the West German role in such matters. Indeed, the anticipated prominence of the Federal Republic as the main European participant in MLF, representing a planned 40 per cent of the total force, contributed to growing anxieties elsewhere in Europe and mounting resistance to the entire project. Such concerns would be magnified all the more if the United States eventually withdrew or relinquished its veto on the use of the force, leaving a European deterrent dominated by West Germany.

Yet a further factor lurking beneath the surface was the European concern that movement from an Alliance MLF toward a European nuclear force could promote decoupling of the United States from its central role in the Alliance's deterrence posture. Indeed, Kennedy drew attention to such a possibility when he observed: 'The day may come when Europe will not need the United States and its guarantees . . . and we would welcome that . . . Once Europe is secure and feels itself secure, then the United States has 400 000 troops there and we would, of course, want to bring them home'.[43] These remarks, delivered shortly after de Gaulle's veto of British membership in the EC and the signing of the Franco-German Treaty, were made in the context of affirming that the United States had no intention of seeking to dominate the affairs of Europe, however much the administration's new MLF policy suggested the opposite. Nevertheless, the allusion to possible US troop withdrawals together with administration suggestions that MLF might evolve toward a European force could not but be linked in European minds.

Despite the administration's revived interest in MLF in January 1963, its intensive focus on the issue was short-lived. As Sorensen recalled: 'Gradually in 1963 the MLF proposal fell from the top of the President's agenda toward the bottom'.[44] Both Sorensen and Schlesinger recorded that zealous State Department promoters of MLF pushed the proposal in Europe more vigorously than the President intended.[45] Schlesinger recollected that Kennedy 'retained a certain skepticism about the MLF' and told Belgian Foreign Minister Spaak in May: 'The whole debate about an atomic force in Europe is really useless, because Berlin is secure, and Europe as a whole is well protected':

> As for the MLF per se, he really considered that, so long as the United States retained its veto (and he never mentioned renunciation as a possibility, though other members of his government did), the MLF was something of a fake. Though he was willing to try it, he could not see why Europeans would be interested in making enormous financial contributions toward a force over which they had no real control.[46]

Moreover, the Bundestag's approval of the Franco-German Treaty in May, including a strong affirmation of the Federal Republic's ties to the United States and NATO, reduced the political importance of MLF as a device for competing with de Gaulle and anchoring West Germany more firmly in the Alliance. Hence, the MLF project stagnated from a combination of presidential neglect and European ambivalence during the remainder of the Kennedy administration. While it enjoyed a vigorous if brief revival during the first year of the Johnson administration, partly due to a mistaken assumption by its supporters that the plan enjoyed strong presidential support, further efforts to promote MLF in Europe were abandoned in December 1964. Although the proposal was not formally withdrawn, the administration in effect reverted to the pre-1963 posture of being prepared to consider a European initiative, which was not forthcoming.

The end result of the failure of the political union talks, the French veto on British membership in the EC, and the only limited prospects for the Franco-German Treaty was to paralyse further progress toward building a European political pillar until de Gaulle's resignation at the end of the decade created possibilities for renewed momentum. In effect, the Kennedy administration's attempt to encourage a Europe with Britain closely tied to the US and de Gaulle's attempt to foster an independent European grouping had checkmated each other.

3 The European Impulse Revived: European Defence Cooperation and the United States, 1968–73

As discussed in Chapters 1 and 2, the end result of the collapse of the proposed European defence and political communities in 1954 and of the political union talks in 1962 was that little progress was achieved through most of the 1960s toward creating a European pillar beyond the economic domain of the EC. The Western European Union was the only European organisation with a mandate to discuss defence issues. Yet the general US and European satisfaction with, or at least acceptance of, existing Alliance structural arrangements meant that during this period the WEU never took itself seriously as a body for the elaboration of distinctively European positions on defence. Indeed, given the prevalence of cold war bipolarity and the primacy of the Atlantic Alliance as the Western pole, the implicit view was that in the area of East–West relations there were no important distinctively European security concerns apart from the Alliance itself. The long-established ethos of indivisible Atlantic area security interests, however much subject to doubt, undermined the rationale for a defence initiative at the European level. Moreover, given occasional indications by US officials that American troops might be withdrawn as Europe strengthened its own defence, European governments were chary of innovations which could lead toward that result. Indeed, by the late 1960s pressures were mounting in Congress for a substantial reduction of US force levels in Europe. The European response to these pressures largely explains the nature and purpose of the modest European defence initiative begun in 1968 known as the Eurogroup, composed of the European members of the Alliance, less France, Iceland and Portugal (though Portugal later joined).[1]

42

The origins of the Eurogroup represent a convergence of several strands of evolution within the Alliance during the late 1960s. On the one hand, the United States, during the Johnson administration, had begun publicly to suggest greater European cooperation within NATO. In December 1967 Secretary of State Rusk stated:

> And we would welcome now, as before, a European caucus, if they want to call it that, in NATO, something like a European defense community, as a full partner in a reconstituted alliance . . . There is nothing in our economic, military, and political relationship that we're not willing to discuss and share in order to accommodate the growing strength and confidence of a uniting Europe.[2]

In a similar vein, Under-Secretary of State Nicholas Katzenbach asserted:

> Europe must be prepared to assume a greater share of the responsibilities and costs of world leadership. America must be willing to accept a less dominant role within the Alliance . . . An assumption of greater responsibility for the planning and direction of the defense of Europe by the Europeans themselves would be a healthy evolution in the structure of our Atlantic alliance.[3]

Former Under-Secretary of State George McGhee, then US Ambassador to West Germany, reaffirmed the Rusk initiative and added: 'In Europe's interest, and in our own, we shall continue to bear large burdens in the defense of that continent for as long as necessary. *And in Europe's interest, and in our own, we shall be happy to turn over these burdens to a united Europe when it is capable of shouldering them alone*'.[4] At about the same time, Secretary of Defence Clark Clifford told NATO defence ministers in Brussels 'not to expect the United States to maintain the present level of its forces in Europe . . . I said the time would come when we've got to begin a withdrawal of those troops'.[5]

In one sense, of course, US encouragement of a European pillar within the Alliance represented a revival of the Kennedy administration's Atlantic partnership concept applied to the defence field, now seemingly more practicable following the French withdrawal from the NATO command structure in 1966. Yet never before (or since) had a US administration been so publicly explicit in suggesting a European defence entity 'as a full partner in a reconstituted alliance'.

The Kennedy administration, while given to occasional speculation about greater European control over a NATO nuclear force, never broached the idea of applying the twin pillar idea to the Alliance as a whole. The new factors accounting for the Johnson administration's position after 1965 were the emerging global retrenchment mood in the country and Congress prompted by growing disenchantment with the Vietnam war, concern over mounting budget and balance of payments deficits partly attributable to overseas troop deployments, a relaxation of East–West tensions in Europe, and a growing belief that European NATO members were not bearing an equitable share of Alliance defence burdens. The coalescence of these factors produced new pressures on the administration to encourage greater European defence efforts linked to the creation of a more cohesive European defence identity.

However, the administration's new devolutionary approach toward Alliance relations suggested a course of change not in accord with most West European preferences, which largely accounts for the exceedingly cautious and modest nature of the subsequent Eurogroup undertaking. The notion that a European group within NATO could become 'a full partner in a reconstituted alliance' raised problematic questions as to what form such a reconstitution might take. The linkage between 'a less dominant [US] role within the Alliance' and greater European responsibilities pointed toward increased European defence burdens and a diminished US role in NATO. This, it was feared, could risk a gradual decoupling of the US from its central role in European defence and an erosion in the credibility of US nuclear deterrence, thus compounding existing European anxieties about the flexible response strategy. In particular, the apparent link between a more visible European defence effort and hints of eventual American troop withdrawals sparked European concerns about the implications of the US initiative.

The pointed American suggestions in 1967/68 for a European defence organisation represented a green light and a goad from Washington for the Europeans to take steps of their own. The first European initiative was advanced by Denis Healey, then British Secretary of State for Defence, who in the autumn of 1968 proposed that the defence ministers of the European members of NATO begin informal consultations among themselves. France declined to participate, suspicious of the idea as being an indirect British attempt to gain entry to the EC, and in any case disinclined to act on the basis of a US initiative for European cooperation.

The immediate political setting of the proposal coincided with the revival of Britain's bid to join the EC, the aftermath of the Soviet intervention in Czechoslovakia, and the prospect of eventual substantial US force reductions in Europe as suggested by the support then evident in the Senate for the Mansfield Resolution. As early as September 1966, 48 senators were reportedly in support of Senator Mansfield's sense of the Senate resolution calling for a substantial reduction of US troops in Europe.[6] The resolution was intended to compel the administration to give serious thought to troop reductions as well as to exert pressure on West European NATO members to improve their own force postures and to begin to assume larger Alliance defence burdens. While Mansfield and his allies initially chose not to seek legislation that would mandate troop cuts, preferring instead to use the proposed resolution as a prod to the administration and the Europeans, it was regarded nevertheless as solid evidence of a basic trend in Senate attitudes. Though the Soviet intervention in Czechoslovakia in August 1968 temporarily weakened support for the measure, Mansfield renewed his call for troop reductions the next month. In sum, the combination of pressure from Washington, new concerns about Soviet policy in Europe, and revived movement toward British EC membership prompted the Healey initiative.

The initial Eurogroup meetings, held in November 1968, were in the manner of informal dinners with no agenda, concluding communiqué or substantive announcement. The defence ministers met again in January 1969, at which time it was decided to commission their permanent representatives to NATO to study matters of defence cooperation and to propose ways in which the European contribution to NATO could be better coordinated and made more effective. In May and December, after Healey had confirmed that the new Nixon administration supported the idea,[7] further Eurogroup dinner meetings were held and discussions focused on possible opportunities for cooperative ventures in military equipment procurement and coordinated logistical support for field units.

From such modest beginnings, Eurogroup remained inconspicuous and low-key until mid-1970. Having been prompted by the political need to manifest the European defence contribution, its very existence tended to configurate a geographical division within NATO which in Europe was feared could undermine the cohesion of the Alliance and weaken the American commitment. With this in mind, Eurogroup was never regarded as an embryo of an eventual alternative to NATO or even as a major European body which might provide a basis for a 'reconstituted alliance'. Indeed, Eurogroup suffered from weak and apprehensive support on both sides of the Atlantic. While the United States favoured a more efficient European utilisation of defence resources, there was concern over the potential impact of European collaboration in military production on US military sales to Europe. Moreover, as Henry Kissinger later recounted, many in the US bureaucracy were concerned that a European defence entity would divide the Alliance and they supported the Eurogroup idea 'weakly and wherever possible surreptitiously opposed its implementation. The other Europeans were ambivalent. They favoured unity in the abstract, but they feared that the attempt to articulate a European identity within NATO might give the United States an excuse for reducing its military establishment in Europe'.[8]

At the same time, however, there was a partly suppressed aspect about Eurogroup characterised by an awareness that the future could bring about major changes in the US–European security relationship, compelling a more concerted European approach to its defence needs. In this sense it was Eurogroup's function to anticipate, while seeking to prevent, such a development. Anticipation implied little more than initiating habits, mechanisms and modest programmes of European defence cooperation and entailed nothing so ambitious as alternative contingency planning for a reduced American role in NATO. It was felt that if Eurogroup were to move too ambitiously and visibly into deliberations on sensitive political and security subjects, it could precipitate the very changes alluded to in American statements that it sought to avoid. This aspect also accounted in part for Eurogroup's virtual obsession with informality and non-institutionalisation, which in addition to facilitating effective working-level consultations, also promoted the desired image of a European defence grouping of limited scope and ambition and firmly committed to NATO in essentially its existing form.

Nevertheless, Eurogroup's pace quickened noticeably during 1970 amid revival of the Mansfield Resolution and growing signs of eventual American troop cuts in Europe. In 1969 Senator John Sherman Cooper, himself an opponent of troop reductions, had warned the Military Committee of the North Atlantic Assembly that approval of the Mansfield Resolution might occur next year. 'If firm steps are not taken by other members to increase the strength and effectiveness of NATO military forces, the demand for the approval of resolutions such as that introduced by Senator Mansfield and others, and of even greater importance, the reduction of funds appropriated to NATO, may very well become successful'.[9] Senator Edward Kennedy told the Assembly that American troop reductions were 'most likely' in view of 'a continuing European reluctance to accept a greater share of the defense burden'.[10] At the NATO ministerial meeting in December 1969, Secretary of Defence Laird was reported to be 'rather gloomy about the trend in the United States', and in his talks with the European defence ministers he 'was trying very intentionally to drive home the point that the current troop level simply cannot be sustained over the years ahead and that the Europeans better get themselves prepared for that'.[11] At the same time, the administration offered assurances that 'essentially' current American force levels would be maintained in Europe through June 1971,[12] with the ominous implication that reductions might take place thereafter. On NBC's *Today Show*, Secretary of State Rogers commented: 'I think probably we are carrying more than our share of the [NATO defence] burden. And, in light of that, we'll give serious consideration to some reduction in the middle of 1971'.[13]

In reaction to the new signals from Washington, the first all-day meeting of Eurogroup defence ministers was held in October 1970, breaking with the previous tradition of meeting only in advance of NATO ministerial sessions. This and subsequent meetings were devoted to shaping the European Defence Improvement Programme (EDIP), which was approved and announced to the NATO Defence Planning Committee in December accompanied by the Eurogroup's first communiqué.

The most salient political aspect of EDIP was the explicit acknowledgement of a quid pro quo linkage between the European defence effort and American pledges not to reduce its own forces in Europe unilaterally. Thus President Nixon's pledge that 'given a similar approach by our Allies' US forces in Europe would be maintained and improved and not reduced except in the context of East–West reciprocity, was matched by the EDIP undertaking 'on the basis that the United States . . . would for its part maintain [its] forces at substantially current levels'.[14] The nature of the bargain left open for continuous review the sufficiency of Europe's 'similar approach' as a claim on the American counterpart pledge. The total size of the EDIP, amounting to approximately $200 million per year for five years, was small in relation to NATO Europe's total annual defence expenditures of approximately $27 billion. Although it represented an 'extra effort' beyond previously planned expenditures, the net effect of the EDIP was an increase of only three-quarters of

1 per cent of the combined defence budgets of the European NATO members.

The recognised modesty of the EDIP 'extra effort' soon became a factor in the continuing transatlantic dialogue on burden-sharing. The European initiative was welcomed in official American statements, and a congressional subcommittee, normally highly sympathetic toward NATO, characterised EDIP as 'a step in the right direction' and 'important for what it said about the change in attitude of the European partners towards their commitment'.[15] However, the same subcommittee remained 'somewhat skeptical' despite the 'fanfare' with which US officials explained EDIP 'as justification that the Allies were indeed ready to take over their fair share of the burden'. A major private study of US forces in Europe characterised the reaction of congressional critics to EDIP as a feeling 'that the ten European defense ministers, after long and arduous consultation, brought forth a mouse'.[16]

In December 1971, Eurogroup ministers announced defence budget increases eventually totaling approximately $1.3 billion for 1972. Known collectively as the Europackage, the increase represented an aggregate 6 per cent rise in Eurogroup defence expenditures above 1971 levels, or approximately 3 per cent in real terms. Though most if not all Eurogroup countries increased their defence expenditures for 1972 in both current and constant price terms, collective current price defence outlays for 1972 as a percentage of gross national product remained at the 1971 level of 4.2 per cent. The Europackage defence increases focused on remedying equipment deficiencies previously identified in NATO studies.

In appraising the significance of the Europackage, it must be kept in mind that one of Eurogroup's major efforts was directed toward maximising the visibility of the European defence contribution to NATO and only marginally toward quantitative increases. The Europackage was acknowledged by Eurogroup staff officials to represent largely pre-planned and scheduled equipment replacement actions (which would have occurred in any case through normal equipment modernisation procurement), and it was unclear how much, if any, of the Europackage was attributable to defence improvement pressures generated within Eurogroup. Though Eurogroup may have played a marginal role as a group pressure organ to extract more generous defence pledges from member governments, its major function in this exercise appears to have been the packaging and projection of significant yet largely routine re-equipment measures in a manner intended to focus attention and recognition on the European defence effort. A second Europackage programme approved for 1973 resulted in a $2.9 billion increase in Eurogroup defence budgets, amounting to a real increase of 3 to 4 per cent over 1972 levels. The great bulk of this increase was borne by Britain and West Germany, again for the most part reflecting pipeline re-equipment programmes nearing completion and thus entailing major expenditure outlays.

Clearly, much of Eurogroup's effort was directed toward influencing US public and congressional perceptions of the magnitude of the European defence contribution in an attempt to forestall US troop reductions. Hence, Eurogroup sought to counter the widespread sentiment in Congress that Europe was enjoying a bargain security ride in NATO at the expense of the American taxpayer and to the aggravation of the US balance of payments deficit. Eurogroup publications were fond of quoting, with evident satisfaction, official US figures which showed that the European NATO members already contributed almost 90 per cent of NATO's ground forces, 80 per cent of its sea-power, and 75 per cent of its air-power.[17] Beyond its defence packaging and public relations activities, Eurogroup also organised into sub-groups tasked with encouraging greater collective development and procurement of weapons systems, including enhanced standardisation and inter-operability, and with improving operational coordination among national military units in such areas as field tactics, logistics, communications, medical services and training. Yet such activities remained focused essentially on rationalisation measures aimed at enhanced defence effectiveness within the framework of largely routine expenditure increases.

Indeed, in a fundamental sense, Eurogroup represented an effort on the part of the European NATO members to make a significant enough collective Alliance contribution to retain the US defence presence at substantially current levels, while avoiding measures that could convey an impression of movement toward European self-reliance which could furnish a rationale or pretext for reducing American force levels. Thus Eurogroup operated between these floor and ceiling constraints on its activity and vision of its role.

A significant aspect of the European response to American pressures was affirmation that any US troop reductions could not be expected to trigger compensatory European force increases. Healey told the North Atlantic Assembly in October 1969 that, facing their own budgetary constraints, the European powers could hardly be expected to respond to a major American force reduction 'by making good the resultant deficiency in conventional power rather than by insisting on greater reliance on the nuclear element in NATO strategy'.[18] Other European officials echoed similar views. While this position may have been entirely genuine, it also served as a tactic to discourage reductions in American forces by rejecting any European alternative to them. Relatedly, the European approach to the troop level issue was to imply the existence of a generally equitable balance in US–European NATO burdens and hence to shift to the United States the responsibility for any consequences resulting from a major reduction of American forces.

As illustrated by Healey's remarks, Europeans advanced the argument that any significant reduction in American force levels would severely weaken the Alliance's conventional military posture, and thereby undermine the strategy of flexible response while lowering still further the tactical nuclear threshold in the direction of the 'tripwire strategy' of the 1950s. In this way, American force reductions were portrayed as leading to the virtual abandonment of the conventional defence component of the flexible response strategy, which had been so vigorously advocated by successive American administrations since the early 1960s. Indeed, the importance of a NATO–Warsaw Pact balance in conventional forces acquired increased emphasis in the thinking of the Nixon administration in the context of emerging US–Soviet strategic parity, which was seen as further diminishing a plausible role for nuclear weapons in the Alliance's defence strategy. On the other hand, as discussed earlier, reversion to a kind of tripwire strategy tended to appeal to a persistent strand of European defence thinking which had always been uncomfortable with the flexible response strategy.

In addition to citing the implications for NATO strategy of a substantial American troop withdrawal, occasional European statements alluded to the consequences of such a development for Western Europe's long-term political orientation in a manner obviously intended to play on US sensitivities. According to this line of reasoning, a major American troop withdrawal would gravely weaken the political cohesion of the Alliance, would stimulate and seemingly vindicate neutralist sentiments in Western Europe, and might lead to a gradual reorientation of Western Europe away from the Atlantic and toward the Soviet Union. For example, Helmut Schmidt, borrowing from Dulles' earlier 'agonizing reappraisal' theme in reverse, warned that 'substantial US withdrawals would sorely undermine public confidence not only in the reliability of the American commitment but also in the basic feasibility of European defense . . . Thus, an American pull-out might indeed cause a psychological landslide and impel a despondent Western Europe toward its first major reorientation since the end of World War II'.[19]

The role of Eurogroup during this period in influencing the outcome of the US debate over troop levels in Europe was significant, albeit not decisive. The first phase of this debate, which encompassed Eurogroup's formative period during 1968–70, as we have seen, was characterised by serious European concerns over the prospect of congressionally mandated reductions in US forces. Concomitantly, there was an awareness of the need to demonstrate the magnitude of the European defence effort and to undertake modest defence improvement programmes to neutralise part of the troop withdrawal rationale of Mansfield's supporters in the Senate.

During the second phase, roughly from late 1970 until early 1973, European concerns over the prospect of US troop withdrawals subsided noticeably. This is explained by several interlocking developments that, however, did not prove entirely durable in the long term. First, Europeans felt reassured by President Nixon's pledge that, given a similar effort by the European allies, US forces would be maintained and strengthened and would not be reduced except through reciprocal East–West action. Second, the several defeats during 1971 of Senate attempts to legislate a substantial withdrawal of US forces from Europe appeared to diminish the immediate cause for concern.

In a first formal test of Senate strength, the Mansfield amendment to the Selective Service Bill, requiring a 50 per cent reduction of US forces in Europe by the end of 1971, was defeated 61–36.[20] Other proposed amendments with a similar intent suffered even more lopsided defeats. Of perhaps decisive importance in explaining the failure of the force reduction amendments was Soviet Chairman Brezhnev's unexpectedly strong endorsement of exploratory East–West force reduction negotiations announced in May, less than a week before the Senate votes. Moreover, the Senate debate, while manifesting strong support for a reduction of US forces, revealed wide differences as to the scope and timing of such a move as well as concerns over the desirability of attempting to impose troop withdrawals through legislative fiat. Nevertheless, the wide margins of defeat for the several force reduction amendments in 1971 tended to obscure the fact, not overlooked in Europe, that Senate sentiment on this issue was much more closely balanced if one compared the total of those who voted against all the amendments with the total of those who voted for at least one amendment. In any event, Europeans drew comforting reassurance from the apparent collapse of the Senate troop withdrawal drive.

Third, as noted above, a major factor of influence in the Senate troop withdrawal debates was increasing optimism regarding prospects for the opening of East–West force reduction negotiations. Though such a possibility had long been used by the administration as an argument against unilateral reductions, the apparent Soviet interest in such talks affirmed during 1971 gave fresh credence to the prospect. The planned beginning in January 1973 of exploratory NATO–Warsaw Pact discussions on force reductions in Central Europe seemingly vindicated the administration's earlier opposition to unilateral withdrawals. It appeared that, at least for the immediate future, the opening of East–West force reduction talks had largely pre-empted and deflected the earlier issue of US troop levels, which had centred around essentially intra-alliance concerns about equitable burden-sharing. Moreover, the general feeling was that the Congress, aware of the complexity of the force reduction issue, was unlikely to push for unilateral cuts as long as the talks appeared to be proceeding with serious intent and there remained any prospect for reciprocal reductions.

Finally, the previously discussed quid pro quo linkage between US and European NATO support efforts, coupled with a sense that recent expenditure increases and Eurogroup activities showed an adequate trend of European effort, reinforced the expectation that American forces in Europe would be maintained at existing levels. Thus, the setback of Senate attempts to legislate unilateral force cuts, the apparent mooting of the intra-alliance troop level issue by long-term East–West force reduction negotiations, and the increase in NATO support from Europe seemingly had forestalled the immediate prospect of unilateral US force reductions. This had always represented a basic aim of Eurogroup, and undoubtedly its contribution to the near-term stabilisation of US force levels was important.

Nevertheless, a third phase of the troop level issue opened early in 1973 with a renewed drive by the Senate Democratic Caucus for a substantial reduction of US forces stationed abroad within the next 18 months. In September the Mansfield amendment, calling for a 40 per cent reduction in US military forces abroad within three years, was narrowly defeated in the Senate (51–44) on a second vote following an initial vote passage by 49–46.[21] A compromise amendment, calling for a 110 000 overseas force reduction by the end of 1975, passed the Senate (48–36) but was subsequently dropped in House–Senate conference action. Nevertheless, it was evident that congressional attitudes on the issue of overseas US force deployments had changed significantly since 1971.

A major factor accounting for the shift was mounting preoccupation with the US balance of payments deficit, which had reached $9.2 billion in 1972, with American military spending in Europe accounting for approximately one-sixth of the total. The general mood of retrenchment accompanying the gradual Vietnam disengagement focused further attention on reducing the size of American overseas military deployments. Additionally, the Congress broke through a major psychological barrier in its relations with the President over control of foreign policy by forcing a halt to the bombing in Cambodia and by passing the war powers legislation over a presidential veto. Finally, whereas the prospect of mutual force reduction negotiations had been used in 1971 to forestall unilateral moves to reduce American forces, the formal opening of the negotiations in 1973 did not impress the Congress as a sufficient reason for postponing unilateral measures that would enable the United States to lessen its balance of payments burden.

The convergence of these factors during 1973 produced the Jackson–Nunn amendment to the defence procurement bill, which was passed by Congress and signed by Nixon in November. The amendment required the President to seek, through bilateral and multilateral channels, payments sufficient to offset fully any balance of payments deficit incurred by the United States during fiscal year 1974 resulting from US force deployments in Europe in fulfilment of NATO obligations.[22] In the event that a full balance of payments offset agreement proved unobtainable within 12 months of enactment, the amendment provided for a reduction in funds for US forces in Europe equivalent to the percentage of the balance of payments deficit that was not offset.

The passage of the Jackson–Nunn amendment reflected a coalescence of congressional attitudes both supportive of and opposed to unilateral US troop withdrawals. Strong consensus for obtaining balance of payments relief represented the common denominator. In effect, the amendment transferred to the European NATO members the responsibility for determining the level of future US force deployments. In so far as the Senate action bespoke continuing congressional dissatisfaction with the levels and trends of European NATO defence spending, the amendment constituted a sharp setback for Eurogroup. Moreover, the amendment's focus on the balance of payments issue represented a major upgrading of US expectations of Europe and a shift from previous understandings that had simply linked the maintenance and improvement of US forces in Europe to 'a similar approach by our Allies'. Thus, the amendment compelled a change in the administration's definition of European defence support sufficiency as a condition for the maintenance of US forces at current levels. In addition to indigenous European force improvements, the core of the previous understandings, the amendment raised the price tag by linking American force levels to the outcome of the payments deficit offset negotiations.

The NATO ministerial meetings in December 1973 acknowledged the new troop level-offset relationship necessitated by the Jackson–Nunn amendment. The Defence Planning Committee reaffirmed the standard formula linking US force levels to continued European force improvements as prescribed by Eurogroup programmes. However, the insufficiency of prior understandings, given the new conditions, was underscored in the recognition that 'the maintenance of United States forces in Europe at their present level calls for a common effort on the part of the allies to achieve a solution to the financial problems which the United States incurs thereby'.[23] Subsequent negotiations between the United States and the NATO allies, principally West Germany, produced offset agreements under the Jackson–Nunn formula sufficient to preclude US troop reductions.

While the Eurogroup initiatives were a significant influence on the outcome of the US troop reduction debate, they were hardly determining factors in themselves. Of more decisive importance in 1971 was the prospective opening of East–West arms reduction talks, which enabled the Nixon administration to argue effectively that unilateral American cuts would weaken the Soviet Union's incentives for negotiating reciprocal reductions. Of decisive importance by 1973 was the troop level–balance of payments offset linkage as an approach to burden-sharing, to which Eurogroup activities were largely irrelevant.

Eurogroup's self-imposed limits on its role coupled with its unwavering Alliance orthodoxy assured it a favourable reaction in Washington, though its close identification with NATO precluded participation by France. This further confined the range of Eurogroup activity inasmuch as there was a general European reluctance to deepen divisions on security matters by creating a major European defence entity without France. This was particularly the case with Eurogroup's efforts to encourage collaborative development of weapons systems. While there was some inclination in Eurogroup to promote such activities without France, partly to exert pressure on France to join, the prevailing view was that a forum acceptable to France was needed as a framework to facilitate joint military projects.

Hence in 1976 it was agreed to establish the Independent European Programme Group (IEPG), a title intended to underscore its separateness from NATO, as the principal body charged with encouraging cooperative European arms procurement projects. Thus with the IEPG's movement into this field, the role of Eurogroup became still more circumscribed. Moreover, other areas of Eurogroup's functional activity, for example, logistics, communications and training, were intrinsically more Alliance-wide in their operational scope and were dealt with increasingly at the NATO level. Nevertheless, despite Eurogroup's attenuated role as a European defence pillar, it was deemed to have a useful purpose in presenting Europe's case in the continuing burden-sharing debate with Washington. Furthermore, as Eurogroup had acquired a certain symbolic status as a European defence pillar, it was felt that its abandonment would send a negative signal to Washington as to the European interest in defence cooperation, which could rekindle pressures for American withdrawals.

It is of particular interest that the ambitious encouragement by US officials in 1967/68 of a European defence community 'as a full partner in a reconstituted alliance' was never seriously followed up by the Nixon administration when it took office in 1969. While the administration welcomed the Eurogroup initiative, provided that it not be used to isolate France, it made no attempt to encourage it to undertake broader tasks beyond practical defence support cooperation. While the administration continued to endorse the traditional rhetoric that 'a stronger and more united European voice will make for a more equitable and hence a more productive Atlantic partnership',[24] there was no further public encouragement for a major European defence pillar within a reconstituted Alliance. Indeed, given the already formidable trade challenge posed by the EC, and the development of the European Political Cooperation process as a mechanism for coordinating the foreign policies of member governments, a European pillar was emerging, though independent of the accustomed framework of the Atlantic Alliance. The Nixon administration's supportive yet measured attitude toward Eurogroup may have reflected a calculated or intuitive hesitancy to encourage an expanded process of European defence collaboration which might eventually blend with the EC, or otherwise present a challenge to US predominance in the Alliance. As will be discussed in Chapter 6, such concerns moved sharply to the forefront during the Atlantic crisis of 1973/74.

4 The European Impulse Revived: The Birth of European Political Cooperation, 1969–73

Unlike the creation of the Eurogroup, which was motivated largely by the possibility of US troop reductions, the movement toward political cooperation was rooted in the longstanding if hitherto failed effort to extend European unity beyond the economic sphere of the EC. Following the aborted Fouchet negotiations in 1962, it had proved impossible to generate sufficient consensus among the six founding members of the EC to revive progress toward political unity or even regularised cooperation on foreign policy matters. The general malaise in this area was compounded by the continued French veto on British membership in the EC and by interruption of the planned supranational evolution in the Council of Ministers whereby many important decisions were to have been taken by weighted majority vote after 1965. Having failed in his earlier attempt during the Fouchet negotiations to shift EC matters under the purview of an intergovernmental union, de Gaulle launched a challenge against the EC institutions themselves by insisting upon a more delimited role for the supranational Commission and by demanding a national veto prerogative within the Council of Ministers. EC business virtually ground to a halt while France boycotted Council proceedings during the so-called 'empty chair' crisis in 1965/66. The resulting settlement, known as the Luxembourg compromise, a compromise in form only, led to a tacit acceptance by other EC governments of the French thesis that when a member declares very important interests to be at stake, deliberations in the Council should be continued until unanimous agreement is reached. The effect, of course, was to encumber and retard the decision-making process in the EC, yet at the same time assuring a more solid EC-wide consensual base for actions taken.

The revived impetus toward establishing political cooperation among EC states in the late 1960s derived from several factors, most conspicuously the resignation of de Gaulle from the French presidency in April 1969. His successor, Georges Pompidou, though a former Gaullist prime minister, was more pragmatic than the General and less suited by style, temperament and political stature to continue his predecessor's more doctrinaire and unyielding approach on such issues as British membership in the EC. While de Gaulle himself had hinted to British Ambassador Soames in January 1969 that he might be prepared to accept Britain into a looser European economic association,[1] he never relented in his basic opposition to British membership in the EC itself. Yet de Gaulle's reported suggestion for a political concert among the major European states – France, Britain, West Germany and Italy – one that would be anchored by close Franco-British cooperation, anticipated Pompidou's subsequent abandonment of opposition to British membership in the EC. In 1967, de Gaulle had shared with British Prime Minister Harold Wilson his pessimism about France's future status in Europe and his apprehension about West Germany's growing economic and political prominence.[2] His tentative opening to Britain in 1969 reflected concerns not unlike those of France during the earlier EDC debate – that a Britain in Europe could be a crucial balancing factor to growing German power on the Continent.

Moreover, the concern that West Germany's increasingly active *Ostpolitik* could stimulate nationalist tendencies and lead to an erosion of its foundations in the West reinforced the case for strengthening the EC as the anchoring framework for the Federal Republic's economic and foreign policy orientation. Indeed, Pompidou told Nixon in 1970 that it was fear of a resurgent Germany that had led him to reverse de Gaulle's policy of opposing British entry to the EC.[3] Britain's reactivation of its bid for membership was partly inspired by similar considerations. West Germany also favoured a strengthened and enlarged EC, partly to reassure its partners that *Ostpolitik* did not portend a weakening of the Federal Republic's ties to the West. As Henry Kissinger later observed, the West German 'opening to the East had the unintended consequence of spurring West European integration. Of the three most important European leaders, two distrusted the tendencies unleashed by the third, and the third needed a gesture by which to assuage these suspicions. British entry into the Common Market provided the mechanism'.[4]

Other factors helped to establish the logic for a more concerted European approach to foreign policy issues. The Pompidou government had come to realise that the scope for an effective independent

French policy, which had been the hallmark of the Gaullist era, was distinctly limited, and that such a course would risk growing French isolation in Europe. Concomitantly, Pompidou saw the possibilities for preserving and advancing French interests through harmonisation and reinforcement at a collective European level. West Germany, likewise seeking to avoid isolation from the West as it pursued its interests in the East, needed a strengthened *Westpolitik* to balance its *Ostpolitik*.[5] Relatedly, a West European structure for foreign policy coordination would mollify concerns about West German unilateralism while reinforcing and legitimising the Federal Republic's policies by giving them a European dimension of expression. Smaller European governments, long accustomed to the limits of their individual influence, also saw advantages to the orchestration of policies within a European structure, particularly since the prospective admission of Britain to the EC, less intimate Franco-German relations, and the end of the Gaullist era had eased concerns about big power domination.

Moreover, the completion of the EC's customs union in 1968, accompanied by the emergence of a common commercial policy toward non-member states, narrowed the gap between economic and foreign policy sectors of activity. Since the EC as a unit was now engaged in negotiating tariff levels and trade agreements with other countries, arrangements with manifestly political implications, the development of EC positions on foreign policy questions acquired increased importance. Thus the EC's own internal development focused attention on the need for a more concerted approach to the foreign policy ramifications of its expanding economic and trade authority.

Furthermore, while the Atlantic Alliance was not questioned as the basis for European defence, notwithstanding France's continued independent nuclear posture and stance outside of NATO, nonetheless the implications for European security of profound change in US–Soviet strategic relations could not be ignored. As discussed in Chapter 2, such concerns had already surfaced during the debate over the flexible response strategy in the early 1960s and were hardly set aside by the formal NATO adoption of the strategy in 1967. This was because flexible response could not adequately address the central European dilemma: in a situation of emerging US–Soviet strategic nuclear parity and mutual vulnerability, implying the likely deterrence neutralisation by each of the strategic nuclear forces of the other, the use of US strategic forces – and hence their threatened use as a deterrent – had become increasingly dubious. Moreover, the likelihood of mutual superpower restraint at the strategic nuclear level implied caution at the tactical nuclear level as well to avoid the risks of escalation that could engulf the United States and the Soviet Union. The beginning of the US–Soviet Strategic Arms Limitation Talks (SALT) in 1969, culminating in the SALT I Treaty in 1972, marked steps toward codifying the new superpower strategic relationship.

Continued US efforts to compensate for weakened nuclear deterrence by increased emphasis on conventional forces only served to heighten European anxieties. Conscious from their own historical experience that conventional forces often fail to deter (though this alleged parallel ignores the risk of nuclear escalation as a factor in deterrence), Europeans were concerned that the emphasis on conventional defence could further weaken deterrence while increasing the risks of war on European soil. Moreover, the US approach seemed to open up, and was perhaps designed to achieve, war-avoidance and escalation-control options uniquely available to it, thus furthering the appearance of American decoupling from an integral role in European defence. In addition, the threat from the East in political terms was deemed not to warrant unpopular conventional force increases which, in the case of West Germany, would have also compromised its new Eastern policy.

The above factors – the troubling significance of US–Soviet strategic nuclear parity and vulnerability for NATO deterrence in Europe, doubts about the implications and need for a strengthened conventional defence focus, and a sense of incipient US–European strategic decoupling – produced a growing European consciousness that there was no satisfactory military solution to its security needs.[6] At the same time, and West Germany's *Ostpolitik* was beginning to point the way, NATO's inadequacies as a military approach to security could be partly compensated for by a stronger West European push for a relaxation of tensions and improved relations with East bloc countries – in short, by *détente*. Indeed, through adoption of the so-called Harmel Report in December 1967, NATO governments had already endorsed the idea of seeking 'realistic measures to further a detente in East–West relations', agreeing that 'military security and a policy of detente are not contradictory but complementary'.[7]

Thus actual and portended changes in the European security environment by the late 1960s, and a growing awareness of the emergence of distinctive European interests, contributed to a reactivation of the unity impulse in 1969. As Pompidou put it in December of that year:

at a time when, as we all know, the superpowers . . . view European problems as they affect their own interests, and cannot but
view them thus, we owe it to our peoples to revive their hopes of
seeing Europe in control of its destiny.[8]

Yet despite NATO's shortcomings as an instrument of military security, and to avoid aggravating them, the Alliance remained the central focus of European *defence* policy, while no longer defining the
boundaries of European *security* policy. Hence, the complementary
approach of seeking enhanced security through the pursuit of *détente*
was to become an early priority of West European foreign policy
cooperation in the early 1970s. Indeed, cooperation among EC governments in shaping joint positions for the Conference on Security and
Cooperation in Europe in 1973, culminating in the Helsinki Final Act
of 1975, represented the most important early success of European
Political Cooperation.

The seminal event initiating renewed movement toward a European pillar in the political field was the EC summit conference at The
Hague in December 1969 which had been proposed by Pompidou.
The key bargain struck at the conference closely linked agreement
to further develop the EC, to enlarge its membership, and to take
steps toward creating a closer political association among member
governments. Consensus was reached on the opening of negotiations
with new applicant states, thus clearing the way for enlargement of
the Community. EC leaders agreed to instruct their foreign ministers
to study the 'best way of achieving progress in the matter of political
unification, within the context of enlargement' and to report by
July 1970.[9]

The reference in the Hague conference communiqué to 'a Europe
composed of states' signalled acceptance of the traditional French
insistence that intergovernmental cooperation be the foundation for
building a political Europe. Indeed, this was implied by the explicit
link between progress toward political unification on the one hand
and enlargement on the other, inasmuch as the new applicant states,
notably Britain, shared France's distaste for creeping supranationalism
in the EC and opposed compromising national sovereignty, particularly
in matters of an expressly political nature.

Ironically, then, the Hague conference agreements represented a
reversion to a situation much as had existed at the time of the collapse
of the Fouchet negotiations in 1962. It will be recalled that at that time
the Belgians and the Dutch had been prepared to accept, at least in the

beginning, de Gaulle's approach toward intergovernmental political organisation in exchange for British admission to the political union and the EC. The acceptance of essentially the same arrangement in 1969 signified the evolution of a stronger consensus for building a political Europe for reasons already discussed. It also reflected a mellowing over time of the earlier sharp polarisation between Gaullism and advocates of rapid progress toward a supranational and quasi-federal EC. De Gaulle's own arrogant style, his Olympian detachment and his unyielding, thunderbolt manner of asserting French interests had of course contributed to the confrontational climate. Moreover, the EC itself, typified by Commission President Walter Hallstein, often appeared headily optimistic and overconfident in seeking to extend the Community's authority. The Luxembourg compromise in 1966, while dealing a setback to advocates of supranationalism, nonetheless helped to narrow the gap between the opposing schools of thought by providing a workable decision-making procedure that would avoid potentially destructive rifts within the Community. Thus by 1969, the great debates of the early 1960s over the nature of the EC and its working methods had subsided and been replaced by greater pragmatism and a softening of ideological division. Hence, a more consensual EC on matters pertaining to the Community treaties likewise facilitated progress toward developing a European political structure.

In response to the Hague conference decision to explore steps toward political unity, a committee of the political directors of the member states' foreign ministries was formed, chaired by Belgium's Etienne Davignon. The committee's recommendations, in the form of the so-called Davignon or Luxembourg Report, were approved by the foreign ministers in Luxembourg in October 1970, thereby formally launching the new procedure known as European Political Cooperation (EPC). The Luxembourg Report[10] endorsed 'the ultimate goal of political union' while accepting the need for a gradual approach to intensify political cooperation among EC member states and in particular to concentrate on the coordination of their foreign policies. It was agreed that governments 'will consult on all important questions of foreign policy' with the aim of 'promoting the harmonization of their views, the co-ordination of their positions, and . . . common actions' where possible and desirable. The mechanism for consultation was to be at least semi-annual meetings of the foreign ministers chaired by the minister having the chair in the Council of the EC. Backstopping the ministers was a Political Committee composed of the political directors in the respective foreign ministries who were to meet at least four times a year to prepare the ministerial meetings and carry out other delegated tasks. EPC consultations were to proceed on the basis of confidentiality, mainly to shield the process from the glare of publicity which would expose national differences and complicate efforts to achieve consensus.

While new members of the EC were to be required to participate in EPC, the two structures were quite distinct and only tangentially related. The EC Commission would be allowed to make known its views if the work of the foreign ministers acting in political cooperation would affect the activities of the EC. An annual reporting procedure was to keep the European Parliament informed of developments in political cooperation, in addition to twice-yearly discussion colloquies between the foreign ministers and the Parliament's political committee.

While the strictly intergovernmental character of political cooperation reflected a clear ideational linkage to the Fouchet Plan, the Luxembourg Report represented a far more modest undertaking. Lacking a statutory base in treaty form, political cooperation was to proceed through the more flexible process of agreements and declarations among governments responding to changing situations and national positions. Gone were the Fouchet Plan's provisions for an elaborate array of permanent institutional structures equipped to take and implement binding decisions. Moreover, while the Luxembourg Report encouraged common actions 'where possible and desirable', absent was a clear commitment to the development of a common foreign policy. In short, the report at best outlined broad goals for political cooperation and established rudimentary machinery to facilitate their achievement.

The initial substantive concerns of European Political Cooperation centred on the Middle East, relations with the United States, and the forthcoming Conference on Security and Cooperation in Europe (CSCE). Only in the latter case, however, were substantial results achieved in developing common positions during the early 1970s. This was facilitated, as already mentioned, by the strong West German interest in establishing a multilateral framework for its Eastern policy and by the absence of major differences in national policy on matters to be addressed at the conference. Moreover, as the Hague summit had emphasised, a goal of political cooperation was the promotion of *détente* and 'rapprochement among all peoples, and first and foremost among those of the entire European continent'. Fortuitously, the organisation of the conference agenda into separate 'baskets' of issues, including one dealing with East–West economic relations, dovetailed with the respective competencies of the EC on the one hand and political cooperation on the other.[11] The absence of defence issues *per se* on the agenda enabled EC governments to focus on broader political and security questions (for example, human rights and principles of relations between states, including renunciation of force, respect for borders and non-intervention in the internal affairs of other states) without risking jurisdictional conflicts with NATO. Thus, in many respects the CSCE represented an ideal forum and opportunity for the elaboration of common European positions.

Nevertheless, the increasingly close EPC deliberations on CSCE matters, which were also being addressed by the United States and other Western countries, raised concerns that divergent positions on key conference issues could emerge within the Alliance. To avoid such a possibility, a liaison procedure was followed enabling regular consultations and coordination of positions between the national delegations to Alliance bodies dealing with CSCE matters and their counterpart groups in EPC. Initial concerns that such a practice could prejudice the development of European unity, by subjecting the formulation of common positions to influence by NATO, proved largely unfounded.[12] Indeed, the relatively marginal interest of the United States in the conference during its early stages enabled the Europeans to assume the lead in the coordination and formulation of Western positions.

The Paris summit conference in October 1972 occasioned the first formal review of EPC at the level of heads of state or government. Following completion of negotiations with the new applicant states, it was the first summit of leaders of the enlarged Community (the original Six plus Britain, Denmark and Ireland). The Paris summit represented at best only a modest advance in the development of political cooperation. European leaders agreed that their foreign ministers would henceforth meet four times a year, instead of twice, to deliberate on political cooperation and that they should produce a second report by June 1973 on methods of improving the process. While it was agreed (again) to attempt to formulate common foreign policy positions 'where possible', the limited commitments and method of political cooperation stood in contrast to the proclaimed intention of EC leaders 'to transform before the end of the present decade the whole complex of their relations into a European Union'.[13] As William Wallace and David Allen observed, the assertion in the summit statement that Europe must be able to make its voice heard in world affairs and must affirm its own views 'masked the continuing inability of the member governments to agree on what that voice should affirm in its dealings with the United States or with the Middle Eastern countries'.[14]

The second report on political cooperation was adopted by EC governments at a meeting of foreign ministers in Copenhagen in July 1973. The so-called Copenhagen Report brought together existing practices in political cooperation as they had evolved since 1970 and sought to chart the course of future development. It represented a comprehensive statement of the nature and provisions of EPC that would guide the process through the 1970s and 1980s.[15] Yet the goal of promoting a harmonisation of views and alignment of positions on foreign policy questions and joint action 'wherever it appears possible and desirable'[16] did not represent a significant semantical advance beyond the language of the Paris summit. However, the recognition of the need to establish Europe's position in the world as 'a distinct entity' to enable 'an original contribution to the international equilibrium' reflected a growing collective self-consciousness that the EPC process itself had helped to engender. As will be discussed in Chapter 6, it also expressed, however mildly, the increasingly confrontational character of US–European relations during the so-called Year of Europe. Moreover, member governments agreed that they 'will consult each other on all important foreign policy questions' and accepted 'as a general rule not to take up final positions without prior consultation with [their] partners within the framework of the political co-operation machinery'. Despite the 'general rule' qualification, leaving a door open for unilateral actions, this provision represented the first formal obligation undertaken to subject the determination of national positions to a prior multilateral consultative process. In fact, this only registered the already existing 'coordination reflex' among EC governments on foreign policy issues that had evolved through EPC since 1970. However, nothing obscured the fact that foreign policy remained quintessentially a national prerogative, and that the commitment to consult carried no assurance that common policies would be achieved, or that member states would allow their partners' views to influence their own positions.

With respect to mechanisms of foreign policy coordination, the Copenhagen Report mostly formalised arrangements that had already materialised pragmatically. The foreign ministers were to meet four times a year in the context of political cooperation and the frequency of meetings of the Political Committee was to increase, in practice to once a month. Working groups of foreign ministry officials were formalised and charged with coordinating national positions in specific issue areas and responsible to the Political Committee. A so-called group of 'European correspondents' was instated, which actually had already begun to function, composed of an official from each of the foreign ministries charged with assisting the Political Committee and monitoring the implementation at the national level of actions taken through political cooperation. The permanent representatives of the EC states to major international organisations such as the United Nations were to consult regularly and, based on their instructions received, seek to formulate and project common positions. It was agreed to establish a confidential communications network between the foreign ministries to facilitate the work of political cooperation.

The linkage between the structure of political cooperation and the institutions of the EC was only modestly strengthened. It was agreed that the foreign ministers and the political committee of the European Parliament would hold four colloquies a year, which would enable discussion of proposals adopted by the Parliament dealing with foreign policy questions. Continuing past practice, the EC Commission would be invited to express its views on matters under deliberation in the framework of political cooperation which affected the activities of the EC. Nevertheless, the Copenhagen Report underscored the separateness of the two mechanisms by noting that political cooperation 'is distinct from and additional to' the activities of the EC pursuant to juridical commitments undertaken through the Treaty of Rome, while affirming that both approaches sought to contribute to the development of European unification. Yet, as a European Parliament study pointed out, the Copenhagen Report for the first time made official the existing dichotomy between EPC and the EC.[17]

The sharp distinction between EPC and the EC reflected the latter's much greater specificity in subject matter competence, its more detailed and obligatory methods of operation, and its more formalised and structured institutional character. Yet it also manifested a commitment to preserve the integrity of the EC's aims and working methods and an equally strong determination to impart a quite different, strictly intergovernmental character to political cooperation. Underlying this position – held most tenaciously by France, Britain and Denmark – was the partly arbitrary yet emotively symbolic distinction between economic issues, managed jointly in the EC, and matters of 'high politics' foreign policy, which remained the guarded preserve of national governments. Sensitivities on this point led to the ludicrous and self-damaging episode in November 1973 when, at the insistence of France, EC foreign ministers met in Copenhagen in the framework of political cooperation and, to avoid the appearance of merging the two processes, adjourned and flew to Brussels the same day to meet as the Council of Ministers of the EC.

The distinctive nature of EPC compared to the EC reflected a realistic assessment of the possibilities for European foreign policy cooperation. Yet despite the limitations inherent in the process, the Copenhagen Report manifested the achievement of substantial progress toward creating an extensive network of regularised political consultations among EC states, a growing adaptation of political and bureaucratic officials to the habit and expectation of consultations, and some progress toward the elaboration of common policies and narrowing areas of disagreement. Given the sketchy beginning of the endeavour at The Hague less than four years before, this was no small accomplishment. Yet the durability of the European search for political cohesion and a distinctive identity would meet an early test in the context of the Nixon administration's policies toward Europe and the Atlantic crisis of 1973/74.

The reciprocal influences of the United States and developments in European defence and political cooperation during the 1968–73 period were significant, though uneven. As discussed in Chapter 3, the main impetus for Eurogroup lay in the growing sentiment in the US Congress favouring unilateral troop reductions, based partly on the alleged insufficiency of the European defence effort. Eurogroup did contribute to the blunting of these pressures in the early 1970s and thus exerted influence on US Alliance policy. Likewise, of course, the Nixon administration's qualified interest in a European defence pillar, its public rhetoric notwithstanding, influenced the character of Eurogroup in its formative years. Thus, Eurogroup was largely an externally responsive initiative and only secondarily linked to indigenous motives for greater European defence cooperation for its own sake. Nevertheless, the internal motives were significant in themselves, including the perceived need for at least a skeletal framework for European defence consultation in the event of a major change in the US commitment, and increased practical defence cooperation to achieve more efficient use of scarce defence resources. However, whether these motives would have been sufficient without the American catalyst is open to question. Clearly, the ethos of Eurogroup, as could be surmised from its early British leadership, was committed to maintaining the Alliance in essentially its present form. There was no interest in encouraging movement toward a real twin-pillar Alliance configuration, since it was feared that this could lead to the very US decoupling from European defence that Eurogroup was established to avoid. Moreover, the central role of the European defence ministries in Eurogroup activities, and their well established ties with NATO bodies, were conducive to the continuance of existing Alliance arrangements. This factor, together with the Eurogroup and later IEPG focus on collaborative procurement ventures, characterised defence cooperation as a specialised though somewhat inbred and cordoned sector of governmental activity with limited influence on other areas of policy.

On the other hand, European Political Cooperation – with its roots in the EC, a more diverse composition including members of the NATO integrated military command but also France and neutral Ireland, and in any case lacking a mandate in defence – necessarily assumed a quite different character. Thus, despite the nearly simultaneous origination of Eurogroup and EPC in 1969/70, there was no direct connection between them. There was an indirect relationship to be sure, to the extent that both initiatives were in part responses to changes in the US–Soviet strategic environment and American retrenchment. Yet unlike Eurogroup, EPC was not responsive to any direct American impulse suggesting or portending major change in US–European relations. And differing from the earlier experience of the Fouchet negotiations, EPC was launched and reasonably consolidated as a process during 1969–72 virtually free of attempted American influence.

Thus in contrast to Eurogroup, from the outset European Political Cooperation possessed a stronger indigenous base – derived partly from the simple fact that it was an independent European undertaking and thus avoided Eurogroup's 'stigma' in some quarters of being little more than an appendage of NATO. Moreover, EPC's roots in the Fouchet Plan negotiations, the longstanding assumption and goal of European 'theology' that some form of political unity must eventually complement economic integration, and EPC's links to the EC itself, all endowed political cooperation with a distinctively European legitimacy lacking in the defence field. EPC did not require an American catalyst; rather, it responded primarily to evolutionary premises and goals within Europe itself which had become more pressing given the foreign policy implications of the EC's common trade identity *vis-à-vis* non-member states. Furthermore, the scope of EPC activity, including liaison with the Commission on EC matters and later ministerial level coordination, required a broad range of national

officials involved with political cooperation, which aided its consolidation as a regularised process at national and Community levels.

None of this, of course, assured EPC of success in the coordination
and harmonisation of member-state foreign policies, let alone the
creation of a common European policy on particular issues. While
EPC was effective in shaping a joint European position toward the
European security conference, this appears to have been the only
substantive success of political cooperation during its early phase.
While a definitive assessment is difficult, given the confidential nature
of EPC proceedings, one may assume that significant outcomes in
other areas, had they occurred, would have been made known.

It is true, as has often been remarked, that EPC largely confined
itself to reacting to external events rather than launching initiatives
of its own. Yet this implied criticism overlooks the fact that most
foreign policy by its very nature is reactive one way or another.
With respect to EPC, this characteristic cut two ways. In the case of
the European security conference, the opportunity to forge common
European positions provided an early laboratory for implementing
the consultation measures set up by the Luxembourg Report. Of
course, converting an opportunity to common policies depended upon
other factors, namely the absence of serious national differences, the
already established EC role with respect to the conference's economic
agenda, and a degree of US deference to European leadership in
coordinating Western positions.

In other cases, where existing national policies differed significantly, external challenges tended to expose and magnify the absence
of consensus. In other words, the lofty goals and mechanisms of EPC
generated expectations of a common European voice that were frequently inconsonant with divergent national views that often resisted
harmonisation at the European level. This inevitably led some observers to disparage the significance of EPC and the consultative process
itself, though such criticism often rested implicitly on unrealistic
standards of performance which did not take due account of the
consensus-shaping limits inherent in the process. In relations with
the United States, for example, the continued force of the Gaullist
legacy in France, despite Pompidou's generally more pragmatic style,
complicated efforts to mold common European positions through
EPC. Moreover, as will be discussed in Chapter 6, Europe's political
cohesion proved on occasion to be embarrassingly fragile when confronted with external challenges that strained the capacity to forge
and sustain a collective position.

5 The Nixon Administration and Europe, 1969–73

Until 1973, the Nixon administration's foreign policy priorities centred on disengagement from the Vietnam war and cultivation of what was labeled a new 'structure of peace'[1] based on movement toward normalising relations with the Peoples Republic of China and building a *détente* relationship with the Soviet Union, the latter premised on the emergence of strategic parity and acceptance of mutual restraint in bilateral relations and in global policy. Given the depth of Soviet–Chinese estrangement at the time, the incipient warming of US–Chinese relations constituted a not too subtle form of pressure against Moscow to move toward improving relations with Washington so as to avoid a more direct US–Chinese alignment against the Soviet Union. While the immediate focus was on achieving a new triangular equilibrium, President Nixon and his assistant for national security affairs, Henry Kissinger were occasionally given to longer range speculation about an emerging pentagonal global order including a unifying Western Europe and Japan. Whether conceived in triangular or pentagonal terms, however, the administration was groping toward a revised global framework of international relations adapted to the circumstances of the relative decline of American power, a more retrenched US global role after Vietnam as sketched in the Nixon Doctrine, and the rise of other power centres.

Yet the place of Europe in the administration's structure of peace design was ambiguous, not surprisingly so given the inchoate nature of Europe's political personality and misgivings engendered by US–EC trade disputes, rooted partly in the experience of the EC as a tough negotiator during the Kennedy round of tariff negotiations concluded in 1968. As then US Ambassador to the EC Robert Schaetzel recalled, 'in a subtle way general American attitudes toward the Community were conditioned by them. For five years America's awareness of the Community was tied to the drama of crises arising out of trade bargaining. The friction of these negotiations became the core of the new American view of the Community as a hard bargainer, an adversary'.[2]

During Nixon's visit to Paris in early 1969, a major effort was exerted to bury past differences with de Gaulle and to stress that the means of building European unity were for the Europeans themselves to determine. Indeed, after pouring effusive praise on de Gaulle as 'the greatest leader of our time', Nixon appears to have embraced a Gaullist view of European political unity and of an independent European role in world affairs. During a press conference in March, Nixon remarked:

> He [de Gaulle] believes that Europe should have an independent position in its own right. And, frankly, I believe that too . . . the world will be a much safer place and, from our standpoint, a much healthier place economically, militarily, and politically, if there were a strong European community to be a balance, basically a balance between the United States and the Soviet Union, rather than to have this polarization of forces in one part of the world or another.[3]

The curious innovation in this passage is Nixon's seeming endorsement of the idea of an independent West European community that would play a balancing role between the United States and the Soviet Union, in sharp contrast to the traditional bipolar concept of Western Europe as part of an East–West balance. However, subsequent clarifications by administration officials denied that this had been Nixon's intent.[4] Thus the remark probably represented a gesture to de Gaulle, whom Nixon much admired, and an effort to find some common ground for improving US–French relations, or perhaps it was simply an ill-considered lapse of thought at the end of a lengthy press conference. Nevertheless later, while speculating on a pentagonal conception of power relationships, Nixon returned to the theme of Europe playing a balancing role in a global context. Equating prolonged periods of peace with the existence of a balance of power, he observed: 'I think it will be a safer world and a better world if we have a strong, healthy United States, Europe, Soviet Union, China, Japan, each balancing the other, not playing one against the other, an even balance'.[5] In any case, as will be discussed in Chapter 6, the notion of a Europe between the superpowers was flatly contradicted by the

Nixon administration's policy toward Europe during the Atlantic crisis of 1973/74.

In general, the Nixon administration's early public rhetoric on US–European relations carried forward the traditional American theme of Atlantic partnership. Nixon's first annual foreign affairs message to Congress[6] included appropriate references to the need for 'a more balanced association and a more genuine partnership' between the US and Western Europe, as the United States moves 'from dominance to partnership'. Favouring 'a definition by Western Europe of a distinct identity', Nixon proclaimed undiminished American support for the strengthening and broadening of the European Community. Recalling the counterproductive effects of earlier US over-involvement in the unity process, he observed that 'the structure of Western Europe itself – the organization of its unity – is fundamentally the concern of the Europeans'. At about the same time, Nixon told the National Security Council that he believed it in the US interest 'to have a strong economic, political and military European community . . . [that would] move independently, going parallel with the United States'.[7] Nevertheless, one gets the impression that Nixon felt comfortable with the idea of European unity as an abstraction, and found it a useful nostrum of Atlantic folklore to articulate, yet he was too solidly entrenched in the premises and practices of Alliance behaviour to seriously contemplate, let alone promote, a genuine transition 'from [American] dominance to partnership'. Moreover, the uncertainties necessarily accompanying efforts to transform relations with the Soviet Union implied a requirement to keep the Western alliance under American leadership to stabilise and guide the process, and to discourage uncoordinated West European moves toward Moscow. Hence, whether by design or habit, the administration's preference for dealing with Europe bilaterally or through the Alliance hampered growth of the European identity and 'the genuine partnership' that it professed to support.

In his foreign policy report to Congress in February 1972, Nixon reaffirmed the goals of European unity and Atlantic partnership, noting that 'political and defense cooperation within Europe will be the fulfillment of European unity', and that the fundamentally parallel nature of US and European interests in defence matters and East–West relations provide sufficient incentive 'for coordinating independent policies'.[8] Acknowledging that competitive Atlantic behaviour had developed in economic relations, the sphere in which

European integration had first been achieved, Nixon nonetheless professed confidence that as European political unity developed, it would 'facilitate cooperation in the wider Atlantic relationship'.

It is difficult to reconcile Nixon's rhetorical support for an independent, unified Europe with his extravagant embrace of de Gaulle, whose policies had blocked the European Community from acquiring the very capability for action which would enable it to play such a role. Yet it is probable that de Gaulle's concept of a loosely unified Europe appealed to Nixon and Kissinger, since it would provide more access points and greater opportunity for US influence than could be expected in dealings with a single European political authority. In *The Troubled Partnership*, Kissinger had written favourably of the Fouchet Plan, arguing that it would 'permit a more flexible arrangement of Atlantic relations than the "twin pillar" concept now in vogue. A confederal Europe would enable the United States to maintain an influence at many centers of decision rather than be forced to stake everything on affecting the views of a single, supranational body'.[9] Moreover, wrote Kissinger, 'a separate identity has usually been established by opposition to a dominant power', and the European sense of identity was unlikely to be an exception to this general rule. A united Europe, Kissinger believed, 'is likely to insist on a specifically European view of world affairs – which is another way of saying that it will challenge American hegemony in Atlantic policy'.[10] Though Kissinger suggested that this might be a worthwhile price to pay for European unity, American policy had suffered by its failure to acknowledge that there was a price to be paid. In the Nixon administration, Kissinger was even less prepared to pay such a price than were his predecessors. He told a Senate committee in 1966 that 'a federal Europe is likely to have the greatest incentives for a policy which we tend to identify as a Gaullist policy, while a confederal Europe would permit us to maintain an influence at many centers and it would probably be, in the long run, less likely to pursue such a policy'.[11] Thus Kissinger's later claim to be 'agnostic'[12] about the form European unity should take stands at variance with his own earlier statements on the subject. Interestingly, Kissinger's conclusions were precisely the opposite of those of both orthodox Atlanticism and Gaullism. Contrary to the traditional American view of Atlantic partnership, Kissinger feared that European separatist tendencies would be magnified by full political union. And, contrary to the Gaullist vision, he believed that de Gaulle's model of a loose, intergovernmental European grouping would (a) preserve opportunities for US influence within an Atlantic framework and (b) provide expression for, while delimiting, the emergent European identity.

Whatever the conceptual ambiguities of the Nixon–Kissinger view of Europe, it hardly mattered during the first Nixon term. For an administration preoccupied with Vietnam and the cultivation of ties with the Soviet Union and China, there was little urgency to deal with a Europe that seemed increasingly absorbed by its own affairs and which posed few compelling problems to command the government's attention.

The big exception, of course, was growing Senate pressure for a reduction of US troops in Europe (see Chapter 3). Yet the administration's handling of this issue offered few additional clues as to its long-term view of US–European relations. Opposition to Senate troop-withdrawal pressures was a necessary corollary of the requirement for dealing with the Soviet Union. The evolution toward US–Soviet strategic parity had strengthened the need for conventional forces in NATO. The 'decoupling' – via mutual deterrence – of strategic nuclear forces from a credible military role in Europe, together with continued escalation uncertainties associated with the use of tactical nuclear weapons, argued against reductions in European conventional force levels. Moreover, the administration insisted that prospects for mutual force reductions in Europe would be jeopardised if the United States embarked upon unilateral withdrawals. Both arguments reflected the view that the United States required a stable East–West military relationship in Europe to underpin its deterrence and arms control policies toward the Soviet Union.

As discussed in Chapter 3, NATO's Eurogroup represented the chief European response to pressures from the administration and Congress for an increased European contribution to Alliance defence. The formation of such a group, as suggested by Secretary of State Rusk in 1967, also seemed consistent with ideas advanced by Kissinger at about the same time. Yet the development of a European nucleus within NATO was never given significant encouragement by the Nixon administration. Though Eurogroup's defence improvement programmes were officially welcomed, the group was seen chiefly as a vehicle for more equitable Alliance burden-sharing and as a means for staving off pressures in Congress for unilateral American force cuts. Despite Kissinger's previous support for 'another force as a balance to ours' in NATO, and Nixon's own speculations about a European pole in a new global balance of power, the administration never encouraged Eurogroup's evolution in such a direction; nor did it show interest in other approaches toward the same end.

In view of France's chosen absence from Eurogroup, efforts to encourage its development as the nucleus of a future European defence community may have been shunned as divisive. However, given Washington's growing reservations about European unity and the increasingly irritable character of US–EC relations, it seems likely that the administration's measured support for Eurogroup reflected an unwillingness to encourage beyond modest limits a defence organisation which could add another problematic dimension to its relations with Europe. In the defence procurement field, for example, Eurogroup agreed to principles of equipment collaboration entailing efforts to coordinate replacement schedules, achieve maximum standardisation, and develop common procurement and follow-on service plans. Though such projects included joint European purchases from the American defence industry (for example, the Lance missile and the F-16), a major purpose of the principles was to restore vitality to European defence industries and to reduce the predominance of US suppliers in the NATO defence market. Thus, a report of the North Atlantic Assembly's military committee cautioned that 'American support for the Eurogroup may wane if the efforts made by European countries to achieve co-operation in armaments production succeed to the point where US equipment sales to Europe suffer . . . When the Eurogroup starts to bite, may not US reaction to it be similar to current American criticisms of the European Community for alleged discrimination and distortion of trade?'[13]

Though relations with the European Community were essentially peripheral to Nixon's global policy during his first term, the administrations's actions contrasted with its ritualistic affirmations of support for European unity. Indeed, the administration had inherited from the Johnson years a growing malaise in US–EC relations, attributable to changes in attitude on both sides of the Atlantic. The romanticised view of European unity and Atlantic partnership characteristic of the Kennedy period had, by the late 1960s, given way to growing American impatience, annoyance and frustration. De Gaulle's predominance, if only negative, over the European unity process left little scope for an active American policy. With European unity indefinitely stalled and with US foreign policy energies increasingly absorbed by Vietnam, the vision of partnership became replaced by Atlantic estrangement, mutual indifference and bickering over trade issues.

The Nixon administration did little to reverse the deterioration of US–EC relations. A predilection for bilateral diplomacy and the cultivation of improved ties with France found its counterpart in devalued relations with Community institutions. J. Robert Schaetzel, US Ambassador to the EC from 1966 to 1972, asserted that 'Washington searched for some alternative approach, for ways of bypassing the Commission and of dealing directly with the member governments'.[14] During Nixon's 1969 visit to Europe, Schaetzel recalled that 'it was touch-and-go whether during his Brussels stopover he would even meet with the European Commission'.[15] The administration's studied neglect of Community institutions, Schaetzel suggested, resulted from a desire not to offend the French and from a view of world politics wherein it would be 'folly' for a major power 'to assist in the organization of what could become an independent coalition of otherwise subordinate European states'.[16] The problem became compounded as the Department of State and its European missions became isolated from the White House-centred policy-making machinery of the Nixon administration. Moreover, the EC's Common Agricultural Policy began to impact on American farm sales to Europe after 1970, generating hostility toward EC trade policies and compelling a more assertive US posture toward the EC on behalf of domestic agricultural interests. US–EC relations were further strained by the Nixon administration's decision in August 1971 to end convertibility of the dollar and to impose a temporary surcharge on imports to deal with the balance of payments crisis, followed by Secretary of the Treasury Connally's peremptory demands upon European finance ministers for trade concessions.

The clear warming trend in US–Soviet relations in the early 1970s proved to be another source of European disquiet. This was in a sense ironic, inasmuch as European leaders had urged the new US administration to embark on such a course in 1969, despite initial scepticism by Nixon and Kissinger.[17] West European *détente* policies were of course well underway by this time, fuelled by West Germany's *Ostpolitik*, which was to become more active later in the year under the new chancellor, Willy Brandt. The new Pompidou government in France, while edgy over the implications of *Ostpolitik*, likewise could not afford to abdicate leadership to West Germany in setting the pace for improved East–West relations. An exchange of visits between Pompidou and Brezhnev in 1970 and 1971, accompanied by bilateral accords on principles of cooperation and consultation in times of tension, moved France into the mainstream of European *détente* policies. As discussed previously, plans for convening an East–West European security conference provided a focus for the orchestration of West European positions toward the East through the new mechanism of European Political Cooperation.

While European leaders had fully supported the thaw in US–Soviet relations – partly to legitimise their own efforts as being consonant with overall Western policy – by 1972 the growing intimacy of US–Soviet contacts, particularly in the area of strategic arms control, gave rise to European apprehensions. While European governments supported the SALT I Treaty concluded in 1972, its symbolism as marking the end of US strategic superiority and the emergence of US–Soviet parity (a fact of life with or without SALT) was bound to accentuate already troubling questions about the credibility of US nuclear deterrence. Moreover, there was European uneasiness over the agreement on Basic Principles of US–Soviet relations reached at the May 1972 Moscow summit, which had not been discussed with the allies.[18] While it resembled the previously concluded Franco–Soviet accord on cooperation, the agreement nonetheless stirred European concerns about the implications of the new US–Soviet cordiality for their own security interests. When coupled with the other US–Soviet cooperative agreements signed at the Moscow summit, the SALT agreement, and previous accords to curb the risks of military confrontation, European anxieties about 'excessive bilateralism' in US–Soviet relations almost inevitably increased.[19]

The US–Soviet agreement on the Prevention of Nuclear War, signed at the Washington summit in June 1973, provoked European criticism as to the secretive manner of its conclusion and the possible implications of its content. The agreement obligated both parties to act so as 'to avoid military confrontations, and as to exclude the outbreak of nuclear war between them' and between either party and other countries.[20] If international circumstances appeared to involve the risk of nuclear conflict, both parties agreed to 'immediately enter into urgent consultations with each other and make every effort to avert this risk'. To allay allied concerns that in a crisis the possible use of US nuclear weapons could be subject to the uncertain outcome of US–Soviet consultations, the agreement stated that it did not impair or affect the obligations of either party towards its allies. Nevertheless, there were misgivings in Europe that in a nuclear 'moment of truth' involving both superpowers, the pledged

US–Soviet crisis management dialogue could take precedence over Alliance consultations.

The agreement itself, which arose from an earlier Soviet proposal for a pledge of 'no first use of nuclear weapons', was viewed by the Nixon administration as an extension of the Moscow Basic Principles by further elaborating objectives and measures of crisis prevention through consultation. While Kissinger himself later disparaged the accord's significance[21] (though at the time he publicly lauded it), nonetheless, as Raymond Garthoff observes: 'It was, however, precisely this element of superpower consultation about potential situations vitally involving third powers that raised concerns in various quarters over a possible emerging US–USSR condominium'.[22] Moreover, US consultations with allied governments had been restricted and perfunctory at best. Only the top leaders of Britain, France and West Germany had been informed in advance[23] and they were pledged to secrecy, thus there was little opportunity for true consultation. NATO ambassadors were advised of the accord only hours before its signing. While European complaints about the insufficiency of US consultations subsided, in November, French Foreign Minister Michel Jobert challenged Kissinger to explain 'how to reconcile the consultations that (NATO) foresees with those foreseen by the accord of 22 June between the two superpowers'.[24] Ironically, Kissinger had ignored his own earlier advice on the conduct of US–European relations: 'Bilateral dealings with the Soviets, from which our Allies are excluded or about which they are informed only at the last moment, are bound to magnify Third Force tendencies'.[25]

6 A Moment of Truth: The 'Year of Europe' and the Atlantic Crisis of 1973/74

THE YEAR OF EUROPE

The European reaction to the Nixon administration's so-called Year of Europe initiative in early 1973, compounded later by the effects of the October Middle East war, constituted a significant watershed in the evolution of US–European relations and of US policy with respect to West European unity. The effect of both developments was to force to the surface the hitherto mostly latent tensions between American notions of Atlantic partnership and the emerging West European identity.

The idea of focusing US foreign policy attention on Western Europe, with the aim of revitalising and imparting clearer direction to US–European relations, germinated within the Nixon administration during the latter half of 1972. With the conclusion of the Moscow summit, the Shanghai communiqué (moving forward the process of US–Chinese normalisation), and the Paris agreements on Indochina, it appeared that significant progress had been achieved on the three major issues of the administration's first term foreign policy agenda. Thus the public designation of 1973 as the Year of Europe signalled the administration's intention to activate consultations on the accumulated issues that had produced growing strains in transatlantic relations. Among these were the need for a coordinated Western approach toward *détente* with the Soviet Union and East–West relations in general, a definition of Alliance security interests and objectives in the current strategic circumstances, and understanding on principles to guide economic relations, including trade negotiations and efforts to reform the international monetary system.[1] Less charitable motives ascribed by some to the administration's initiative included Nixon's need for a diversion from the deepening quagmire of Watergate, an effort to reaffirm American leadership of the Alliance to bolster the US position *vis-à-vis* the Soviet Union and the coming Washington summit, and an attempt to gain economic concessions from the allies leveraged by European security dependence on the United States. In any case, there was irritation in Europe at what some regarded as the Nixon administration's presumptuous and condescending arrogance in assigning Europe its 'turn' on the agenda of American diplomacy.

Nevertheless, the sense of need for a high-level review of trans-atlantic relations initially drew support from European leaders, particularly in the context of their concerns over the implications of US–Soviet *détente* after the Moscow summit and American domestic pressures for troop withdrawals from Europe. Moreover, the enlargement of the EC and the beginning of political cooperation among the Nine (Belgium, Britain, Denmark, the Federal Republic of Germany, France, the Republic of Ireland, Italy, Luxembourg, the Netherlands) pointed to the need for a review of Atlantic relations in light of developing European unity. Indeed, in December, French President Pompidou suggested consultations 'at the highest level' to consider the emerging changes in Atlantic and East–West relations.[2]

However the 'Year of Europe', formally initiated by Kissinger's proposal for a new Atlantic charter in April 1973, in fact gave rise to an unprecedented period of acrimony in US–European relations and revealed a wide chasm between the essentially traditional American Atlanticist outlook and the testy, if uneven, assertiveness of the emerging European entity. With characteristically sardonic humour, Kissinger would later end his lengthy memoir chapter describing the episode with a section titled 'The Year That Never Was'.

Despite Kissinger's earlier support for increased European autonomy, and his later claim that the administration 'had no difficulty with the concept that Europe should be free to conduct its own policy',[3] his diplomacy identified him as a partisan of the very hegemonic attitude toward Europe that he had earlier criticised as harmful to Atlantic cohesion. Moreover, the years of neglect in US–European relations, the isolation of State Department 'Europeans' from the administration's policy-making process, and the often confusing signals from Europe led to undervaluations by Washington of the European mood following de Gaulle's resignation. The growth of the European Community's political consultations since the 1969 Hague conference, the completion of the membership enlargement negotiations, and the ambitious (albeit ill-fated) commitment at the 1972 Paris summit to achieve union by 1980 had produced a Europe whose attitude on Atlantic issues could no longer be taken for granted. The Nixon administration was so unprepared for the European reaction that Kissinger later acknowledged: 'it took us a long time to accept that there was a serious argument going on'.[4]

Yet if this was so, the administration clearly blinded itself to preliminary signs of the European reaction that surfaced during conversations with key European leaders prior to Kissinger's Atlantic charter address. Britain's Prime Minister Edward Heath, no devotee of the traditional Anglo-American 'special relationship', was intent on establishing Britain's 'European' credentials and preferred delaying any elaboration of Atlantic relations until European institutions had matured further. In any case, as Kissinger later recounted, the revitalisation of Atlantic relations was not a priority for Heath and he wanted any European response to American initiatives in this area to come from Europe as a unit.[5] West Germany's Chancellor Brandt, intent on pursuing the opening to the East through his already successful *Ostpolitik*, was lukewarm toward any Atlantic level of policy coordination in East–West relations that might restrict West Germany's flexibility toward the East. Brandt, too, saw advantage in linking Bonn's policy to a broader European consensus, later noting that the heads of European governments no longer represented solely their own countries but acted 'to a certain degree, as a representative of the European Community as well'.[6] France, though initially noncommittal (probably because of the earlier broadly similar proposal by Pompidou), would later voice deep mistrust of the US initiative.

Kissinger's Atlantic charter proposal aimed at developing a set of principles to redefine and revitalise US–European relations in order to face the economic, political and strategic circumstances of the 1970s. Conceived as a rather unproblematic undertaking, it was proposed that the declaration be completed for signature in conjunction with President Nixon's European trip, planned for the autumn. The proposal was deliberately meagre in substance, in order to allow for European input and avoid the appearance of American dictation, yet its overall tone met a sceptical and suspicious European audience.

For one thing, despite earlier conversations with selected European leaders about the general aims of the administration's plan, the tone and substance of Kissinger's address, embracing the full spectrum of US–European relations, came as something of a surprise.

The State Department was not involved in the drafting of the speech, and Secretary of State Rogers had no advance notice of its content.[7] US missions abroad were uninformed about the address and could not answer questions about its meaning. Moreover, at a time when Europeans were enjoying a heady self-confidence, Kissinger's condescending reference to Europe's regional interests (contrasted with America's global interests and responsibilities) proved insensitive and irritating. And, at a time of renewed European optimism and commitment to achieve union by 1980, Kissinger seemed to subordinate the goal of European unity to the requirement of Atlantic solidarity: 'For us, European unity is what it has always been: not an end in itself but a means to the strengthening of the West. We shall continue to support European unity *as a component of a larger Atlantic partnership*'.[8] Though such language has limited meaning in the abstract, it implied conditional US support for European unity, the practical significance of which became clear during the sharp Atlantic exchanges in the aftermath of the October 1973 Middle East war.

Moreover, many Europeans suspected that the administration sought their agreement to the general principle of 'linkage' among economic, monetary and security issues, which could then be used by Washington to support demands upon Europe for trade concessions and increased defence expenditures under threat of US force reductions. Since the linkage approach had been frequently asserted, or connoted, by US officials beginning with President Kennedy (and actually applied in the Jackson–Nunn amendment), there was reason for European concern as to Washington's intentions. Indeed, Kissinger's April speech strongly implied that the recent European defence improvement efforts coordinated by Eurogroup, amounting to $4.2 billion in budget increases for 1972 and 1973, were still insufficient. Noting that Alliance defence burdens must be equitably shared, Kissinger pledged: '*When* this is achieved [emphasis added], the necessary American forces will be maintained in Europe'. In addition to suggesting new US demands for European defence budget increases, Kissinger (with an eye on the Senate) spoke only of maintaining the 'necessary' American forces in Europe, thus qualifying previous US assurances which stated or implied that forces would be maintained at current levels.

Finally, Kissinger alluded to problems of Alliance defence 'in radically different strategic conditions', the full implications of which had yet to be faced. The administration had previously acknowledged the declining credibility of nuclear threats in the context of US–Soviet strategic parity. This factor, coupled with the previously discussed Nixon–Brezhnev Agreement on Prevention of Nuclear War, further clouded the atmosphere for the proposed Atlantic declaration.

The European reaction to Kissinger's address crystallised early around French and British resistance to linking trade, monetary and security issues in a single forum and declaration. Moreover, Heath and Pompidou agreed in May 1973 that an Atlantic summit meeting was premature in advance of agreements on the specific issues to be included in any common declaration. There was a general European reluctance to negotiate a set of principles which could bind the future at a time of major intra-European change and when American intentions (with regard to linkage) were widely suspect. The inclination in Europe was to accept the US proposal as the beginning of an extended Atlantic dialogue which *could* result in summit agreements, depending upon the outcome of substantive negotiations.

The European determination to avoid linkage contributed to a decision by EC foreign ministers at Copenhagen in July to draft a proposed declaration on relations with the United States embodying areas of the Community's competence, while excluding security issues which would be dealt with in the framework of the Alliance. Thus by insisting on two distinct negotiating fora, the Europeans signaled an intention to strengthen their own collective voice *vis-à-vis* the US on EC matters, while insisting that defence burden-sharing questions be addressed separately and not be linked to possible European concessions in the trade field. The EC action, about which Kissinger claimed the United States was not consulted, had the immediate effect of subdividing the dialogue into areas of US–EC relations on the one hand, and Atlantic security issues on the other. Kissinger accepted the two-level approach on the assumption that the two declarations would be signed 'essentially simultaneously' so as to preserve a sense of commonality in total effect.[9] In addition to the proposed declaration on US–EC relations, work also began on a statement of the European identity, later approved by EC foreign ministers in December.

The manner of the EC's internal consultations on the proposed declaration provoked further strains with the Nixon administration. The United States was not to be consulted in the formulation of the EC draft and was to be apprised of its contents only upon agreement by the Nine. At that point, the European position would be presented to the US by the presiding chair of the EC foreign ministers who had no authority to negotiate on its substance. Hence, an inevitably cumbersome transatlantic negotiation would ensue whereby any American reaction to the EC draft would have to be reconsidered by the Nine, whose spokesman would again lack authority to negotiate with the US. Reacting to the Community's new procedure, a clearly outraged Nixon wrote to Brandt after the Copenhagen meeting: 'I must honestly tell you that I find it astonishing that an endeavor whose purpose was to create a new spirit of Atlantic solidarity and whose essence should have been that it was collaborative at all stages should now be turned almost into a European–American confrontation'.[10]

Despite continued European scepticism as to the value and implications of the whole exercise, there was a general reluctance to offend the Nixon administration by not appearing responsive to its initiative on Atlantic relations. Indeed, in the context of the uncertainties generated by the US–Soviet Washington summit and pressures for American troop withdrawals, most governments saw value in the reaffirmation of US–European ties.

As it turned out, the EC proposal for a joint declaration on US–EC relations agreed to in September was a document of generalities and platitudes that contained little basis for objection or for substantive negotiation.[11] Its chief value lay in its very existence as the first agreement among the Nine on proposed principles of their relations with the United States. The form of the declaration throughout emphasised the United States on the one side and the European Community and its member states on the other. One key paragraph provided that the United States 'welcome the intention of the nine to insure that the Community establishes its position in world affairs as a distinct entity'. This was hardly a novel proposition as both the United States and EC governments had said much the same thing on numerous previous occasions.

The generally banal nature of the EC text, citing *inter alia* lofty principles of East–West relations, international cooperation, trade, monetary reform and the environment, reflected the widespread European perspective on the Atlantic declaration project from the outset. It was an opportunity to state some general principles, on which all could readily agree (including the Nine among themselves), which could provide a basis for later US–European negotiations on concrete particulars. However, given the still developing character

of the EC itself, and the still early stages of its political cooperation, it was premature to lock in firm agreements with the United
States across the range of issues on the Atlantic agenda. Indeed,
there was some European suspicion that the Nixon administration
sought to consolidate American hegemony through the Atlantic
declarations, leveraged by Europe's security dependence, *before*
the EC's economic and political cohesion had advanced to the
point of strengthening Europe's position in the Atlantic relationship.
Moreover, the Nine were divided among themselves over reconciling
their own efforts to establish a distinct European identity in world
affairs with a new affirmation of Atlantic partnership, particularly
given the traditional connotations of the term often implying American hegemony in Atlantic relations. Given such considerations,
European governments essentially turned the Atlantic declaration
exercise into an opportunity to reaffirm their own distinct identity
vis-à-vis the United States, coupled with broad principles which in
no way mortgaged the future of the US–European relationship.

At the same time, however, differences among the Nine over relations with the United States, the inchoate nature of the EC's political
identity, and Europe's security vulnerability, set practical limits to its
posture of individualisation from the US. Indeed, it was recognised
that the linkage between Europe's political cohesion and transatlantic
relations cut two ways, each with a partly neutralising effect on the
other. European concerns over the possibility of American troop
withdrawals, doubts about the efficacy of US nuclear deterrence,
and anxieties about the implications of US–Soviet *détente*, inevitably
led European leaders to a more concerted effort to consider their
own position in light of actual or potentially changing circumstances.
Yet these very factors, as we saw in the Eurogroup discussion in
Chapter 3, also militated against any major change in the Atlantic
status quo and argued for a reaffirmation of Atlantic ties as a means
of arresting their potential erosion.

Ironically, nonetheless, the short-term result of Kissinger's proposal for a declaration of Atlantic principles was to stimulate increased
European cohesion, which altered the context of the original initiative. In form, the European response was a model of the Atlantic
partnership expectations of growing political unity and structure in
Europe, in accordance with Nixon's and Kissinger's own public
positions. But the manner and context of its emergence set the stage
for protracted Atlantic acrimony which, for Kissinger, vindicated his
earlier reservations about the partnership's evolution.

THE MIDDLE EAST WAR AND THE OIL CRISIS

In an important sense, the Atlantic crisis that transpired following the outbreak of the October Middle East war was the first US-'European' crisis in that the United States confronted a fledgling European political entity seeking to establish, albeit imperfectly, an independent position on issues that also directly engaged the United States. The Middle East war, begun by Egyptian and Syrian attacks against Israeli forces, aggravated the already strained dialogue on the Atlantic declarations. As Kissinger later recounted: 'Europe, it emerged increasingly, wanted the option to conduct a policy separate from the United States and in the case of the Middle East objectively in conflict with us'.[12] In broad terms, the Europeans sought to minimise friction with both the Arab states and the Soviet Union: with the former because of heavy dependence on Middle East oil supplies, and with the latter to avoid disruption of *détente* in Europe and a revival of East–West confrontation. The United States, more committed domestically to Israel and less dependent on Arab oil, saw its interests in a different light. Moreover, the United States derived less substantive benefit from *détente*, and thus risked less from a situational confrontation with the Soviet Union, assuming the military hazards could be controlled. In any case, the Nixon administration believed that Soviet behaviour in the crisis challenged an agreed understanding of the US–Soviet *détente* – that neither side would seek unilateral advantage at the expense of the other. Such differences of interest were at the root of the US–European divergences that surfaced quickly in October.

During the first week of the war, the Nixon administration was annoyed by Britain's refusal to sponsor a UN Security Council resolution calling for a cease-fire. Britain had made independent soundings and had determined that Egypt would not accept a cease-fire and that the Soviet Union would veto the measure. Thus, according to one official, Britain decided 'not to play the fall guy for the US'.[13] Later, following Prime Minister Heath's demand for a 'cover story' in connection with Kissinger's request for use of a base in Britain or Cyprus (from which to conduct aerial reconnaissance of battlefield conditions), Kissinger ordered a ban on US intelligence reports to Britain.[14] Kissinger also showed resentment at the British–French refusal to support the United States in its opposition to sending in a joint Soviet–American police force, which had been proposed by Moscow. Kissinger's irritation deepened when the European NATO members balked at Ambassador Rumsfeld's request that they chill their political and trade relations with the Soviet Union as a means of pressure.[15] Reportedly, the Europeans felt that East–West relations had not deteriorated to the point that such measures were warranted.

Moreover, a rare public breach with Bonn occurred when the West German foreign ministry requested that the United States cease loading military supplies aboard an Israeli freighter in Bremerhaven. Though Bonn had tacitly acquiesced in previous US supply operations from West German territory, press reportage of the activity embarrassed Bonn, spotlighting a seeming compromise of West Germany's avowed neutralist position. Additionally, the United States was piqued at the refusal of nearly all European NATO members to permit landing or overflight rights for American aircraft engaged in resupplying Israel. Only Portugal was singled out as having been fully cooperative with the United States throughout the crisis.

On the other hand, Europeans were disquieted over the United States' calling of a military alert (to deter possible unilateral Soviet intervention, as had been hinted privately by Brezhnev), without prior consultation or notification of the NATO allies. Though European leaders did not publicly challenge the action itself, their isolation from a decision which could have impacted upon European security only increased their sense of impotence in the crisis. The European reaction was most sharply expressed by French Foreign Minister Jobert, who complained that Europe was 'treated like a nonperson, humiliated all along the line' while the United States and the Soviet Union armed their respective allies and then pursued secret negotiations toward a cease-fire.[16] American spokesmen countered that the need to respond quickly to a possible Soviet military move precluded consultation. Kissinger ventilated his own frustration over Europe's crisis behaviour in an aside following testimony before a congressional committee: 'I don't care what happens to NATO, I'm so disgusted'.[17]

American calls for Western solidarity in the crisis, particularly with regard to possible direct Soviet intervention, were countered by European assertions that the Middle East was outside the range of common Alliance responsibility, thus, by inference, providing both scope and rationale for an independent European position. This was also, of course, in keeping with the general European desire to minimise the effects of the Middle East conflict on the wider fabric of East–West relations and particularly on the course of *détente* in Europe. Such views prompted a sharp message from Nixon to Brandt that conveyed the essence of the US criticism of the European perspective and foreshadowed similar divergences that would appear in other crises in later years (see Chapter 7). Replying to Brandt's explanation of the West German decision to disallow Israeli supply shipments from German depots, Nixon wrote:

> You note that this crisis was not a case of common responsibility for the Alliance, and that military supplies for Israel were for purposes which are not part of the Alliance responsibility. I do not believe we can draw such a fine line when the USSR was and is so deeply involved, and when the crisis threatened to spread to the whole gamut of East–West relations. It seems to me that the Alliance cannot operate on a double standard in which US relations with the USSR are separated from the policies that our Allies conduct toward the Soviet Union . . . A differentiated detente in which the Allies hope to insulate their relations with the USSR can only divide the Alliance and ultimately produce disastrous consequences for Europe.[18]

The wide European dissociation from US policy toward Israel and the Soviet Union, compounded by frustration at being only marginal to a crisis in an area of their own earlier pre-eminence, led to efforts to formulate an independent European position on the Middle East – a project that had been attempted unsuccessfully before the war. On 6 November, EC foreign ministers announced an agreed statement on the Middle East which urged that 'the forces of both sides in the Middle East conflict should return immediately to the positions they occupied on 22 October' (the cease-fire line more favourable to Egypt), and that a peace agreement should include an end to the occupation of Arab territories maintained by Israel since the 1967 war.[19] The EC statement, about which the US had not been consulted, undercut Kissinger's efforts at that time to negotiate a disengagement of Egyptian and Israeli forces by calling for greater Israeli concessions than the Egyptians themselves were demanding. Thus the EC position had the effect of further exacerbating already strained relations with Washington, alienating Israel, and embarrassing Egyptian President Anwar Sadat, who was made to appear less demanding for the Arab cause than were the Europeans themselves.

The immediate effect of the Middle East crisis on European unity was mixed – though on balance, negative. Manifestations of unity in formal declarations and spasmodic appeals were often dissipated by countervailing pulls at the national level as EC countries scrambled for bilateral oil deals to secure their energy supplies and shield themselves from an oil embargo. Moreover, the EC's statement on the Middle East contrasted with the spectacle of the member states failing to aid the Netherlands when it was subjected to a complete Arab oil embargo for its alleged pro-Israeli attitude. Community members argued that aiding the Netherlands would have risked a total embargo against the Nine, which the Arabs had threatened and which would have created a far worse situation. The Dutch crisis was mitigated through the rerouting by oil companies of non-Arab shipments to Rotterdam, and by the Dutch threat to cut off supplies of natural gas to its European partners. Nevertheless, the crisis demonstrated the fragility of European unity when critical national interests were held to be at stake.

The crisis spurred completion of the EC's declaration on the European identity, agreed on at Copenhagen in December 1973. Though generally an unexceptional document, it reflected European concerns developing out of the recent crisis: 'International developments and the growing concentration of power and responsibility in the hands of a very small number of great powers mean that Europe must unite and speak increasingly with a single voice if it wants to make itself heard and play its proper role in the world'.[20] The Nine reaffirmed that they 'should progressively define common positions in the sphere of foreign policy' and pledged themselves to 'increasingly act on the basis of agreed common positions'. Yet the declaration's homage to the need for unity and a distinctive European world role contrasted with the acknowledgement that 'in present circumstances there is no alternative to the security provided by the nuclear weapons of the United States and by the presence of North American forces in Europe'. Thus, the reaffirmation that European security would continue to depend upon the Alliance and US military power signalled limits to the quest for a distinctive European identity and an enhanced European role in world affairs.

Moreover, the significance of the Copenhagen declaration was mocked by the demeaning episode of foreign ministers from several Arab states appearing before the European foreign ministers to demand that the EC increase pressure on Israel to withdraw from all occupied Arab territories. By allowing direct presentation of the

Arab case in such a forum, EC ministers had granted to Arab governments an access to EC deliberations that had been consistently denied
to the United States. This spectacle, combined with the declaration's
affirmation of the indispensability of US defence protection, only
served to underscore Europe's weakness and dependence in the vital
areas of military and energy security.

The February 1974 Washington Energy Conference of industrialised states again tested the strength of European unity, and
again the overall result was mixed. In his December 1973 speech
to the Pilgrims Society in London, Kissinger had proposed the
creation of an energy action group of the major industrialised
countries to develop an action programme for collaboration in all
areas of the energy problem. Yet in an apparent rebuff to the
Kissinger proposal a week before the conference, the EC foreign
ministers adopted a position stating that 'the Washington conference
cannot, above all in its present composition, be transformed into a
permanent organisation . . . it should not serve to institutionalise
a new framework of international cooperation reserved for the
most industrialized countries'.[21] The European Community should
'reserve its total freedom' to decide the form of its energy policy
and its relations with producer countries.

The statement bore the strong imprint of the French view that
the oil-producing states should be involved in energy consultations
at the outset to avoid polarisation between producing and consuming
countries which might further jeopardise European oil supplies. Moreover, Jobert professed to see American hegemonic designs behind
an organisation of industrialised countries in which American economic strength and greater energy self-sufficiency would necessarily
make its influence preponderant. In addition, France was opposed
to any collective action which could restrain the establishment of
bilateral oil and cooperation arrangements with oil-producing states
(which France had already begun to develop). Thus, French opposition to the US proposals was matched by resistance to meaningful
cooperation at the EC level which also might have tied French
hands.

Nevertheless, the facade of European unity crumbled quickly
at the Washington conference when Community members, with
France alone dissenting, agreed to the establishment of an energy
coordinating group, substantially along the lines of the Kissinger proposal. The rigid and blatantly self-serving French position, rejecting
virtually any form of cooperation as proposed by Washington,

contributed to the breakdown of the Community's fragile front, the isolation of France, and the alignment of the conference with the American position. The US proposal to share its own oil supplies in the event of emergency or prolonged shortages contrasted sharply with France's go-it-alone approach and helped build support for the American position. Moreover, the global importance of the American economy, less afflicted by the oil crisis than were the European and Japanese economies, provided added incentive for cooperating with Washington. Finally, the security issue was an underlying reminder of Washington's trump card in any negotiation on interdependence with its allies. President Nixon pointedly told the conference that 'security and economic considerations are inevitably linked and energy cannot be separated from either'.[22]

The European Community's open division at the Washington conference was partly healed by an agreement announced shortly afterward to propose a plan of long-term economic, technical and cultural cooperation with Arab states, the so-called Euro-Arab Dialogue. An eventual meeting was envisaged at the level of foreign ministers, thus giving the dialogue an expressly political character. Though the plan did not include oil-access provisions, the Nixon administration resented its exclusion from the EC's deliberations on a matter of relations between oil-consuming and producing states that had just been discussed at the Washington conference, as well as the manner of the EC action presented as a *fait accompli*. EC governments had been pulled between competing French and American approaches to dealing with the energy crisis which led them to abandon France and align with Washington at the energy conference, only to repair relations later with France and alienate the US in endorsing the Euro-Arab Dialogue.

In the Nixon administration's view, the European Community initiative was the culmination of a long series of adverse European actions since October 1973 – systematic exclusion of the US from EC policy deliberations, nonsupport of US–Israeli resupply efforts, uneven cooperation in shaping UN cease-fire resolutions, the pro-Arab tilt of the Community's position on the Middle East, and the scramble for separate oil and cooperation agreements with Arab states – all of which demonstrated fundamental US–European divergencies in responding to the crisis. In an apparent vindication of European apprehensions about US linkage diplomacy, President Nixon delivered an unusually harsh public assessment following the European proposal to the Arab states:

Now the Europeans cannot have it both ways. They cannot have the United States participation and cooperation on the security front and then proceed to have confrontation and even hostility on the economic and political fronts . . . it is the time when the Europeans as well as we must sit down and determine that we are either going to go along together on both the security and economic and political fronts or we will go separately. . . . In the event that Congress gets the idea that we are going to be faced with economic confrontation and hostility from the Nine, you will find it almost impossible to get Congressional support for continued American presence at present levels on the security front. . . . We are not going to be faced with a situation where the Nine countries of Europe gang up against the United States – the United States which is their guarantee for their security. That we cannot have.[23]

THE CRISIS AND ATLANTIC RELATIONS: OUTCOME AND ASSESSMENT

The effect of the Middle East crisis on the negotiation of the two Atlantic declarations was dramatic, if slow to unfold. In the aftermath of the US military alert and American criticism of European behaviour during the crisis, European NATO members chose to suspend work temporarily on the Atlantic security declaration. However, the consequences for the proposed US–European Community declaration of principles were ultimately more significant. The Atlantic discord generated by the crisis increased the French-led European resistance to inclusion of any reference to partnership, interdependence, or the Atlantic Alliance in the declaration, as proposed by the United States.[24] The European draft stressed the separateness of the European entity and confined its substance to areas of EC competence. Potentially entangling Atlanticist references, with their implications of linkage among security, trade and monetary issues, were avoided.

By December 1973, the cumulative effects of Atlantic declaration diplomacy, the Middle East crisis, and Europe's assertiveness had produced a marked change in the Nixon administration's attitude toward European unity. In his address to the Pilgrims Society in London,[25] Kissinger warned: 'Europe's unity must not be at the expense of Atlantic community. . . . I would be less than frank were I to conceal our uneasiness about some of the recent practices of the European Community in the political field. To present the decisions of a unifying Europe to us as faits accomplis not subject to effective discussion is alien to the tradition of US–European relations'. Explaining the United States' occasional failure to consult adequately as 'a deviation from official policy and established practice – usually under pressure of necessity', Kissinger observed: 'The attitude of the unifying Europe, by contrast, seems to attempt to elevate refusal to consult into a principle defining European identity. To judge from recent experience, consultation with us before a decision is precluded, and consultation after the fact has been drained of content'. Kissinger argued that 'as an old ally the United States should be given an opportunity to express its concerns before final decisions affecting its interests are taken'. Then he warned that the United States 'cannot be indifferent to the tendency to justify European identity as facilitating separateness from the United States'.

Whereas Kissinger's Pilgrims speech reaffirmed US support for European unity 'in all its dimensions, political as well as economic', it was also made clear that such a Europe 'must strengthen trans-Atlantic ties'. Thus, not just any unified Europe would do – but one that would (a) remain accessible to American influence prior to the taking of decisions, (b) acknowledge a debt for US military protection in its security, trade and monetary policies, (c) accept American leadership in the management of East–West crises, and (d) commit the cause of European unity to the higher loyalty of Atlantic solidarity. Following US complaints over the European proposal for cooperation with Arab states, Kissinger remarked at a meeting of congressmen's wives: 'The United States has no objection whatever to an independent European policy. It does have an objection when independence takes the form of basic hostility to the United States. It does have an objection when, in a crisis which can only be dealt with cooperatively, the Europeans deliberately adopt a competitive posture'.[26] Kissinger appeared astonishingly blind to the contradiction of supporting European unity and independence, only so long as such independence was exercised in harmony with US interests.

By March 1974, the Nixon administration had ceased to press for completion of the declaration on relations with the European Community and suspended its involvement in the drafting exercise.[27] Officials let it be known that they believed Europe was drifting toward Gaullism and that the domestic weakness of most European governments prevented them from effectively opposing French policies. Whereas the administration would be prepared to support 'the right kind of united Western Europe', a White House official explained that 'we made a pragmatic judgment that this was not achievable as a practical matter'.[28] In light of the seeming emergence of a Gaullist Europe, further efforts to consolidate a 'partnership' Europe seemed pointless and likely only to exacerbate tensions.

After Washington's complaints about the EC's initiative toward the Arab states, and in view of apparent American indifference over the conclusion of the Atlantic declarations, Bonn sought to repair the damage. Addressing a key complaint voiced in Kissinger's Pilgrims speech, West Germany proposed that the Nine's Political Committee consult with US officials on all proposals affecting American interests, prior to the adoption of recommendations to be considered by the Council of Ministers in the framework of political cooperation. While Kissinger gave Bonn a green light to explore the plan with other EC governments, France predictably opposed the idea on grounds that it would facilitate US interference in the Nine's decision-making process and perpetuate American dominance over Europe.

However, Harold Wilson's newly elected Labour government in Britain, more inclined to conciliate the United States than Prime Minister Heath had been, insisted that its approval for implementing the Community's plan for cooperation with the Arab states would be contingent upon the establishment of adequate consultation provisions with the United States. Defining the approach of the new government, Foreign Minister James Callaghan echoed many of Kissinger's criticisms when he told the House of Commons: 'We repudiate the view that Europe will emerge only out of a process of struggle with the United States'.[29] Professing to be 'very much concerned' about 'the political direction the Community is taking', Callaghan pledged that Britain would resist political consultations within the European Community that take on 'an anti-American tinge'. Faced with a British veto of the French-inspired plan, Foreign Minister Jobert indicated France's acceptance of a modified form of the West German proposal for Community consultation with the United States. The new arrangement was approved by EC foreign ministers in April 1974 at Schloss Gymnich near Bonn, and hence was labelled the 'Gymnich formula'.[30] The agreement provided that any member government could request consultation with the United States at any stage of the Community's decision-making process. Holding such consultations would require unanimous consent of the member governments, though reportedly a gentlemen's agreement was reached to treat requests for consultation with a 'maximum of good will'.[31] The country holding the six month rotating Presidency of the EC Council was authorised to conduct consultations on behalf of the Nine. Moreover, any member government would be free to take up questions bilaterally with the United States or other countries. The Gymnich accord was significant in that it established for the first time an informal procedure for US–EC consultations in the context of European Political Cooperation that continues to apply. The practice developed of holding consultations between State Department officials and the EPC Presidency prior to meetings of EC foreign ministers on matters of common interest to the United States and Europe.[32]

The negotiations for a statement of Atlantic security principles had encountered less difficulty from the start, and a declaration on Atlantic relations was concluded by NATO foreign ministers at a meeting in Ottawa during June.[33] Drawing heavily from a French draft submitted in November 1973, the declaration was unexceptional in that it reaffirmed familiar Alliance verities at a level of abstraction which committed the signatories to little beyond good intentions. Nevertheless, to an unprecedented degree, the declaration reflected a distinctive European presence as a component of the Alliance. Thus, whereas an indivisible common defence was reaffirmed, it was recognised that the near equilibrium of the US–Soviet strategic relationship had caused European defence problems to assume 'a different and more distinct character'. For the first time in a joint Alliance statement, the French and British nuclear forces were alluded to as 'capable of playing a deterrent role of their own contributing to the over-all strengthening of the deterrence of the alliance'.

The 1973 Middle East crisis resulted in divergent US and West European assessments of its significance and implications for their own interests. The Nixon administration viewed the conflict not only in Middle East regional terms but also as a major East–West crisis, which risked an abrupt increase of Soviet influence among the Arab states that 'would have fundamentally altered the East–West political and military balance, with incalculable results'.[34] European leaders, on the other hand, generally did not fully share this view, particularly since the alleged threat of Soviet military intervention had eased by the time they were informed as to why the United States had found it necessary to alert its forces. Different US and European perceptions of the nature of the crisis were compounded by widely differing US and West European dependencies on Middle East oil. Western Europe obtained 72 per cent of its oil and 47 per cent of its total energy requirements from Arab oil-producing countries, in contrast to 19 per cent and 2 per cent, respectively, for the United States.[35] Hence, the Europeans were naturally inclined toward policies least likely to offend the Arab states and toward a posture resentful of unilateral American measures in support of Israel which might alienate the Arabs and implicate Europe.

Divergencies on such substantive issues led to recriminations on the procedural level. The United States, arguing that the rush of events precluded consultations before calling the alert, also appeared to have assumed that the Europeans would concur with the American version of the crisis and accept US leadership in crisis management. When this did not occur, invectives were rapidly traded, against the United States for not consulting, for acting unilaterally and for failing to take into account European interests, against Europe for obstructing US efforts to support Israel and for not consulting prior to undertaking its own Middle East initiatives.

The bickering over lack of consultation was also symptomatic of different perceptions of the respective US and European roles and interests in the Middle East. Kissinger had already piqued European sensitivities in his Atlantic charter speech when he referred condescendingly to the global interests and responsibilities of the United States, compared with Western Europe's regional interests, with the implication that on issues outside of Europe the West Europeans should follow the American lead. Moreover, Kissinger learned that consultation itself provided no assurance that underlying differences could be overcome. Noting that there was no automatic relationship between consultation and agreement, Kissinger observed: 'It is a root fact of the situation that the countries that were most consulted proved among the most difficult in their cooperation and those countries that were most cooperative were least consulted'.[36]

The American assumption that Western Europe would fall into line with US policy in the Middle East came at an untimely moment in view of Western Europe's own recent stirrings toward political cohesion. The European Community had been buoyed by completion of the membership enlargement negotiations and the conclusion of free-trade area agreements linking the remaining members of the European Free Trade Association to the expanded Community of the Nine. The Community was in the process of consolidating and extending its procedures for political consultation, and at the 1972 Paris summit the Nine 'affirmed their intention to transform the whole complex of their relations into a European union by the end of this decade'. Responding to US Atlantic initiatives in 1973, moreover, the Nine became obsessed with defining their own identity as a distinct economic and political entity. The seeming revival of the Community's progress had not yet been dashed by the oil embargo, prolonged recession and monetary disruptions, which were to paralyse the momentum of the early 1970s. In such a setting of optimism and confidence, Europe was in no mood to be leaned on and taken for granted by US attitudes and behaviour which many felt had not adjusted to the European Community's new consciousness and strivings toward unity.

Ironically, 1973/74 witnessed dismaying European impotence and disarray, yet never before had Washington been so annoyed at Europe's attempted displays of unity. The deterioration in Atlantic relations forced a moment of truth as to the compatibility of US notions of Atlantic partnership with the direction of West European unity as perceived by the Nixon administration. The harder the United States pushed its ideas of partnership and their incorporation in statements of Atlantic principles, the harder Western Europe pushed back with expressions of its own identity and independently developed positions. And when the Community proved able to forge a common position, thereby fulfilling a longstanding *abstract* goal of US policy, its efforts met with mounting US suspicion and President Nixon's charge that Western Europe was attempting to 'gang up' against the United States. Thus while US policy had traditionally supported progress toward West European political unity, the Nixon administration was not prepared to accept its attendant implications and risks – namely, that with unity would inevitably come attitudes of self-assertiveness and independence in which European positions might often diverge and even conflict with those of the United States.

The EC agreement on consultations with the United States and the conclusion of the declaration on Atlantic relations were facilitated by leadership changes in Britain and France during the first half of 1974. A new Labour government in Britain declined to support France in its policy of confrontation with the United States and predicated its support of the Euro-Arab initiative on the improvement of Atlantic consultations. The death of President Pompidou in April, the narrow Gaullist victory in the spring elections, the departure of Jobert from the foreign ministry and the more pragmatic leadership style of President Giscard d'Estaing led to a new flexibility in French diplomacy on Atlantic relations. Nevertheless, both agreements bore strong marks of a salvage operation to rescue some measure of consensus from months of Atlantic discord. Neither signified a major *démarche* in US–European relations, despite improvement in procedural consultations via the Gymnich agreement.

Moreover, the Community's growth optimism, typified by the 1972 Paris summit communiqué, proved unable to withstand the economic and monetary shocks brought on by the oil crisis and the upheaval in Atlantic relations. The Community's embryonic monetary snake was an early casualty as the French and Italian economies, facing pressures on their reserves from higher import costs, proved incapable of sustaining their currency parities. Wide disparities in the effects of inflation, recession and unemployment among member countries militated against Community-level measures and tilted governments toward national solutions. The global scope of the energy problem argued for approaches transcending the membership and competence of the European Community. With evident relief, Kissinger later remarked: 'The period in which Europe was attempting to define itself is at least temporarily over. We are now closer to the Atlantic partnership that we envisaged with the year of Europe in 1973'.[37]

Other factors did not augur well for increased political unity in Western Europe. As the European Community's internal momentum dissipated after 1972, major domestic changes in Europe's southern tier resulted in a second phase of enlargement diplomacy intended to stabilise and anchor the newly established democratic systems in Greece, Portugal and Spain. Yet, as suggested by the Community's first enlargement experience, it would prove difficult to reconcile the horizontal broadening of membership with the achievement of deeper vertical integration.

Moreover, the West European position in the wider setting of East–West relations posed other issues which operated to retard unity. Whereas the earlier concern over possible US troop withdrawals produced wary calls for a more concerted European approach to defence problems, by the mid-1970s there was little talk of this and the acceptance of European security dependence on the Alliance became reinforced. In a reversal of the French emphasis on the need for West European defence unity in 1973, Giscard d'Estaing later repudiated such efforts as (a) premature in the absence of political unity and (b) provocative to the Soviet Union and thus damaging to *détente*.[38] Furthermore, prolonged uncertainties over the outcome and implications of the SALT and Mutual and Balanced Force Reduction (MBFR) negotiations militated against structural change in the Alliance. West Germany's potential role as a catalyst for unity was tempered by its own distaste for such a role, for historical reasons, and by wariness among the Nine as to the implications of the Federal Republic's economic preponderance in the Community. Moreover, West Germany's role in the West was partly mortgaged to its interests in the East, where Bonn remained essentially a supplicant. West German aims in the East – including normalisation with East Germany, safeguarding the position of West Berlin and facilitating emigration of ethnic Germans to the Federal Republic – rendered it vulnerable to pressure, should it be inclined to assume a more vigorous role in promoting West European unity.

As discussed in Chapter 2, the traditional US policy of support for West European unity within an Atlantic partnership was developed at a time when Western Europe remained politically divided, essentially impotent and (France excepted) generally accepting of American leadership. Under the Nixon administration, US attitudes changed when the European Community began to behave in a more cohesive and autonomous manner and became more resistant to the American lead. The Nixon administration's handling of Atlantic relations suggests that US support for West European unity was regarded as a necessary part of the political foundation of Atlantic ties, but not to be taken too seriously. As in the early 1950s debate over West German rearmament and the proposed European Defence Community, Europe in 1973 was faced with external pressures which strained its fragile unity. In the latter period, however, there was an established context of Atlantic trade rivalry and a real movement toward the development of a distinctive European political personality, and these posed challenges to the Nixon administration's concept of partnership. This concept, as former Ambassador Schaetzel observed, assumed 'a docile, client-Europe whose proxy would be in the hands of American officials as they went about their negotiations, whether with the Russians or the Arabs'.[39] As West European unity progressed from the abstract to the concrete, it forced to the surface the hitherto mostly latent contradictions of the American concept of partnership. Kissinger's Atlantic charter initiative, the Middle East war, and the oil crisis were external stimuli which both accelerated and confused the European unity momentum that had been slowly under way. Despite Europe's spasmodic and laboured assertiveness, the effects of the crisis dealt a setback to European unity, while Atlantic political relations remained fundamentally unchanged. However, the United States was put on notice that, in cases where the European Community proved able to muster a common position, its alignment with the American point of view could no longer be taken for granted.

The foregoing analysis suggests that the Atlantic crisis was as much a product of conflicting approaches, styles, personalities, timing and situational political constellations as it was the result of differences over issues of substance. The substantive areas of difference in themselves did not compel the escalating pyrotechnics that resulted. Yet the sheer simultaneity of the Atlanticist and European political initiatives was bound to generate debate over the compatibility of the two visions. The Middle East conflict and the oil crisis furnished a highly charged arena conducive to the amplification of what had been only moderately energised differences. The Nixon administration was the first to confront a Europe attempting to speak with a single political voice – and thus a Europe in a position to vindicate or challenge traditional American assumptions about Atlantic partnership. The administration's emphasis upon US–Soviet ties, its secretive diplomatic style, its lapses in Alliance consultation at key points and its tendency to take European concurrence for granted all encouraged responses that aggravated the latent rivalry between the Atlantic and European ideas. In effect, the Nixon administration unwittingly helped to create, if only briefly, the very kind of Europe that was antithetical to its own notions of partnership.

7 The United States and the European Pillar in the late 1970s and the 1980s

AMERICAN AMBIVALENCE TOWARD EUROPEAN UNITY

With the development of the EC's political cooperation since the early 1970s, and with movement toward West European defence cooperation as well, US support for a European pillar in an Atlantic framework continued as a staple of US public diplomacy. As in earlier formulations linking the Atlantic and European ideas, US statements typically have included assumptions and expectations that the emerging West European pillar(s) would reinforce the overall solidarity and strength of the West. Barely more than two years after the bruising Atlantic crisis had challenged the proposition, Henry Kissinger, still Secretary of State during the Ford administration, could affirm to European audiences that the most meaningful Atlantic cooperation 'will occur only after Europe has achieved political unity' (ignoring the earlier pain to the US of European attempts to do just that), and that 'European unity and Atlantic partnership are both essential and mutually reinforcing'.[1] In his address to the European Parliament in 1985, President Reagan invoked Kennedy's Atlantic partnership theme, including its twin pillar imagery, as a continuing aim of US policy.[2] In two major speeches in 1987, Reagan stated that 'the Alliance must become more and more an alliance among equals' and that the US must 'welcome a European identity in defense which . . . is bound to spur Atlantic cooperation'.[3] And while in Europe for the NATO summit in May 1989, President Bush affirmed that the drive toward European unity 'and the transatlantic partnership reinforce each other'.[4]

However, despite the constancy of official US public support for European political unity since the early 1950s, the assumptions and qualifications associated with that support have offered a clearer indication of actual American policy. And the twin pillar model of evolving US–West European relations is at a level of abstraction that provides only limited and often misleading guidance. Public rhetoric notwithstanding, US policy has often manifested reserve, suspicion and even hostility toward the idea of a European pillar, particularly though not exclusively in matters of security and defence – traditionally the turf of NATO. This was particularly the case after the 1973/74 Atlantic crisis and in response to developments in West European political and defence cooperation during the 1970s and 1980s.

Thus during the Ford administration, State Department Counselor Helmut Sonnenfeldt affirmed that the United States would continue to work with European institutions and respond to European initiatives as they emerge, but cautioned that the American attitude would be 'determined by the contribution which can be made to the promotion of our *common* interests'.[5] Thomas Enders, US Ambassador to the EC during the early part of the Reagan administration, captured the essence of American ambivalence toward EC actions in the political field. Noting that the EC had generally taken positions supportive of or complementary to those of the US, he also observed:

> Nevertheless, from the US point of view, the new dynamism of political cooperation is a two-sided development. Where interests or tactics differ, it may work to dramatize differences. More subtly, political cooperation may reinforce the existing European tendency to emphasize political as against security measures, because this is the only avenue open to Europe to act together beyond its borders. And political cooperation caters to the desire of some EC members to define their positions in the world at least partly in opposition to the US.[6]

In 1983, Richard Burt, then Assistant Secretary of State for European Affairs, noted the efforts by EC countries to expand their political cooperation to seek common positions on security issues also of concern to NATO. Then, in what clearly amounted to both a description and an expectation, he observed that the EC countries 'have been careful to insure, however, that questions of defense are left to NATO. The EC does not have, and does not foresee acquiring, an independent defense capability. Our partners clearly understand that the Atlantic alliance is the vital underpinning of Western security'.[7]

Official US support for the revival of the Western European Union in 1984 (see Chapter 9) was qualified by clear signals that Washington would not welcome a European defence caucus should it undermine multilateral NATO consultations by fostering independently developed European positions on matters of Alliance-wide concern. Thus a senior US official remarked: 'We would have reservations [about WEU] if there was the slightest evidence that this would in any way detract from NATO. But everyone has made clear that it will not'.[8] Reportedly, in 1985 the Reagan administration informed the seven WEU members 'in blunt and direct terms that the US saw no need to revitalize the Western European Union, and that any larger European role in defense should take place within NATO'.[9] Similarly, the US made known its reservations should the WEU attempt to develop its own position, apart from NATO, as to the strategic and defence implications of President Reagan's Strategic Defence Initiative.

And in an unusually frank assessment, if not a warning, Stephen Ledogar, then US Deputy Permanent Representative to NATO, wrote in 1986:

> It seems axiomatic . . . that there is very little tolerance . . . for separate uncoordinated initiatives on major East/West security matters by sub-groups of European NATO Allies . . . *there is no way that a sub-caucus of Western European NATO Allies could proceed beyond internal discussions to take up rigid positions* vis-à-vis *the East on arms control matters – departing significantly from those agreed in NATO – without violating the security rights of the US.*[10]

Indeed, Ledogar opined that by and large 'European defense cooperation is not appropriate in what from NATO's perspective is the political spectrum of East/West relations'. Ledogar allowed that after their own meetings, European NATO members could 'sing out in public on a well-known Atlantic tune, provided they stick closely to the score'.

How does one explain the American ambivalence, reserve and even hostility toward significant expansion of the European pillar idea beyond the economic sphere as represented by the EC? Through a combination of instinct, calculation and experience, US policy has seemed attentive to the previously quoted perspective expressed by Henry Kissinger 25 years ago. Noting that 'a separate identity has usually been established by opposition to a dominant power', and that the European sense of identity was unlikely to be an exception to this general rule, Kissinger argued that a united Europe 'is likely to insist on a specifically European view of world affairs – which is another way of saying that it will challenge American hegemony in

Atlantic policy'. Kissinger speculated that a loose intergovernmental European political union would

> permit a more flexible arrangement of Atlantic relations than the "twin pillar" concept now in vogue. A confederal Europe would enable the United States to maintain an influence at many centers of decision rather than be forced to stake everything on affecting the views of a single supranational body . . . a federal Europe is likely to have the greatest incentives for a policy which we tend to identify as a Gaullist [independent] policy, while a confederal Europe would permit us to maintain an influence at many centers and it would probably be, in the long run, less likely to pursue such a policy.[11]

The often made assumption and expectation that the interests and policies of the US and a unifying Western Europe would be broadly convergent and reinforcing bears closer examination in light of the experience during the 1970s and 1980s, as already underscored by the Atlantic crisis discussed in the previous chapter. Indeed, as Richard Burt (then US Ambassador to West Germany) observed after the American bombing raid against Libya in 1986, 'over the past 20 years, however, nearly every crisis in the third world has produced major trans-Atlantic strains: the Vietnam War, the 1973 Middle East conflict, the Iranian hostage crisis, the Soviet invasion of Afghanistan and now Libya'.[12] In Burt's view, the chief cause of the difficulty lay in differing US and West European capabilities for action which led to divergent crisis perceptions and prescriptions.

> In each case, the dominant American impulse was to do something about a situation that Washington was not prepared to accept. In contrast, the Europeans' dominant impulse was to insulate European interests from the consequences of events that they felt powerless to influence directly.
>
> The key to these divergent responses is the differing perceptions of the United States and its allies about their respective capacities to exercise power. For the average American, the lesson of 20th century history has been that our country can wield substantial influence at great distances. Throughout the same period, European nations have seen their power steadily diminish and their overseas role dwindle.

Noting that 'the strains and resentments may be cumulative and seem to be occurring with increasing frequency', Burt warned of the possibility 'that at some point the Western alliance will be undermined in a fundamental and irreversible way'.

> The answer seems clear: a more united and influential Western Europe. . . . A strong and confident Europe would be able to meet, with the United States, common security challenges. A united Europe, of course, might not always agree with the United States, but at least Europe's basic impulse to action, when facing external challenges, would be more like the American impulse, because its capabilities would be more like those of the United States.

Burt's analysis of the problem argued the mainstream official US view since the early 1960s, namely that increased European political unity would facilitate a stronger identity of views at the Atlantic level because the two entities would possess more comparable capabilities. Of course, part of Burt's analysis represents virtually a truism: that a politically more unified Western Europe would feel a stronger impulse to action. But the track record of instances in which Western Europe has been able to act more or less as one challenges the other conclusion by Burt that a unified Europe's impulse to action would be more like that of the United States. It is not at all clear why a politically more unified Western Europe would be conducive to greater harmony in Atlantic relations when numerous examples of collective European action have resulted in striking Atlantic discord. Moreover, Burt's basic premise – that a united Europe's impulse to action when facing external challenges would be similar to America's because of similar *capabilities* is flawed – because it takes inadequate account that Europe's understanding of its *interests*, often divergent from America's, will determine how its capabilities will be applied. This was already apparent from the 1973/74 Atlantic crisis and was further exemplified through US–European encounters in the 1970s and 1980s over specific issues to be examined below. The synopses portray varying US and European reactions to several critical episodes in Atlantic relations. The position of each side had merit within its own frame of reference, though the differences challenge the view that a unifying Western Europe and the United States would develop closer alignment on global issues (see assessment in Chapter 10).

AT ISSUE: THE IRAN HOSTAGE CRISIS

The seizure and captivity of 50 Americans and violation of US embassy grounds by Iranian militants in November 1979 provoked prompt protests by European governments and an EC call for release of the hostages. In response to press reports that the Europeans had been insufficiently supportive of US interests, the State Department disclosed in late November that West European countries had been 'completely forthcoming and cooperative in their response' and that all US requests for support had been met.[13] Yet when Secretary of State Vance met with European leaders in December to explore the possibility of economic sanctions against Iran, the European response was non-committal, though generally supportive of considering sanctions through UN Security Council action. European reservations about imposing economic sanctions at this stage included worries about likely Iranian reprisals in the form of a cutoff of oil supplies, possible disruption of international financial and trade markets, and concern that sanctions would be counterproductive to the aim of securing release of the hostages.

While Vance reportedly did not seek a firm European commitment to sanctions, an administration official stated frankly: 'We're trying to impress upon our allies that unless they cooperate in resolving this crisis, we may be forced to resort to arms, and that would have serious consequences for them as well as us'.[14] President Carter later recalled that it soon became apparent that 'even our closest allies in Europe were not going to expose themselves to potential oil boycotts or endanger their diplomatic arrangements for the sake of American hostages. . . . Only the direct threat of further moves by the United States would have any real effect on some of our friends and on the Iranians'.[15] Significantly, shortly after the Vance visit, EC foreign ministers agreed that they should only act together with respect to sanctions policy toward Iran,[16] thereby shielding individual countries from US pressures to apply sanctions.

The Soviet Union vetoed in the Security Council a US resolution introduced on 10 January 1980 calling for sweeping economic sanctions against Iran, including a suspension of all exports (except food and medical supplies) and a ban on new loans, credits and most new service contracts. The US proposal was supported by Britain and France, the only EC permanent members of the Security Council. In view of the previous EC decision to seek joint action on sanctions policy, it seems likely that the EC as a whole supported the British and

French position. Nevertheless, given the general European reluctance to impose sweeping sanctions against Iran, and the likelihood of a Soviet veto of the measure as had been earlier announced, it is possible that EC countries adopted this course to demonstrate political solidarity with Washington in the expectation that the sanctions themselves would not be applied. As *The Economist* later put it, the Europeans 'have been trying to devise ways not so much of putting pressure on Iran as of demonstrating to the Americans that Europe is a reliable ally'.[17] The immediate US reaction to the Soviet veto was to seek allied support for imposing sanctions anyway, though European resistance to this approach contributed to persuading the administration to delay further measures for the time being.[18] Nevertheless, the administration's initial push for allied agreement on sanctions, followed by postponement of its own action without prior notice, created irritation and confusion in Europe as to the direction and consistency of US policy.[19]

On 7 April, amid continued frustration of attempts to secure the hostages' release, the Carter administration sought to escalate pressure against Iran by severing diplomatic relations, denying new entry visas to Iranian citizens and prohibiting further exports to Iran. Concurrently, the administration sought allied support in the form of suspending or downgrading their own economic and diplomatic ties with Iran. Carter personally advised France's President Giscard d'Estaing that the United States would soon have to take more forceful steps, including military action, and that combined European pressure on Iran could be effective in securing an early resolution of the crisis.[20]

The initial European response was disappointing to the Carter administration. On 10 April, EC foreign ministers issued a declaration that repeated earlier condemnations of Iranian behaviour and regret that the hostages had not been released, though no sanctions were mentioned. However, the way was held open for future action following consideration of a report mandated from EC ambassadors in Tehran on the likelihood of early release of the hostages. There was a continued widespread European view that sanctions might harm prospects for the hostages' release and that the economic and diplomatic isolation of Iran from the West would only serve to push it closer to the Soviet Union. Moreover, though EC dependence on Iranian oil supplies had dropped from 16 per cent in 1978 to under 10 per cent by 1980, an Iranian threat to ban oil exports to countries that participated in economic sanctions contributed to

European hesitations. British officials, concerned about the effect of sanctions on London's international banking relations with Iran, cited domestic legal obstacles to such measures unless authorised by formal Security Council action. West Germany, still Iran's largest trade partner, was reluctant to back sanctions as were other EC states, some of whom also cited domestic legal obstacles. However, it was France, determined not to be 'stampeded into economic warfare with Iran',[21] as one official put it, that spearheaded the weak ministerial declaration. Yet given the earlier determination by EC governments to attempt to act jointly on sanctions policy, France's insistence on a minimalist response appears to have provided not unwelcome cover for other governments which in varying degrees shared the French position, or were not prepared to oppose it.

The Carter administration promptly stepped up pressure on its allies to take further steps against Iran, including a formal break in relations, if the hostages were not soon freed. Stressing that it was 'not a matter of many weeks'[22] for economic and diplomatic measures to show results, for the first time Carter spoke openly about the possible use of military force to resolve the crisis. Such measures could be avoided, Carter pointedly stated, 'to the extent that the allies can join with us in making effective the additional diplomatic and economic pressures' leading to the release of the hostages. Allied leaders were given a specific date, reportedly in the first part of May, for these measures to be effective, after which military means would likely be employed.

Clearly under new and intensified US pressure to act, on 22 April EC foreign ministers agreed to a set of phased economic and diplomatic sanctions against Iran in accordance with the vetoed 10 January Security Council resolution. The decision to impose sanctions on Iran represented the first EC action taken through political cooperation that went beyond mere declaratory statements of position.[23] The first stage, to begin immediately, included a ban on new export and service contracts, suspension of military sales, a reduction of member states' diplomatic staffs in Tehran and of Iranian representation in Europe, and new visa requirements for Iranians travelling to EC countries. The second stage, to be implemented by 17 May if decisive progress had not been achieved toward releasing the hostages, entailed a full embargo on all exports to Iran except for food and medicine. The Carter administration declared that it was pleased with the EC measures, though 'stronger and more immediate action' would have been preferred.

However, European scepticism as to the utility of sanctions had not changed. A major motive for the EC decision was the sense of need to demonstrate solidarity with Washington and avoid damage to the political cohesion of the Alliance. Whereas in the 1973/74 Middle East crisis the Nixon administration had publicly linked expected European solidarity with the preservation of US Alliance commitments, the Carter administration's linkage approach was largely implicit, though no less clearly understood in Europe. Indeed, reportedly one high US official sought to influence West Germany's attitude by pointedly comparing the importance of European solidarity with the US on the hostage issue with American solidarity in support of West Berlin.[24] Reflecting its unique vulnerability to such pressures, West German officials let it be known that Bonn was prepared to impose sanctions unilaterally if need be.

Nevertheless, the most important factor leading to the EC's reluctant embrace of sanctions was the hope that stronger European measures would influence Washington not to resort to force against Iran. This did not reflect EC confidence that sanctions would facilitate release of the hostages, but rather an acquiescence to the American position that Western solidarity on sanctions might preclude or at least delay US military measures. And by supporting Washington on sanctions, the Europeans hoped to gain some influence over any future US consideration of the use of force. Moreover, if EC governments had not endorsed sanctions and the US resorted to force against Iran, the Europeans would have been open to criticism that their lack of support for economic and diplomatic pressure had left Washington no choice but to escalate the crisis.

The aborted US attempt to rescue the hostages, within days after the EC decision to impose sanctions, irritated European governments, though open criticism was muted by a desire not to aggravate Washington's latest setback over the hostage issue. Thus there was a tendency to accept the Carter administration's distinction between a humanitarian rescue attempt and punitive military measures against Iran which Europeans believed their sanctions had at least succeeded in postponing.

Nevertheless, EC countries sharply equivocated as the 17 May date for their imposition of full economic sanctions against Iran drew near. Several countries cited legal difficulties that could expose them to claims for compensation for cancelled merchandise and service contracts that pre-dated the seizure of the hostages. On 18 May, EC foreign ministers substantially diluted their previous position on sanctions by agreeing that the trade embargo would apply only to export contracts signed after 4 November 1979, the date of the seizure of the hostages. The vetoed Security Council resolution of 10 January, which nonetheless, at US request, had guided the EC sanctions decision of 22 April, included an export ban on 'all items, commodities or products' (excepting food and medicines) without distinction as to existing or future contracts, though the ban on services was limited to new contracts. Indeed, the amended EC sanctions were largely symbolic in nature, since by one estimate they were expected to reduce EC exports to Iran by only 8 per cent.[25] Britain broke ranks even on these limited measures, as vigorous domestic opposition to the abrogation of existing agreements forced the Thatcher government to limit sanctions to the prohibition of new contracts with Iran. In any case, the EC trade measures against Iran were taken so late as to be barely implemented before the hostages were released.[26]

AT ISSUE: THE SOVIET INVASION OF AFGHANISTAN

In many respects, US and European responses to the Soviet invasion of Afghanistan in December 1979 paralleled reactions to the largely contemporaneous Iran hostage crisis and the 1973 Middle East war. In all three cases Washington and most European capitals viewed the crises in different terms; the US took steps widely seen in Europe as needlessly confrontational and counterproductive; European reactions tended to oscillate between pressures to show solidarity with the US and strong reservations about following the American lead; and efforts at collective European action were often compromised by internal EC differences.

However, the Afghanistan crisis posed more direct and fundamental questions about overall Western relations with the Soviet Union at a time when the US–Soviet *détente* of the early 1970s had already begun to unravel. As early as 1976, President Ford had declined to use the term *détente* to characterise US–Soviet relations. By the late 1970s, there was a widespread American perception that *détente* had been largely a one way street of technological and agricultural benefits to the Soviet Union, indirectly subsidising the Soviet military buildup without corresponding advantages accruing to the United States. An active and expansionist Soviet global diplomacy belied earlier US expectations that *détente* would yield more restrained Soviet international behaviour. The strategic arms control process, which had been somewhat insulated from the general cooling of US–Soviet relations in the late 1970s, itself fell victim to the demise of *détente* as prospects for Senate ratification of the SALT II Treaty dimmed even before the Soviet invasion of Afghanistan. The announcement of the Carter Doctrine in January 1980, threatening military force against any power seeking to gain control of the Persian Gulf region, accompanied by a wide array of sanctions against the Soviet Union, signalled the formal ending of the US–Soviet *détente* and the US return to a containment strategy emphasis in dealing with the Soviet Union.

The European response to the Soviet invasion was characterised by efforts to demonstrate Western solidarity in denouncing the action, while avoiding punitive measures against the Soviet Union that might risk further damage to *détente*. In contrast to the American experience, *détente* was working in Europe and there was a clear reluctance to jeopardise its gains and prospects by joining Washington in a renewed confrontational posture toward the Soviet Union.

In particular, West Germany's *Ostpolitik* had produced tangible progress in transforming the Federal Republic's relations with its Eastern neighbours. The normalisation of diplomatic relations, the stabilisation of West Berlin's status and ties to the West, increased inter-German travel and contacts, the repatriation of nearly 300 000 ethnic Germans from the east to the Federal Republic in the 1970s, and expanded trade and investment relations with Soviet bloc countries had established a major West German stake in the preservation of *détente* in Europe. As West German Chancellor Helmut Schmidt warned: 'All this could come to a standstill. So you will understand that the divided nation of Germans . . . is not in a position to act as a spearhead or as a forerunner in a conflict between two superpowers'.[27] Thus the continued success of *Ostpolitik*, including movement toward ending or humanising the German division, was seen as dependent on sustained progress in East–West *détente* in Europe with the necessary cooperation of the Soviet Union.

Moreover, European assessments of Soviet motives differed from those prevalent in the Carter administration. No European leader echoed President Carter's characterisation of the Soviet invasion as 'the greatest threat to peace since the Second World War' which, if unchecked, would no doubt tempt the Soviet Union 'to move again and again until they reached warm water ports or until they acquired control over a major portion of the world's oil supplies'.[28] While not directly challenging US assessments of the crisis, Europeans tended to view the Soviet Union as motivated more by the need to restore its crumbling position in Afghanistan and stabilise its own bordering Islamic regions against the tide of Iranian inspired religious fundamentalism, than as a harbinger of a new Soviet expansionist thrust toward the Persian Gulf.

Given divergent US and West European perceptions of the significance of the crisis and differing value commitments to *détente*, it is hardly surprising that the Soviet invasion of Afghanistan resulted in uneven responses within the Alliance. Beneath the veneer of allied solidarity in denouncing the invasion and calling for a Soviet withdrawal, France and West Germany tended to downplay the crisis and avoided full association with the Carter administration's more confrontational approach. Schmidt warned of the 'deadly game' that could ensue from American plans for a military containment response in the Persian Gulf region to the Soviet presence in Afghanistan.[29] On 5 February, Schmidt and French President Giscard d'Estaing declared that '*détente* could not withstand a further shock of the same magnitude',[30] thus implicitly acknowledging that in their view *détente* had survived the Soviet invasion. Indeed, in June, Schmidt candidly told a Social Democratic Party Congress: 'We have made great efforts in past months to make sure that, despite intensified tensions in the world, the *détente* process in Europe would not be damaged but further strengthened'.[31]

France, less constrained than West Germany by security dependence on the US, opposed American efforts to build a Western consensus for sanctions against the Soviet Union and to use Alliance consultations for this purpose. Thus France rejected participation in a meeting of several Alliance foreign ministers planned for 20 February in Bonn to consider further steps in response to the crisis. On 20 January, President Carter had announced his intention to call for a boycott of the summer 1980 Olympic Games scheduled in Moscow if Soviet troops were not withdrawn from Afghanistan within a month. French officials viewed the Bonn meeting as a further American effort to muster European support behind the US sanctions approach, despite the fact that France had already made known its opposition to an Olympic boycott. Moreover, in the French view efforts to orchestrate a collective Alliance response would unwisely transform the crisis into an East–West confrontation, facilitate American domination in determining Western policy, and limit the flexibility of European governments to choose options in light of their own perceptions of interest. In a classic expression of traditional Gaullist views, Giscard expressed irritation at efforts to push France toward alignment and disparaged 'the reconstitution of the system of blocs that increase tension . . . and eliminate the margin for maneuver and the influence of France's foreign policy. . . . Any meeting that would result in a bloc approach to the current situation will not win French participation'.[32]

Indeed, it often appeared that the main European problem was not so much how to respond to the Soviet invasion as how to respond to American pressures for strong sanctions against the Soviet Union. The conflicting pull between US expectations of Alliance solidarity behind punitive measures against Moscow and the European preference for caution and restraint led to ambiguity in European public statements. Thus on 15 January, EC foreign ministers declared their continued support for *détente* while acknowledging, in line with the US view, that '*détente* is indivisible and has a global dimension',[33] thereby implying that European *détente* could not be isolated from the effects of the Afghanistan crisis. Yet the interest in European immunity was evident in the EC characterisation of the Soviet action as 'a threat to peace, security and stability in the region, including the Indian subcontinent, the Middle East and the Arab World' (that is, not necessarily to Europe).

The main initial US sanctions, announced by President Carter on 4 January, included a suspension of further high technology and other strategic exports to the Soviet Union, an embargo on the sale of 17 million tons of grain in excess of the 8 million tons that the US was obligated to sell to Moscow under terms of a previous bilateral agreement, severe curtailment of Soviet fishing rights in American waters, and the deferral of most Soviet–American cultural exchange programmes.

On 15 January EC foreign ministers endorsed the principle that Community agricultural exports to the Soviet Union must not replace, directly or indirectly, agricultural commodities included in the US embargo. The EC also agreed to a temporary suspension of subsidised sales of butter to the Soviet Union and to end its food aid programme to Afghanistan since the intended destination to the Afghan people could not be guaranteed. The EC no-substitution pledge on embargoed US farm exports included assurance that 'traditional patterns' of agricultural trade with the Soviet Union would be respected. However, given the highly erratic nature of recent EC farm exports to the Soviet Union, it was hard to determine what this pledge actually meant. Outside the agricultural sector, there was also general agreement that EC countries would not undercut the US embargo on high technology exports to the Soviet Union with replacement contracts of their own.

Nevertheless, US officials expressed disappointment that the EC was unwilling to go beyond its no-substitution policy to apply punitive economic measures of its own. Indeed, EC countries reaped major benefits in exports to the Soviet Union in the wake of the US sanctions policy. While US–Soviet trade dropped by 60 per cent in 1980, Franco-Soviet trade increased by 100 per cent, West German–Soviet trade by 65 per cent, and Italian–Soviet trade by 35 per cent.[34] A report later issued by the European Parliament charged that the EC Commission had allowed a major expansion of farm exports to the Soviet Union in 1980 beyond the average for the previous three years.[35] However, while substantial increases in most EC agricultural exports to the Soviet Union did occur in 1980, they appear largely attributable to the fulfilment of previously signed contracts.

EC governments remained divided on whether to take additional collective measures beyond those announced on 15 January. While Britain supported firmer EC backing of the US position, and took some unilateral steps of its own, France and West Germany resisted sanctions that went beyond the Community's no-substitution pledge for embargoed American farm products. While there were widespread European misgivings as to the appropriateness of threatening to boycott the Moscow Olympics, the Western solidarity argument likely would have prevailed had it not been for resolute French opposition. Thus EC foreign ministers, meeting in Rome on 19 February, the day before Carter's proposed deadline for announcing the Olympic boycott, were unable to agree on unified support of the US position. In the end West Germany, alone among major West European governments, agreed to back Washington in boycotting the Moscow Olympics. Despite Bonn's own strong reservations about the boycott, West Germany's unique security vulnerability and dependence virtually compelled alignment with Washington on the issue. As Foreign Minister Genscher frankly stated the West German motivation: 'We expect solidarity from the United States in the Berlin question and we will not deny them our solidarity in the question of the Olympic Games'.[36]

The general European reluctance to join the US in punitive sanctions against Moscow was partly offset by a willingness of some countries to undertake positive measures to promote stability in the region such as through increased economic support for Pakistan, India and Turkey. Politically, internal EC differences over the Olympics boycott issue at the Rome ministerial meeting contrasted with unanimous support for a British plan to propose a Soviet troop withdrawal in the context of a neutralised Afghanistan under international guarantees. The US endorsed the idea, indeed Carter himself had earlier suggested it, though it was not viewed by Washington as a viable initiative nor as a substitute for the stiffer measures the Europeans were being asked to adopt. Indeed, in one respect the EC proposal ran counter to the American strategy, since the desire for a favourable reaction from Moscow to the neutralisation idea could be used as a justification for the EC not to take additional sanction measures. Presidential National Security Affairs Advisor Zbigniew Brzezinski later publicly urged the allies to take more 'tangible actions' against the Soviet Union, remarking that a policy of 'rhetorical unity and substantive passivity'[37] was not acceptable.

AT ISSUE: THE POLISH CRISIS OF 1981/82

Initial US and European reactions to the declaration of martial law in Poland on 13 December 1981 were broadly similar. In the absence of evidence of Soviet involvement, the action of the Jaruzelski government was deplored but characterised as an internal affair. Whereas a year earlier NATO governments had developed contingency plans for responding to a possible Soviet intervention in Poland, there was little anticipation that the growing political unrest in the country would be met with a crackdown from within. Caught by surprise, the initial collective reaction of EC foreign ministers on 15 December was merely an expression of 'concern' over the imposition of martial law coupled with a call to refrain from outside interference in the internal affairs of Poland.

On 23 December President Reagan, in announcing a range of economic sanctions to be imposed on Poland, also moved to directly implicate Moscow, charging that the events in Poland had been 'precipitated by public and secret pressure from the Soviet Union'.[38] Insisting that the Soviet Union bore 'a major share of blame for the developments in Poland', Reagan warned of political and economic measures against the Soviet Union if the repression continued. British and French leaders also asserted a measure of Soviet responsibility for the crackdown, though in milder terms.[39] However the West German reaction, while strongly critical of the establishment of martial law, continued to avoid public accusations of Soviet responsibility and resisted moves toward sanctions against Poland or the Soviet Union. Closely paralleling earlier West German policy during the Afghanistan crisis, the Schmidt government appeared intent on minimising damage to its *Ostpolitik* by avoiding measures that could further aggravate East–West tensions. Thus an EC statement issued on the day of Reagan's announced sanctions, while stronger in its condemnation of repression in Poland, was silent on the issues of sanctions and Soviet responsibility. EC countries did agree to suspend official food aid shipments to Poland, pending assurances that deliveries would be made directly to the Polish people.

On 29 December, citing heavy and direct Soviet responsibility for continued repression in Poland, Reagan announced unilateral US sanctions against the Soviet Union including suspension of export licences for computers, electronic equipment and other high-technology materials; suspension of new licences for sales of oil and gas equipment, including that needed for construction of the Soviet natural gas pipeline to Western Europe; closing of the Soviet Purchasing Commission office in New York; postponement of negotiations for a new long-term US–Soviet grain purchase agreement and maritime accord; the non-renewal of several soon-to-expire science and technology and exchange agreements; and suspension of Soviet airline flights to the United States.[40] US allies were asked to take parallel measures or at least not to allow the American actions to be undermined. Despite the sweeping nature of the sanctions, their immediate impact on US–Soviet trade was marginal, affecting only around 12 per cent of US sales. This was because the Carter administration's restrictions on grain shipments to the Soviet Union, which represented about two-thirds of US exports, had been lifted in April 1981 and were unaffected by the new measures.

Faced with mounting pressure from the US and some European leaders for a firmer stand on the Polish crisis, the Schmidt government yielded on the issue of Soviet responsibility. At a special meeting on the crisis on 4 January 1982, EC foreign ministers noted their concern and disapproval of 'the serious external pressure and the campaign directed by the USSR and other Eastern European countries against the efforts for renewal in Poland' and issued a 'solemn warning' against any open intervention by the Warsaw Pact.[41] However, on the matter of economic sanctions, the EC declined to follow the American lead, agreeing only to avoid measures that could undermine the effects of US sanctions. Closely mirroring their response to the Afghanistan crisis, EC governments thus agreed not to allow replacement of American contracts barred by US sanction measures. Indeed, once again the EC provided a useful framework for orchestrating a collective position and reducing the vulnerability of individual European countries to bilateral pressure from Washington.

US–European alignment on responses to the Polish crisis was advanced at a special NATO ministerial session on 11 January, though only modestly with respect to the Soviet Union.[42] With regard to Poland, it was agreed to suspend future commercial credits for non-food purchases and to postpone negotiations relating to possible rescheduling of payments due on Poland's official foreign debts. However, Alliance members agreed only to 'examine' their economic and commercial relations with the Soviet Union. While identifying certain sanction measures that might be taken, it was recognised that any action would be in accordance with the 'situation and laws' of each country. Indeed, during the two month period following the NATO meeting, West Germany approved government guaranteed loans for exports to the Soviet Union totalling over $500 million.[43] Working within Cocom, the organisation of industrial states that regulates sales of sensitive products to communist countries, the US did secure allied agreement on restricting sales of some computer and electronic equipment, though European members opposed export restrictions on ten critical technologies as proposed by the United States.[44]

Nevertheless, EC countries did move somewhat closer to the Reagan administration's position on sanctions toward the Soviet Union. Preceded by largely symbolic diplomatic and economic restrictions on relations with Moscow announced by Britain and West Germany, EC foreign ministers agreed in February to limit imports from the Soviet Union as a gesture of disapproval of its support for martial law in Poland. However, as eventually approved, the restrictions applied to only about 1.4 per cent of EC imports from the Soviet Union.[45] While the Reagan administration's own sanctions had only a limited impact on the Soviet Union and US export interests, it is clear that European governments were even more unprepared to accept damage to their trade relations with the Soviet Union. In addition, despite tough US talk about punishing Moscow, Europeans were more impressed by the Reagan administration's unwillingness to harm American farm interests by embargoing grain sales to the Soviet Union.

AT ISSUE: THE SOVIET GAS PIPELINE DISPUTE

Overarching the Atlantic debate on the Afghanistan and Polish crises was the festering dispute over the proposed Soviet natural gas pipeline to Western Europe. Upon completion, initially anticipated by 1984, the pipeline was expected eventually to supply five member states of the EC with nearly one-third of their gas needs or almost 6 per cent of their overall energy consumption. As the largest East–West commercial deal ever attempted, the pipeline project offered lucrative equipment contracts for European industries, profits for European lending institutions, and the prospect of new jobs to alleviate the highest European unemployment levels since World War II. Moreover, Soviet gas supplies promised to reduce European energy dependence on uncertain and costly Middle East oil. Finally, the pipeline project would reinforce West European efforts to strengthen *détente* by forging a structure of economic interdependence with the Soviet Union which, in the European view, would contribute to reducing East–West tensions.

European discussions with the Soviet Union, underway since 1978, reached a decisive stage in November 1981 with the conclusion of a major agreement between Moscow and West Germany's largest gas distributor providing for approximately $45 billion in Soviet gas deliveries over the next 25 years, nearly doubling West German dependence on Soviet gas supplies. France followed suit in January 1982 with a similar though smaller accord with Moscow, after President Reagan had announced US sanctions against the Soviet Union, including an embargo on gas and oil equipment, in response to the alleged Soviet complicity in the establishment of martial law in Poland. Italy also announced agreement in principle on a gas supply contract with Moscow.

The Reagan administration, which had tried unsuccessfully to block the pipeline plan by encouraging Europe to adopt energy alternatives, mounted pressure against the European allies to reconsider their commitments to the project and also to implement restrictive export credit policies toward Moscow. US sanctions imposed in the wake of the Polish crisis had already stopped plans by several American companies to supply equipment for the pipeline. In the administration's view, the gas supply and export credit issues had become litmus tests of the allies' willingness to adopt an appropriate response to recent Soviet actions in Afghanistan and Poland. Given the hesitant and limited nature of concrete European measures endorsed thus far, a business as usual approach on the pipeline project would send the wrong message to Moscow, while underscoring the European interest in preserving and strengthening *détente* in spite of recent Soviet behaviour and the sharp deterioration in US–Soviet relations. In addition, US officials argued that substantial dependence on Soviet energy supplies would further disincline European governments from taking stern measures toward Moscow should a future crisis arise, while increasing European vulnerability to threats, intimidation or subtle pressures by the Soviet Union.

Finally, the administration warned of the beneficial effects on the Soviet economy of its gas sales to Europe at a time of deepening East–West tension and expanding Soviet military programmes. Already dependent on oil and gas exports for the great bulk of its hard currency earnings, prospective new gas sales from the pipeline would enable the Soviet Union to sustain strong export earnings by cushioning the effects of projected declining revenues from oil sales. This, in turn, would strengthen the Soviet economy by enabling acquisition of advanced equipment and technologies from the West, while aiding the Soviet military buildup by permitting deferral of hard choices in resource allocations between the military and civilian sectors of the economy.

The summit conference of industrialised countries, meeting at Versailles in early June 1982, appeared to have produced an understanding, though not so stated in the communiqué, that the US would not take further steps to block the pipeline project in exchange for the allies' willingness to adopt more stringent export credit policies toward the Soviet Union.[46] However on 18 June President Reagan announced the extension of previous US sanction measures to include foreign companies or subsidiaries of American companies producing equipment for the pipeline under US licenses.[47] Acting under its interpretation of authority under the 1979 Export Administration Act, the administration's move had a direct application to several European companies that had already contracted for production of pipeline equipment. At issue was the administration's assertion of US trade policy jurisdiction over foreign subsidiaries or licensees of American companies, including the requirement that they comply with any trade sanctions as invoked unilaterally by the United States. Such companies that violated the ban by shipping pipeline equipment to the Soviet Union would be subject to denial of any exports or data from the United States, whether or not related to oil or gas, as well as other possible penalties including fines.

The immediate effect of the Reagan action was to widen the scope of the Atlantic debate beyond the coordination and management of East–West relations in the context of the Polish crisis. At issue now for European governments was the far more provocative matter of the US assertion of extraterritorial jurisdiction over the activities of companies located within their own sovereign borders. The European reaction was quick and sharp. On 23 June EC foreign ministers declared that the new US measures, taken without any consultation with the EC, were 'contrary to the principles of international law' and 'unacceptable' to the Community.[48] In July, major European governments took steps to oppose the US action and to signal their determination to proceed with the pipeline project. Britain invoked a trade law that placed the Thatcher government in a position to take legal steps to prevent the US embargo from affecting British companies. West German banks, backed by government guarantees, agreed to extend $1.6 billion in export credits to the Soviet Union for pipeline equipment at substantially lower interest rates than had been urged by the Reagan administration for commercial contracts with Moscow. France led the way in direct defiance of the new US embargo by instructing French companies to fulfil their contracts for pipeline equipment. Italy, Britain and West Germany later followed suit and ordered or encouraged their companies to fulfil contracts in defiance of the American ban. France's Foreign Minister Claude Cheysson spoke openly of a 'progressive divorce' developing between the US and its European allies and warned that the Reagan action 'could well go down as the beginning of the end of the Atlantic Alliance'.[49]

The European reaction was fuelled by anger that the main burden of the new American sanctions would fall on Europe rather than the United States, where far smaller commercial interests were at stake. And Europeans found not a little hypocrisy in the Reagan administration's attempt to deny important economic advantages to Europe, while it had restored commercial benefits to American farmers by ending the Soviet grain embargo in 1981 and reaching a new grain accord with Moscow shortly after announcing its most recent pipeline sanctions. Europeans were generally unimpressed by the administration's distinction between the gas supply deal, which would enable the Soviet Union to earn hard currency from the West, and grain sales, which would force Moscow to spend it.

In a strongly worded official protest delivered to the Reagan administration on 14 July, the EC called for withdrawal of the embargo as applied to European firms and reiterated that the US action could not be accepted by the Community.[50] In a lengthy critique of the administration's action delivered in mid-August, the EC argued that the 'sweeping extensions of US jurisdiction' were contrary to international law and constituted 'an unacceptable interference in the independent commercial policy of the EC'.[51] Moreover, the EC argued that the US measures would be unlikely to delay materially the pipeline's construction since the Soviet Union could produce the equipment components denied by the American embargo. Thus a perverse effect of the US action could be to encourage expansion of Soviet manufacturing capabilities in energy-related equipment, thereby neutralising the effects of the embargo while promoting Soviet technological independence from the West. Citing the 'seriously damaging' effects on European interests, the EC warned that the US action could jeopardise future technological links between European and American companies, if contracts could be nullified unilaterally by the US government.

Atlantic tensions heightened in late August, when the Reagan administration announced sanctions against two French companies and a British firm for defying the embargo on orders from their governments. Placed on a temporary denial list, the companies were barred from acquiring US oil and gas technology and equipment. In the weeks that followed, other European firms were blacklisted for defying the embargo.

Nevertheless, the united EC stance against the extraterritorial extension of the embargo, combined with mounting congressional opposition to all US pipeline sanctions, prodded the administration to search for ways to avoid further confrontation over the issue. After weeks of negotiations, in November President Reagan announced the ending of the US pipeline embargo in the context of 'substantial agreement' with the allies on an overall economic strategy toward the Soviet Union.[52] Agreement was reported not to engage in trade which would enhance the military or strategic advantage of the Soviet Union or preferentially aid its economy, and to strengthen existing controls on the transfer of strategic items to the Soviet Union. No new contracts for purchase of Soviet natural gas were to be concluded pending the outcome of a feasibility study on energy alternatives. It was further agreed to establish procedures for monitoring financial relations with the Soviet Union and to seek to harmonise export credit policies.

It is clear that the Reagan administration had come to recognise, albeit belatedly, that its sanctions policy was producing deep divisions within the Alliance, alienating the American business community, and provoking resistance in Congress, while achieving little more than some delay in the eventual completion of the pipeline. A Central Intelligence Agency (CIA) study completed in August, substantially corroborating conclusions reached by the EC, forecast that the Soviet Union 'will succeed in meeting its gas delivery commitments to Western Europe through the 1980s', and that problems posed by the American sanctions in building the new pipeline 'should delay commencement of deliveries till no later than the end of 1985'.[53]

While the November accord was portrayed as a consensus for stronger and more effective allied economic measures toward the Soviet Union, thereby justifying an end to Washington's own pipeline sanctions, the substance of the agreement was modest. Given the Soviet–West European gas supply arrangements made during the previous 12 months, the agreement to temporarily not conclude new contracts may simply have barred what was unlikely to occur in any case during the relatively short expected time-frame of the study on energy alternatives. And beyond the establishment of procedures to monitor financial relations with the Soviet Union, the agreement did little more than articulate largely uncontroversial principles with the specifics left for future determination. Nevertheless, the agreement enabled the Reagan administration to make a face-saving retreat from its sanctions policy through the claim of restored allied unity on economic policy toward the Soviet Union. France struck a dissonant note by publicly dissociating itself from the agreement, charging that it had not been finalised and that Reagan's announcement had been premature. The Mitterrand government had rejected Washington's linkage between the ending of US sanctions and the new allied agreement, insisting that the unilaterally imposed American sanctions should also be lifted unilaterally without the appearance of quid pro quo concessions from the allies. Nonetheless, France did not dissent from the main substance of the agreement.

AT ISSUE: THE US BOMBING RAID ON LIBYA

US–European differences over responding to Libyan supported terrorism had been a continuing though low-keyed Atlantic issue years before the US bombing of suspected Libyan terrorist support facilities in April 1986. While US–Libyan relations had deteriorated since the burning of the US embassy in Tripoli in 1979, by mid-1981 the new Reagan administration was determined to pursue a more confrontational approach in opposition to the policies of Libya's leader Col. Muammar Qaddafi, including reports of plots to assassinate high US officials. In May, Libyan diplomatic personnel in the US were expelled, remaining US diplomats in Libya were withdrawn, and Americans were advised not to travel to or remain in Libya. In August, US Navy jets shot down two Libyan fighters in disputed airspace over the Gulf of Sidra after being fired on by one of the Libyan aircraft. By December, the Reagan administration had stepped up pressure on Americans to leave Libya and was considering other measures, including a possible oil boycott.

The European response to American efforts to isolate and pressure Qaddafi was uniformly non-supportive in 1981. In September, EC foreign ministers agreed not to take any measures against Libya,[54] a move which dashed the Reagan administration's hopes for concerted allied action while casting doubt on the practicality of further unilateral American moves. Europeans doubted the effectiveness of confrontational policies in moderating Libyan behaviour and believed that efforts to isolate the country would likely exacerbate rather than blunt Qaddafi's radical tendencies. European scepticism of the utility of economic sanctions, also evident in the Afghanistan, Polish and Iranian hostage crises, argued against such an approach toward Libya as well. Libya's position as the tenth most important exporter to the EC, Italy's main oil supplier and West Germany's third largest, and the some 40 000 Europeans employed in Libyan industries also inclined the EC toward a more moderate stance than Washington.

Nevertheless, the Reagan administration continued to curtail ties with Libya through the banning first of crude oil imports in 1982 and eventually of refined petroleum products in 1985. Libya was acutely vulnerable to economic pressure, though not by American means alone. Libyan oil sales, the source of 90 per cent of its export earnings, had dropped from $20 billion in 1980 to $8 billion in 1985 due to price declines, sharply reducing available financing for government programmes.[55] Moreover, approximately 80 per cent of Libyan oil was exported to European countries, mainly Italy and West Germany. Thus cooperation from Europe would be essential to the success of any effort to exert economic coercion on Qaddafi.

In January 1986, the Reagan administration initiated a more intensive campaign of economic, diplomatic and military pressure against Qaddafi in response to alleged Libyan responsibility for terrorist bombing attacks in December at the Rome and Vienna airports which killed 19 people, including 5 Americans. On 7 January Reagan imposed a total ban on all non-humanitarian trade and commercial transactions with Libya, a prohibition on travel to Libya except for journalists, and ordered remaining Americans to leave the country. While in the early 1980s the administration had not pressed for supportive European action against Libya, on this occasion Reagan denounced Qaddafi as a 'pariah in the world community' and called on 'our friends in Western Europe and elsewhere to join with us in isolating him'.[56] Given the progressive diminution of US–Libyan economic links over the 1981–85 period, clearly the new American sanctions in themselves would have a negligible effect on the Libyan economy. In the following weeks, the administration conducted a vigorous though unsuccessful effort to secure European alignment with the American position. Deputy-Secretary of State John Whitehead presented the administration's case to European leaders in January, though while making a strong circumstantial case for Libyan involvement, other US officials acknowledged that conclusive 'smoking gun' evidence was lacking.[57]

Even before Reagan's announcement of sanctions, European governments made known their distaste for Washington's latest campaign against Qaddafi, particularly in the absence of what to them was conclusive evidence of Libyan responsibility for the airport bombings. Within a week after the attacks West Germany, Libya's second largest European trading partner, announced its disapproval of economic sanctions, citing their ineffectiveness and often counterproductive results. Italy, which received 20 per cent of its total energy needs from Libyan oil and gas exports and was its largest European trading partner, was also unwilling to impose sanctions. Moreover the nearly 15 000 Italians working in Libya and Italy's geographic vulnerability to possible Libyan retaliation contributed to the government's cautious approach. Similar scepticism as to the advisability of sanctions was voiced by Britain and France. Furthermore, Europeans were concerned that the sharply confrontational American posture could aggravate East–West tensions, as the Soviet Union had accused the United States of using the airport bombings as a pretext for escalating pressure against Libya with whom Moscow had close ties. Europeans also believed that punitive US measures against Qaddafi would evoke a David and Goliath image of the confrontation, producing sympathy for Libya and eliciting expressions of solidarity from other Arab governments. Concern for the fate of their hostages held in the Middle East was a further source of European caution.

As in the other cases studied of US–European policy differences, the reaction of European governments was to seek to channel bilateral American pressures for action into the multilateral political coopera- tion machinery of the EC. By invoking the theme of European unity as the appropriate framework for their response – a longstanding professed aim of Washington as well – European governments could be shielded from American pressures to act individually against their instincts while multilaterally diffusing responsibility for whatever col- lective position should emerge.

The results of the first EC foreign ministers' meeting on the Libyan crisis on 27 January were a sharp if not unexpected disappointment for the Reagan administration. While condemning the Rome and Vienna bombings and terrorism in general, the EC statement omitted any reference to Libya at the insistence of Greece and Spain with support from France and Italy.[58] The EC agreement not to export arms to countries 'clearly implicated in supporting terrorism', again without naming Libya, left it to each country to determine to whom the arms embargo would apply, notwithstanding the explanation of some officials that the intent was to ban arms sales to Libya. In any case, the agreement essentially only transformed existing practice into EC policy since only Italy had exported significant quantities of arms to Libya since 1984, and such sales were stopped following the Rome airport bombing (a move which challenged the consistency of the later Italian reluctance to name Libya as a country support- ing terrorism). Closely paralleling their response to US sanctions in the other crises studied, EC governments agreed to do all in their power to prevent their businesses from taking commercial advan- tage of measures adopted by other countries in response to terrorist activities.

A major reason for the tempered European stance toward Libya, as well as a major concern over the direction of American pol- icy, was that attempts to isolate and punish Qaddafi could provoke increased terrorist activity and an escalation of violence in Europe and the Mediterranean. It is ironic that the EC position contributed unwittingly to the very outcome it sought to avoid by increasing the Reagan administration's sense of frustration and isolation in dealing with Qaddafi, hence encouraging it toward unilateral military measures. Given its inability to muster support for broad Western diplomatic and economic sanctions against Libya, the administration was persuaded that its only recourse was increased military pressure. The result was not long in coming.

In March, US ships and planes clashed with Libyan forces in the Gulf of Sidra, having crossed Qaddafi's so-called 'Line of Death' into territorial waters claimed by Libya, though regarded as international waters by the United States and West European governments. While the US action was explained as an assertion of the right of free passage through international waters, American officials acknowledged that its purpose was less to uphold a principle of international law than to provoke Qaddafi,[59] while signalling to European governments that more punitive military actions might be taken if they refrained from meaningful sanctions against Libya.[60] The European reaction was mixed. While most governments did not question the right of US naval forces to operate in the Gulf of Sidra, concern was expressed about the military confrontation that had occurred and the potential for a further spiralling of hostilities. However Italy, angered by the use of its ports for the American move against Libya, openly criticised the American action as a provocative military escalation and called on Washington to refrain from similar moves in the future. Wishing to minimise the public airing of allied differences, the administration chose not to seek a declaration of support for its position from the North Atlantic Council.

Tensions heightened following the death of two people and injury of over 200 persons, including 64 Americans, in the 5 April bombing of a discotheque in West Berlin, believed to have been directed from the Libyan mission in East Berlin. Amid widespread reports that the United States was considering military reprisals against Libya, accompanied by American naval movements toward the Libyan coast, EC foreign ministers held an emergency meeting on 14 April. The meeting was also prompted by a recent threat from Qaddafi to strike at US and NATO bases in southern Europe should the United States attack Libya. Indeed, Qaddafi later carried out the threat in a limited way immediately following the American bombing raid by the firing of two missiles at a US Coast Guard navigation station on an Italian island.

Given the conflicting EC interests at play, and plagued by its own internal divisions, the EC meeting could produce but meagre results. While most governments at this stage found US evidence of Libyan complicity in the West Berlin bombing inconclusive, and thus were unwilling to join Washington's punitive measures, they also did not wish to appear intimidated by Qaddafi's threats of reprisals against Europe and the vulnerability of their own citizens in Libya. Still firmly opposed to military and economic pressures, they also wanted to demonstrate a measure of solidarity with the United States and head-off further US military action which could trigger Libyan retaliation against Europe.

The result of these disparate tendencies was agreement on a package of relatively mild measures[61] which fell well short of American calls for more punitive action. EC ministers did agree for the first time to name Libya as a country clearly implicated in supporting terrorism. It was also determined to impose stricter visa requirements for Libyans desiring to enter EC countries and to reduce the staffs of Libyan diplomatic and consular missions while restricting the movement of remaining personnel. Most EC members opposed a Dutch proposal, supported by Britain, that all Libyan diplomatic missions in the EC be closed. Economic sanctions were not even discussed. Qaddafi's threats against EC member states were rejected as unacceptable, and Libya was warned that any such action would be met with a vigorous and appropriate response. In a clear reference to possible US military action against Libya, EC ministers called for 'restraint on all sides' to avoid further escalation of tensions. Despite expressions of hope by European officials that their moves would forestall direct US military action, there was probably little confidence that this would be the case. Indeed some EC governments, notably Britain, France and Spain, had been broadly apprised of US military intentions days before the EC meeting in connection with efforts to secure operational support including overflight rights for the mission.[62]

The American bombing of Libyan terrorist targets, within hours after the 14 April EC meeting, provoked generally negative reactions from European publics and their governments.[63] Only Britain's Prime Minister Thatcher, who had consented to the use of American bases in Britain for the launching of the raid, provided full public support. The French and Spanish governments, which had denied permission for US aircraft to overfly their territories *en route* to Libya, were openly critical, while the most vocal condemnation came from Italy and Greece. One European official characterised the US action as 'a slap in the face for Europe' while Italian Prime Minister Craxi, alluding to the EC's tightened diplomatic restrictions toward Libya, complained that 'the position adopted by Europe was ignored'.[64] Many Europeans viewed the bombing as a Rambo-style reaction and, with memories of Grenada still in mind, typifying the administration's excessive reliance on military force as an instrument of foreign policy. US public attitudes were heavily weighted in support of the raid and even more sharply critical of what was widely perceived as European weakness in responding to terrorism. While the Reagan administration generally sought to play down the rift in public, one senior official acknowledged that it had been 'absolutely disappointed' with the allied response to Qaddafi and professed 'anger and disgust'[65] that more support had not been received.

Despite the sharp flurry of acrimony across the Atlantic, an early outcome of the Libyan raid was the adoption by EC governments of somewhat stronger measures to combat terrorism. Building upon the limited actions taken on 14 April, the Twelve (Belgium, Britain, Denmark, the Federal Republic of Germany, France, Greece, the Republic of Ireland, Italy, Luxembourg, the Netherlands, Portugal, Spain) agreed to reduce to a minimum the size of Libyan diplomatic and consular staffs while similarly cutting EC member governments' staffs in Libya.[66] Tighter restrictions were agreed on Libyan diplomats in the EC as well as tougher visa requirements for other Libyan citizens. EC coordination in the sharing of intelligence information about suspected terrorist activities was expanded, as were procedures for information exchanges with the US and other non-EC countries. Some commercial contracts with Libya were cancelled, government supported financing and guarantees for trade were ended, and imports of Libyan oil were reduced by most countries. The general Western tightening of diplomatic, economic and internal security measures toward Libya was accompanied by a sharp short-term decrease in terrorist incidents in Europe believed to be of Middle East origin.[67] According to Department of State statistics, international terrorist attacks in Europe dropped from 218 in 1985 to 137 in 1987,[68] though of course the extent of Libyan responsibility, either for restraint or perpetration, was typically problematic, as was the extent to which that decrease was attributable to Western policies.

The European shift to a somewhat stronger anti-terrorism stance, particularly toward Libya, was motivated in major part by a recognition that the EC measures adopted previously had been too little and too late to forestall direct US military action. While it is unclear what other, if any, European measures might have averted the air strike, continued US hints after the attack that further military moves against Qaddafi might be taken clearly prompted EC leaders toward stronger and more concerted steps of their own. Moreover, many European governments found evidence of Libyan involvement in terrorist actions, including the West Berlin bombing, increasingly persuasive.

Nevertheless, important US–European differences in approach remained. EC countries, except for Britain, preserved direct diplomatic contacts with Libya; trade continued, though at lower levels, and European workers remained in the country, though in smaller numbers. A renewed American effort in September to encourage tighter European sanctions was rebuffed. In contrast to the American strategy of seeking to isolate and intimidate Qaddafi through punitive economic, military and diplomatic means, the Europeans continued a more nuanced and variegated approach of maintaining contacts while strengthening internal security measures to detect and thwart possible terrorist threats. The American emphasis on dealing with Libyan-inspired terrorism 'at the source', intrinsically problematic due to the difficulty in marshalling conclusive evidence of responsibility, contrasted with the European emphasis on reducing the risks of terrorism and stronger and more concerted management of anti-terrorist operations within Europe. The focus on reducing the risks of terrorism also influenced the general European approach toward the Arab–Israeli conflict to be discussed in the next chapter. Moreover, Europeans resented American insinuations that they lacked courage in dealing with terrorism, pointing out that various forms of radical violence had been part of the European domestic experience for years (for example, the Red Brigades in Italy and the Baader–Meinhof gang in Germany in the 1970s), and that they had been dealt with effectively without overreaction and excessive use of force.

Soon after the US confrontation with Libya had subsided, another development transpired which further illustrated the differing US–European approaches to dealing with terrorism. In early 1987, the Reagan administration expanded its military presence in the eastern Mediterranean as a warning to terrorists in Lebanon who were holding several Americans as hostages, as well as hostages from three European countries. While the administration sought to quell concerns that it intended military action, it nonetheless acknowledged that American aircraft carriers were equipped with detailed plans for bombing dozens of suspected terrorist targets in Lebanon should a strike be ordered in retaliation for the killing of American hostages.[69] In this context, Britain, France and West Germany rebuffed a US proposal to hold a conference of officials from the seven main industrialised democracies to discuss coordinated responses to the continued hostage-taking in Lebanon.[70] While the Reagan administration denied that the purpose of the meeting was to elicit a joint strategy or plans for military action, the European countries felt nonetheless that their participation in the conference would associate them with the American policy of military pressure which they believed could be provocative and counterproductive. In particular, it was generally felt that diplomatic efforts should be pursued to obtain release of the hostages, that military pressure would only worsen the atmosphere for negotiations, and that military action would risk the lives of the hostages and produce excessive collateral damage likely to alienate Arab opinion and increase tensions in the region.

8 Other Regional Issues

CENTRAL AMERICA

US–European differences over Central America during the early and mid-1980s resembled the earlier Vietnam experience in several respects. In both cases, the United States had far stronger strategic interests (or at least commitments) at stake as compared to Europe which, coupled with European security dependence on the US through NATO, set practical bounds to European dissent and independence from American policies. Both cases involved the direct or indirect use of American military power to effect or prevent change in Third World situations, thus invoking the issue of US political judgement and morality in the use of force against less-developed societies. Relatedly, with respect to both Vietnam and Central America, there was a European tendency to identify American policies with opposition to the expression of indigenous nationalism (Vietnam) or with efforts to prop up or advance the cause of governments or groups which were not genuinely committed to fundamental political, economic and social change (for example, South Vietnam and El Salvador). Moreover, as also in the cases of the 1973 Middle East war and the Soviet invasion of Afghanistan, Europeans often criticised the United States for an excessive propensity to view primarily regional or domestic conflicts through the lens of East–West confrontation while, in the case of Central America, attributing exaggerated influence to the Soviet Union as a cause of regional disturbance. Such perspectives reinforced and validated the view, however oversimplified, of the United States as a 'military power' in contrast to the more favourable image of Europe as a 'civilian power', one which uses instruments of diplomacy, development aid, trade preferences and programmes of regional cooperation to foster constructive modernisation in the Third World.

Furthermore, European governments were disturbed that popular European distaste for American policies in Vietnam and Central America could weaken domestic support in other issue areas, such as involving NATO, that were conspicuously associated with the United States. In addition, there was some concern that US preoccupation in Southeast Asia and later Central America, reinforced by the growing

American commercial outreach to the Pacific, could divert US attention and resources from Alliance security interests in Europe. This
factor was mitigated, however, by the broadly improving trend of
East–West relations in Europe since the early 1970s, despite interruption by occasional setbacks, and by the growing sense that the Soviet
Union represented a declining security threat to Western Europe.
Nevertheless, as Michael Harrison observed, the Central American
crisis intensified 'the bipolar struggle between the United States and
the USSR, reducing West European room for maneuver and increasing the prospect for an outbreak of actual conflict somewhere that
[might] have ramifications in Europe itself'.[1]

Also, both Vietnam and Central America lay outside the formal
geographic scope of NATO, hence US efforts to obtain support for
its policies, or to minimise possible harm to them (as in the case of
other issues studied), had to be based on a broader appeal for political
solidarity justified by America's global strategic responsibilities and
leadership of the Alliance. Such an interpretation of the Alliance,
which implied a European acceptance of American predominance in
determining responses on 'out-of-area' issues, was often resisted by
European governments. Nevertheless, with respect to both Vietnam
and Central America, as well as with the other cases studied, the
United States and European NATO members generally sought to
minimise the impact of their out-of-area differences on their relations
in the Alliance itself.

Yet the differences between Vietnam and Central America as
issues in US–European relations are also noteworthy. If the Vietnam war was the catalyst for a more critical and morally judgment-
tal European view of America, in the eyes of many the Reagan
administration's policies in Central America provided its confirmation. Indeed, to a significant extent the Vietnam war had altered
European expectations as to future American foreign policy behaviour. As Stanley Sloan observed, the war was 'the event which gal-
vanized the new, more critical, European analysis of the United
States'.[2] While the United States was in a general retrenchment mode
through most of the 1970s, culminating with the Carter administration, the election of Ronald Reagan in 1980 and his administration's
early emphasis on combating communism in Central America revived
European concerns that had been largely dormant since the Vietnam war. Whereas there was general European satisfaction with the
Reagan administration's commitment to the restoration of American
power, there were attendant anxieties that its sharply ideological

view of the world could lead to excesses in the use of that power reminiscent of the Vietnam war period. Hence it was natural, particularly among the European left, to view US policy in Central America through the prism of Vietnam and to focus on this issue as a major element of criticism of the Reagan administration's overall foreign policy orientation. Of course a strongly countervailing factor, particularly at the level of official policy, was the far greater US historical and geopolitical security interest in the Western Hemisphere, compared to Southeast Asia, which encouraged European governments to defer to American actions and limit their dissent from American policies, however much they might disagree with them.

In addition, European countries had a more fully developed set of relations with Central America during the early 1980s than they had with Southeast Asia during the Vietnam war period. Overall, EC states represented the second largest market and investment source for Central America.[3] Eleven states in the Caribbean region maintained trade and development ties to the EC through the Lomé Conventions. Moreover, bilateral links were significant, including activities of some West European churches, trade unions and political parties with counterpart groups in the region.[4] The West German Christian and Social Democratic parties became particularly active in Central America, as were other European parties affiliated through their respective international associations. Such groups typically worked to advance democracy in the region, to promote international legitimation of opposition groups, and to stabilise post-revolutionary governments.[5] West Germany, in particular, found it useful to encourage such non-governmental groups to minimise official bilateral friction with Washington, since their activities were often criticised by the United States and governments in the region as 'subversive' or overly identified with revolutionary movements.[6]

France and Spain were the most active West European countries in Central America at the official bilateral level. The Mitterrand government found a natural affinity with Central American socialist parties through personal associations and the Socialist International. In August 1981, France and Mexico signed a joint declaration expressing support for two leftist opposition groups in El Salvador, characterising them as a 'representative political force'[7] and urging the Duarte government to negotiate with them. Later France, joined by Denmark, Greece and the Netherlands, co-sponsored a UN General Assembly resolution calling for negotiations before the holding of elections. In 1982, France announced a military aid programme for the Sandinista government in Nicaragua, including helicopters, naval reconnaissance craft and 7000 air-to-surface rockets.[8] For its part, Spain exerted leadership in encouraging EC endorsement of the Contadora regional peace initiative beginning in 1983.

Divergent US and West European attitudes toward the crisis in Central America became increasingly apparent in the early 1980s and were manifested at both the US–EC and bilateral levels. European governments were convinced that the problems of Central America were rooted in widespread poverty, rigid social and political stratification, economic underdevelopment, and overdependence by some governments on entrenched landowner, military and business elites that made them resistant to meaningful domestic reform and hence indirect perpetrators of domestic tension and unrest which invited a continuing climate of violence. Europeans generally did not share the Reagan administration's fixation on the Sandinistas and their Soviet and Cuban supporters as the chief source of instability in the region. While the administration also acknowledged – and to an extent addressed – the domestic causes of Central American unrest, its preoccupation with resisting Soviet expansion and its sharply ideological view of global power relations and of domestic political configurations was the dominant feature of its policy. In the administration's perspective, ending Soviet, Cuban and Nicaraguan intervention in neighbouring Central American countries was a precondition for achieving domestic stabilisation, democratisation and economic and social reform. Europeans, on the other hand, tended toward the view that domestic problems should be addressed first, and in a regional context, in order to blunt the appeal of externally abetted domestic radical forces.

The differing views on the nature of the problem in Central America, and the nearly inverse prioritisation on how to deal with it, were bound to lead to tensions in US–European relations. In March 1981, EC foreign ministers approved a food and medical aid package for El Salvador, despite US opposition on grounds that deliveries might fall into the hands of the Salvadorian guerrillas.[9] The Reagan administration expressed opposition to an EC plan to aid construction of an airport in Grenada, a signatory of the Lomé Convention, on grounds that the left-wing government of Maurice Bishop might allow its use as a military base for Cuban operations in the region or Africa.[10] US annoyance at EC aid plans was matched by European irritation at the Reagan administration's attempts to influence EC policy deliberations. In 1982 France, the Republic of Ireland and Spain supported a Nicaraguan initiated resolution in the UN Security Council, vetoed by the United States, that implicitly appealed to the US to refrain from the overt or covert use of force against Nicaragua.[11] France later publicly criticised the United States for holding military manoeuvres in Honduras, which was being used as a staging area and sanctuary for US-backed Contra military operations against the Sandinista government.[12]

The Reagan administration protested a high-level European rebuke of its policies which was implicit in the statement of EC leaders at the June 1983 Stuttgart summit meeting that they were 'convinced that the problems of Central America cannot be solved by military means, but only by a political solution springing from the region itself'.[13] On the latter point, the Ten (Belgium, Britain, Denmark, the Federal Republic of Germany, France, Greece, the Republic of Ireland, Italy, Luxembourg and the Netherlands) formally endorsed the aims of the Contadora group, a regional initiative by Colombia, Mexico, Panama and Venezuela to encourage a Central American peace accord based on the objectives of ending all cross-border military and other subversive actions, the withdrawal of foreign military bases and advisers, controlling arms in the region, full pluralist democracy and respect for human rights. The Reagan administration formally welcomed the Contadora initiative, since it embraced several of its own objectives and because it did not want to be isolated from a regional peace initiative that gained wide support among Central and South American countries. Yet the administration's unwillingness to abandon the option of military pressure against the Sandinistas led it to adopt only a lukewarm attitude at best toward the Contadora process.

To be sure, by the end of 1983 European attitudes toward the Sandinistas had noticeably cooled, while support for the Salvadorian guerrillas also declined following the increased legitimacy acquired by the Duarte government as a result of the 1984 elections. With regard to Nicaragua, European governments were critical of the Sandinistas' close ties with Soviet bloc states and Libya and its suppression of human rights, including religious and press freedoms. Spain, whose socialist Prime Minister Felipe Gonzalez was a strong advocate of the Contadora initiative, was nevertheless concerned about reports that the Sandinistas had aided the Basque separatist movement in Spain, which had taken responsibility for terrorist acts. France ended military support for Nicaragua in 1983, in deference to the Contadora process (but also reflecting the Mitterrand government's more critical attitude toward the Sandinistas), while West Germany discontinued new development aid programmes to Nicaragua in the same year.

Nevertheless, strong differences over Central America persisted between the United States and Western Europe, particularly with respect to the Reagan administration's use of economic pressure and military power in the region. There was widespread European criticism of the US invasion of Grenada in 1983, though this was somewhat abbreviated by the quick success of the operation and mitigated by shared European concerns about the possible strategic use of the island by Cuba, for example to transport its troops to Angola. Yet Britain, despite the Thatcher government's usual alignment with the administration on East–West issues, was probably offended by the only pro-forma consultations by US officials immediately prior to the invasion of a British Commonwealth state, and embarrassed by the action itself. In any event, no European government approved the Grenada invasion, and France voted for a UN Security Council resolution that 'deeply deplored' the operation, while Britain abstained.[14] Most European governments condemned or deplored the US mining of Nicaraguan ports in 1984, and the following year criticised the US imposition of trade and other economic sanctions against Nicaragua on grounds that they would be ineffective and would likely push the Sandinista government toward still closer dependence on the Soviet bloc.

Continued strains in US–European relations resulting from different assessments and policies toward the problems of Central America contributed to a significant shift in approach by EC governments beginning in 1984. As we have seen in several cases previously studied, European governments found it useful to reduce their vulnerability to bilateral pressures from Washington by channelling foreign policy responses into the multilateral framework of the Community, embracing both European Political Cooperation and the EC itself. Moreover, such an approach could add a broader measure of European legitimacy and greater collective weight to any initiatives undertaken, while giving fuller scope to the competencies of the EC already established in commercial policy and trade/development ties to Central America through the Lomé Conventions. A more visible Community economic and political involvement in Central America would also help meet domestic pressures for a European alternative to the Reagan administration's policies by giving further expression to the satisfying image of Europe as a civilian power

devoted to the worthy aims of non-intervention, political pacification, democratisation, economic and social justice, and human rights.
In addition, by focusing EC efforts on regional cooperation within
Central America, the interdependence of the area's economic and
political problems could be better addressed, while providing some
cover for continued European assistance to Nicaragua. Also, the
EC's own experience with regional economic integration led it to
encourage similar movements elsewhere by channelling its initiatives through other regional bodies. Finally, the substance of the
new European approach, essentially one of regularised political dialogue and economic cooperation, offered a way of reducing tensions with Washington by focusing on positive programmatic aims
also generally shared by the US, hence to a degree displacing an
atmosphere often dominated by European criticisms of American
policies.

In September 1984 in Costa Rica, EC governments (plus future
members Portugal and Spain) agreed with the Central American
states and the Contadora countries to inaugurate 'a new structure of
political and economic dialogue between Europe and Central America'.[15] The 'structure' was to include regular meetings at ministerial or
other official levels to discuss and advance cooperation in economic,
political and cultural relations. The dialogue was later institutionalised through the Final Act of a ministerial conference in Luxembourg
in November 1985, which provided for annual ministerial meetings,
also including the Contadora countries. It was the first time that EC
political consultations with non-member countries were based on a
formal act signed by the foreign ministers,[16] assigning a status to the
political dialogue never accorded to EPC–US consultations. Exemp-
lifying the new EC approach, it was agreed in Costa Rica to move
toward an interregional framework cooperation agreement between
the EC and member states of the Central American Economic Council
(concluded in 1985). Relatedly, EC governments agreed to increase
Community aid for development projects to be provided through the
Central American Bank for Economic Integration. With respect to
conflict in Central America, the foreign ministers 'were united in the
view that the problems of the region cannot be solved by armed force
itself' (the 'itself' emphasis rendering the statement unobjectionable
to the Reagan administration). Support was reiterated for regional
pacification through the Contadora process, including an indirect
appeal to the United States to implement any such agreement that
might be reached.

Nevertheless, the Costa Rica accord produced new tensions in US–European relations as a result of the inclusion of Nicaragua in the new interregional dialogue, once again revealing fundamental US–European differences in dealing with the Sandinistas. While there was broad agreement over the importance of containing Nicaragua, the US emphasis on economic and military pressure to destabilise and eventually to replace the Sandinistas contrasted with the European emphasis on economic and political inducements to encourage domestic reform in a setting of regional cooperation. Hence, EC governments turned aside a strong plea by Secretary of State George Shultz that the interregional dialogue launched at Costa Rica 'not lead to increased economic aid or any political support for the Sandinistas'.[17] In November 1985 the EC states, plus Spain and Portugal, concluded a five-year trade and cooperation accord with the countries of Central America and agreed to a substantial increase in EC development aid, with a particular emphasis on regional projects.[18] Earlier, shortly after the US imposition of economic sanctions against Nicaragua, the EC agreed to help finance a $5.2 million programme to expand Nicaragua's grain warehouses and export facilities.[19] Indeed, in the mid-1980s, Nicaragua was the largest recipient of EC economic aid to Central America.

Despite continuing US–European differences over Central America, there was a clear desire on both sides not to treat it as an Alliance problem, to contain the quarrel within manageable bounds, and to limit the potential of disagreements to worsen other aspects of transatlantic relations. European governments were constrained by the sharp imbalance in US–European interests in the area, by their limited capability to influence either American policy or regional pacification, by their sharing of some US concerns about the Sandinistas, by their reluctance to challenge the Reagan administration in what it had identified as a vital policy issue, and by a desire not to risk undermining an Alliance relationship on which European security depended. The Reagan administration, while resentful of European support for Nicaragua and what it regarded as European meddling in a region of primary American influence, nonetheless also wanted to contain the Central American problem as far as overall US–European relations were concerned. Significantly, however, European attitudes reinforced the still more influential resistance in Congress to any contemplation of direct US military action against Nicaragua. The administration could hardly ignore the perspective expressed by Spanish Foreign Minister Morán that massive US 'intervention would strengthen neutralist and pacifist movements to such an extent [in Europe] that it could jeopardize the continued participation in NATO of some of its members, especially Spain'.[20]

During the later 1980s, continued European support for the interregional dialogue and the Contadora process corresponded with growing pressure from the US Congress to end military aid to the Contras, eventually terminated in 1988. With a military option against Nicaragua effectively denied, the administration became more attentive to the possibilities of regionally focused solutions (for example, the 1987 Arias plan) which somewhat narrowed the gap between US and European approaches. Moreover, the congressional cut-off of US military aid to the Contras virtually ended the military pressure aspect of American policy that had been a focal point of European criticism. Thus by the late 1980s, US–European differences over Central America were reduced significantly, somewhat resembling the evolution of US and European policies toward the Middle East to be considered next.

THE MIDDLE EAST

As discussed above, the predominance of the US role and interests engaged in the conflicts in Vietnam and Central America reduced the scope for significant European influence. This was also the case with respect to the Arab–Israeli conflict in the Middle East, though in a different way. West European ties with the Arab world, based on geographic proximity, recent historical involvement and economic interdependence, were far more extensive than those with Southeast Asia or Central America. Indeed, as we have seen, the early years of European Political Cooperation were marked by efforts of EC governments to forge a common stance toward the Middle East. Moreover, US involvement in the Middle East was primarily of a diplomatic rather than a military nature which, combined with the absence of a regional security structure on which to base its appeals, meant that the nature of the US role in the Middle East was of a different character than in either Southeast Asia or Central America. For one thing, the pervasive societal influence of Islam, combined with Arab nationalism, limited the appeal and opportunities for domestic communist-type movements which typically had triggered US interventions in other areas. On the other hand, the United States had long supported Israel as a bulwark of its strategic position in the

Middle East and as a counter to Soviet influence with Arab states that were hostile to Israel. Despite the preservation of diplomatic openings with moderate Arab governments, the potency of American domestic support for Israel limited US options in seeking a resolution to the Arab–Israeli conflict over Palestine. Nevertheless, the stronger American strategic posture in the region – both unilaterally and in conjunction with Israeli military superiority – combined with some influence with moderate Arab governments and at least potential leverage with Israel, underscored the more favourable position of the United States, compared to Europe, as an influence on the Middle East peace process.

US–European divergences with respect to the Arab–Israeli conflict, extensively foreshadowed during the 1973/74 Atlantic crisis, continued through the 1970s culminating with the EC's Venice Declaration in 1980, which represented the Nine's most forthright statement in support of the Palestinian people's right to self-determination. While Roy Ginsberg's view that Europe's disarray in 1973/74 'was – in hindsight – the most important external spur to common policy since the Soviet threat to Western Europe helped create NATO in 1949 and the ECSC in 1951'[21] may be exaggerated, it is nonetheless true that the EC was able to forge a consensus on Middle East policy, particularly with respect to the Palestinian dimension of the Arab–Israeli conflict. EC governments were increasingly convinced that resolution of the Palestinian problem through a comprehensive settlement between Israel and its Arab neighbours was the central requirement for peace in the Middle East. Nevertheless, the EC resisted Arab efforts to politicise the Euro-Arab Dialogue begun in 1974 (see Chapter 6) by refusing to accept the Palestine Liberation Organisation (PLO) as a recognised participant in negotiations. Instead, through the so-called Dublin formula adopted in 1975, it was agreed that the dialogue would be conducted through two homogeneous groups – the EC and the Arab League, the latter including PLO participation as part of its delegation. Despite this *modus vivendi*, and the European attempt to keep political questions related to the Arab–Israeli conflict out of the dialogue, the clear tendency of European positions was toward increased support for the Palestinians, which placed the EC on a collision course with both Israel and the United States.

Thus in June 1977 at London, EC leaders approved a statement that 'a solution to the conflict in the Middle East will be possible only if the legitimate right of the Palestinian people to give effective expression to its national identity is translated into fact, which would take into account the need for a homeland for the Palestinian people'.[22] By embracing the concept of a Palestinian 'homeland', for the first time EC governments gave concrete expression to their November 1973 statement on the Middle East which had merely endorsed 'the legitimate rights of the Palestinians'. Moreover, in calling for involvement of representatives of all parties concerned, 'including the Palestinian people', in negotiations leading to an overall settlement, the statement anticipated the more explicit position of the Nine on Palestinian representation in the Venice Declaration three years later. The envisaged settlement encompassed Israeli recognition of Palestinian rights, including now 'homeland' rights, and Arab recognition of Israel's right to live in peace within secure and recognised boundaries. The London statement marked the first formal EC recognition that the Palestinian people had the right to some form of national self-determination and to be directly involved in negotiating its establishment.

The London statement also reiterated EC support for UN Security Council Resolution 242, approved after the 1967 Middle East war, which endorsed principles for a Middle East settlement including: Israeli withdrawal of its forces from territories occupied in the war and an end to the state of belligerency and acceptance of 'the sovereignty, territorial integrity and political independence of every State in the area and their right to live in peace within secure and recognized boundaries free from threats or acts of force'. The resolution called for 'achieving a just settlement of the refugee problem', a formulation which, however, had become obsolete as a serious basis for discussing the Palestinian issue by the mid-1970s. The deliberate ambiguity of the resolution on the issue of Israeli withdrawal, itself a basis for its acceptance by the Arab states and Israel, lay in the meaning of withdrawal. Thus the Arab states, citing the resolution's reference to 'the inadmissibility of the acquisition of territory by war', asserted that Israel must withdraw from all the occupied territories as a condition for a general settlement. Israel, on the other hand, citing the resolution's reference to the right of states to live 'within secure and recognized boundaries free from threats or acts of force', insisted that it be interpreted so as to permit Israel to retain enough captured land to insure defensible borders.

In mid-1977, US and EC positions on the issues addressed by Resolution 242 were broadly similar, though not identical. The Carter administration called for Israeli withdrawal from all fronts in the Middle East dispute – the Sinai, Golan, the West Bank, and Gaza – with the exact borders and security arrangements to be negotiated, thus allowing for the possibility of a less than total Israeli withdrawal.[23] Yet neither had EC positions on the Middle East, including the 1977 London statement, explicitly called for a complete Israeli withdrawal from all occupied territories, though its stance on this issue was less flexible than that of Washington. On the Palestinian question, the administration spoke of 'the need for a homeland for the Palestinians whose exact nature should be negotiated between the parties',[24] a formulation closely approximating the EC's London statement.

Egyptian President Anwar Sadat's historic visit to Israel in November 1977, beginning a bilateral dialogue culminating with the Camp David accords the following September, also set the stage for growing US–European divergence on Middle East policy. The launching of an Egyptian–Israeli dialogue on Middle East peace, an approach strongly encouraged by the United States, though repudiated by most Arab states, threatened to split the Arab front in opposing Israel and seemed pointed toward a piecemeal resolution of Egyptian–Israeli differences that would not adequately address the Palestinian problem. France was particularly sensitive to the Arab reaction to the Sadat visit and opposed a US request that the EC provide strong endorsement for it, which France viewed as American interference in the EC's policy deliberations. While other European governments shared reservations about the implications of the Sadat visit, France blocked a proposed EC declaration that expressed 'deep satisfaction' about Sadat's 'courageous and constructive' initiative in going to Israel.[25] Instead, EC foreign ministers later approved a statement that merely cited Sadat's 'courageous initiatives' with the hope that the new dialogue would facilitate 'comprehensive negotiations leading to a just and lasting overall settlement taking account of the rights and concerns of all the interested parties'.[26] The language of the EC statement reflected apprehension that the new dialogue might be restricted to Egyptian–Israeli political and territorial issues while leaving unresolved the questions of Israeli occupation of Golan, the West Bank, Gaza, and the Palestinian problem.

The Camp David accords signed in September 1978 culminated the Egyptian–Israel *rapprochement* initiated by Sadat's visit to Israel the previous year. The agreements were in two separate parts, one addressing bilateral relations and envisaging an Egyptian–Israeli peace treaty, and the other defining a general framework for resolving the West Bank, Gaza and Palestinian problems. The framework accord, based on Security Council Resolution 242 (and its companion

Resolution 338 adopted after the 1973 war), provided that Egypt, Israel, Jordan and 'the representatives of the Palestinian people' should undertake negotiations on the resolution of all aspects of the Palestinian problem. The agreement, recognising 'the legitimate rights of the Palestinian people and their just requirements' (hence going beyond the UN resolutions), called for a freely elected self-governing authority (administrative council) for the West Bank and Gaza to be followed by withdrawal of the Israeli military government and its civilian administration. The modalities for establishing the self-governing authority were to be agreed by Egypt, Israel and Jordan – with the negotiating delegations of Egypt and Jordan allowed to include Palestinians from the West Bank and Gaza 'or other Palestinians as mutually agreed'. Thus the nature of Palestinian participation in the negotiations would be subject to Israeli concurrence. Following the establishment of the self-governing authority, a five-year transitional period was to begin during which the final status of the West Bank and Gaza was to be determined through negotiations between Egypt, Israel, Jordan and the elected representatives from the West Bank and Gaza. It is significant that the call for participation in negotiations by representatives of the Palestinian people was similar to the Nine's London statement as to procedure, while different from that of the Nine as to the aim of negotiations (that is, the homeland issue).

The EC reaction to the Camp David accords was one of qualified support. On the one hand, the Nine could hardly refrain from welcoming the agreements as offering at least some hope of progress toward a comprehensive Middle East settlement. Their own one-sided (in the Israeli view) support for the Arab states and the Palestinians (for example, the London statement call for a homeland) in effect had placed the Nine out of the picture as a major influence in the Middle East peace process. Moreover, as with some of the crises previously studied, the broader European strategic dependence on the United States constrained the Europeans from policies that could risk an open breach with Washington on an issue of major American political investment. As a British diplomat with long experience in the Middle East and EC political cooperation described the European dilemma: 'how to reconcile their own perception of the right way forward in the Middle East with the need to avoid a major disagreement with the United States that could have wider strategic consequences . . . the Middle East also illustrates very vividly the acute difficulty faced by the EC in seeking to pursue a regional policy on its merits while at the same time taking full account of the interests of the United States, on which Europe's own security depends'.[27]

Nevertheless, the carefully worded EC statement issued in response to the Camp David accords, while congratulating the participants, refrained from any explicit endorsement of the agreements themselves.[28] Instead, it recalled the London statement as the basis for the EC's position and expressed the 'hope' that the outcome of Camp David would lead to a just and 'comprehensive' peace involving participation by all parties concerned. West German Foreign Minister Genscher, speaking on behalf of the Nine at the UN General Assembly, stressed 'the view that a peace settlement in the Middle East will be possible only if the legitimate right of the Palestinian people to give effective expression to its national identity is translated into fact [taking into account] the need for a homeland for the Palestinian people'.[29] While the EC position on the Palestinian question did not differ significantly from the US statement in mid-1977, the Carter administration had implicitly qualified its own 'homeland' position through association with the Camp David accords that envisaged only an administrative council in the West Bank and Gaza.

Subsequent developments appeared to vindicate European scepticism about the Camp David approach. Despite US and Egyptian claims that the bilateral accords aimed at a comprehensive settlement, the more telling point was the absence of direct linkage between the two. Thus the Egyptian–Israeli peace treaty was concluded in March 1979, leading to Israel's return of the Sinai to Egypt, which was completed in 1982. At the same time, however, the issue of reaching agreement on a self-governing authority for the West Bank and Gaza, as a prelude to an Israeli withdrawal, became indefinitely stalemated. Israel refused to accept the Palestine Liberation Organisation as a participant in the negotiations, given the PLO's rejection of the Camp David accords and its public hostility toward Israel. Other West Bank Palestinians were too disorganised, lacking in support, or fearful of PLO reprisals to step forward as 'representatives of the Palestinian people' to participate in the negotiations.

Further European distancing from Camp David was apparent in the EC reaction to the Egyptian–Israeli peace treaty. The Carter administration had sought an expression of unified EC support for the treaty with the hope of influencing the attitude of key Middle Eastern states and reducing Egypt's isolation within the Arab world.[30] France, which viewed the treaty as a separate peace that effectively abandoned the

Palestinian cause, blocked a strong EC statement of support on its behalf. However some other EC governments, albeit less outspokenly, shared French reservations in keeping with previous EC attitudes toward the Camp David process. Thus the Nine's reserved statement on the treaty noted merely that it represented a 'correct application' of the principles of Resolution 242 to Egyptian–Israeli relations,[31] and that it must be considered only as a first step toward a comprehensive settlement that must include provision for a Palestinian homeland. The deeper European concern of course was that the normalisation of Egyptian–Israeli relations, which the Camp David accords had envisaged as an example for future relations between Israel and other Arab states as well, would encourage Israel to insist on such a model in any future negotiations, while retaining an effective veto power over the implementation of the West Bank–Gaza provisions of the accords. In this view, the Egyptian–Israeli treaty vindicated European reservations about Camp David, with the two agreements likely to produce a prolonged impasse in achieving a comprehensive Middle East peace. Moreover, Israel's settlements policy in the occupied territories, strongly criticised by the EC, was viewed as bad faith with respect to Resolution 242 and the Camp David accords and evidence of Israeli determination to harden a status quo that those agreements sought to alter.

During the year following the Egyptian–Israeli treaty, the growing European perception that the Camp David process had stalled, and in any case was deficient, combined with the Iranian and Afghanistan crises and the second oil shock to produce momentum for a European Middle East initiative which was pursued at both national levels and through the EC's political cooperation. European governments became convinced that Islamic support for achieving a satisfactory solution in Afghanistan required more positive Western support on behalf of the Palestinians, an easy assessment to make since it furnished an additional rationale for the Nine's existing position. In line with the EC's London statement, these efforts focused primarily on the Palestinian issue which was widely viewed as neglected by Camp David. France, typically out in front on the Palestinian question, advocated EC recognition of the PLO.[32] West German Foreign Minister Genscher called for Palestinian self-determination, a formulation that went beyond the EC's previous 'homeland' position and anticipated the June 1980 Venice Declaration. The concept of a 'homeland', though nebulous, was not necessarily inconsistent with the Camp David provision for a self-governing authority in the West

Bank and Gaza; however, this would not constitute an independent Palestinian state as clearly implied by the term self-determination.

Moving toward confrontation with Washington, in early 1980 EC governments reportedly agreed on a new strategy to deal with the Palestinian issue aimed at supplementing Resolution 242 with an annex that would expressly recognise the Palestinians' right to a homeland, combined with an international conference to address the problem guided by the revised resolution.[33] Anxious to avoid the appearance of thwarting the Camp David process, pending the outcome of US mediated negotiations for West Bank–Gaza autonomy, the EC plan was held in abeyance. However, there was little European confidence that the negotiations would succeed, particularly given American election year politics which were expected to constrain the Carter administration from exerting pressure on Israel. Meanwhile, led by Britain and France, EC coalescence strengthened in support of Palestinian self-determination and PLO participation in the peace process.

The United States, in line with the Israeli position, was firmly opposed to dealing with the PLO as long as it remained publicly committed to the destruction of Israel. Hence, the Carter administration viewed the emerging European position as undercutting its Camp David diplomacy.[34] In the US view, if the EC approach became a formal initiative, it would discourage Palestinian interest in the Camp David process by providing international backing for the EC's more advantageous homeland/self-determination formula. Of course, European officials often denied any intention of undermining Camp David and sought to portray their position as helpful to the process by offering a more realistic basis for Palestinian participation. However, given the more limited concept of Palestinian self-rule already enshrined in the Camp David accords, beyond which Israel would not budge, the EC approach offered no prospect of moving the negotiations forward. On the other hand, as Europeans often pointed out, the Camp David formula provided inadequate inducement to attract sufficient support from Palestinians and most Arab governments to achieve progress toward an overall settlement, thus allowing the Palestinian problem to fester and risk growing turbulence in the region.

Disregarding US opposition to the emerging European approach, in April EC leaders instructed their foreign ministers to submit a report on the Middle East problem to the next EC Council session in Venice, amid clear indications that a new European move was imminent. In May, President Carter sent newly appointed Secretary of State Edmund Muskie to Europe in an effort to dissuade European governments from taking a Middle East initiative, and later publicly threatened to veto any attempt to modify Resolution 242.[35] In a 'Face the Nation' interview on 1 June, Carter depicted Resolution 242 and the Camp David document as 'almost like a Bible now' and criticised any European attempt to circumvent or replace the Camp David process.[36] Publicly pledging 'to prevent any damage to UN Resolution 242', Carter discouraged the European allies 'from injecting themselves into this process as long as we are engaged in negotiations which might lead to success'. Muskie told the Washington Press Club on 9 June that, while the administration had no objection to a new initiative that would further the Camp David process, 'we will strongly oppose any efforts that would derail that process'.[37]

Despite anger at the blunt US opposition to their planned initiative, the Europeans had little choice but to yield. Faced with the certainty of an American veto, and wishing to avoid widening the breach with Washington, the Nine abandoned their earlier plan to seek revision of the UN resolution. Following a meeting with President Carter on 11 June, Italian Foreign Minister Emilio Colombo stated on behalf of the Nine that they did not intend to propose an initiative that might be interpreted as an 'alternative in contradiction with the Camp David formula'.[38] In later statements, Carter commented on US efforts 'to make sure that they [the EC] don't do anything that would interfere with or subvert the progress of the Camp David procedure', and noted with satisfaction that 'good progress' had been made 'in stopping a purported European drive' to amend Resolution 242.[39]

While the EC Council's Venice Declaration of 13 June 1980 manifested a less innovative position than had previously been envisaged, it nonetheless represented an important achievement for political cooperation among the Nine by breaking new ground in four areas of policy. For the first time in a collective statement, EC leaders professed support for the Palestinian people 'to exercise fully its right to self-determination', noting in a barb at Resolution 242 that the Palestinian problem 'is not simply one of refugees'.[40] Second, while stopping short of calling for a Palestinian state and formally recognising the PLO, the Nine affirmed for the first time that the PLO 'will have to be associated with negotiations' leading to an overall Middle East settlement, though a call for PLO 'participation' was dropped from the final text.[41] Hence, by using language that referred to the Palestinian people *and* the PLO, the declaration carefully avoided recognising the PLO as *the* representative of the Palestinian people. Third, the Venice Declaration included an operational dimension whereby, through the presiding EC Presidency, the Nine would make contact with the parties concerned to ascertain their views on the principles of the declaration to determine if a basis existed for further action by the Nine to advance the peace process. Fourth, in their first collective move in security policy implying military commitments, the Nine declared their willingness to participate in a system of concrete and binding international guarantees, including on the ground, within the framework of a comprehensive settlement. While the chief aim of the Venice Declaration was to promote a solution to the Palestinian problem, the requirement for balance in the document was addressed through reaffirmation that all countries in the region 'are entitled to live in peace within secure, recognised and guaranteed borders'.

Beyond the specifics of the Venice Declaration, the evolution of the Nine's policy on the Middle East since the Camp David agreements was in part a function of their intensive consultations through political cooperation. As observed in the other cases studied, the accepted value of at least attempting to forge a common EC position, coupled with extensive and regularised consultative mechanisms for doing so, exerted a pull on individual governments to adjust their own positions in the interest of acquiring greater influence through collectivity than any could achieve alone. Moreover, the value of reaching consensus at the European level could be cited domestically as justification for shifts in national position. This was particularly the case with the Netherlands, Denmark and, to some extent, West Germany which had traditionally followed policies more fully in support of Israel. While it is generally true that the Venice Declaration reflected an evolving European alignment with French Middle Eastern policy, France, too, had to compromise (for example, with respect to recognising the PLO) in the interest of agreement at the Community level as the best hope of achieving some progress on the Palestinian question. Nevertheless, it can also be argued that the European positions expressed in joint statements were primarily the result of shifts in national position largely independent of any pressures for consensus operating within the Nine's political consultations.

The US reaction to the Venice Declaration, though described by one knowledgeable observer as 'profoundly unhappy',[42] was nevertheless one of general relief that the Nine had not gone further with respect to support for the PLO and proposing changes to Resolution 242. In any case, given the absence of any formal European role in the

Middle East negotiations, and the fact that Israel totally rejected the declaration while the PLO criticised it for not going far enough, the European initiative had little immediate effect on Middle East diplomacy. Nonetheless, by drawing attention to the Palestinian question as a central issue in the Middle East peace process, the Venice Declaration helped to keep the subject of Palestinian rights, however those rights might be interpreted, at the forefront of subsequent Middle East diplomatic initiatives. Moreover, when viewed in light of the evolving policies of EC governments since the early 1970s – particularly the launching of the Euro-Arab Dialogue, the 1977 London statement, and criticism of Israeli policy in the occupied territories – the Venice Declaration marked a further step toward forging an EC consensus on policy toward the Middle East. In addition, together with EC reactions to the concurrent Afghanistan and Iran hostage crises, the Venice Council statement manifested a growing European readiness to adopt positions independent of those of the United States. Indeed, in July EC governments resisted US pressures to vote against a UN General Assembly Resolution which endorsed the right of the Palestinian people 'to establish its own independent sovereign state', while omitting any guarantees of Israel's security and legitimacy.[43] The Nine only abstained on the resolution, though in previous Assembly sessions most had voted against resolutions containing milder formulations of Palestinian rights.

Nevertheless, the Venice Declaration proved to be the high point of the effort to establish a more influential EC political role in the Middle East. The exploratory fact-finding mission to the area came to naught, partly because Israel refused to allow it to meet with Palestinian leaders in the West Bank. Yet the European retreat from the ambition to play a larger collective role in the Middle East, already signalled by the Venice Declaration itself, was the result of factors endemic to the nature of European Political Cooperation, as well as factors over which the Europeans had no control. With respect to EPC itself, the inefficient procedure of six-month rotating presidencies impaired consistent and sustained Community attention to the problem. Luxembourg, which held the presidency during the crucial six-month post-Venice period, was made to carry most of the weight of implementing the fact-finding mission. The Netherlands, given its traditionally strong support for Israel, was naturally disinclined to push the Nine's initiative when it assumed the presidency during the first half of 1981. Moreover, shifts in national position inevitably altered the practical meaning of the Community's unified stance at Venice. For example, Britain's Prime Minister Margaret Thatcher, after Ronald Reagan's election to the American presidency in November 1980, reportedly backed away at least temporarily from supporting further European Middle East moves in the interest of cultivating understanding with the new administration on the need for tougher policies toward the Soviet Union.[44] As will be seen France, too, later abandoned support for collective European initiatives for other reasons.

The Reagan administration's emphasis on countering the Soviet threat resulted in efforts to strengthen the American military presence in the Middle East and to develop a new 'strategic consensus' with Israel to limit Soviet influence in the region. As the Middle East came to be regarded increasingly as a theatre in the US–Soviet confrontation, American policy toward the Arab–Israeli conflict was viewed initially primarily in that context. While the administration could have chosen (and later did) to approach the problem by seeking resolution of the Palestinian question (thus weakening the basis for Soviet ties with radical Arab states), it chose instead to strengthen relations with Israel and moderate Arab states in the region. This led to an implicit downgrading of attempts to address the Arab–Israeli conflict on its own terms and hostility toward any European attempts to do so.

Despite the post-Venice loss of momentum for the European peace initiative, Britain and France attempted to revive the idea in talks with the Reagan administration early in 1981. Based on tentative internal EC agreement, a working paper containing several options called for total Israeli withdrawal to its pre-1967 borders, dismantlement of all post-1967 settlements in the occupied lands, creation of a Palestinian entity to be administered by a transitional authority while the Palestinians determined their own future (for example, by voting for an independent state or federation with Jordan or with Jordan and Israel) and Western military guarantees for all states in the region.[45] Though the plan did not mention the PLO, in an effort to avoid triggering an automatic Israeli rejection, the earlier expressed European view that the PLO would have to be associated with the settlement process could hardly be ignored. As with previous European peace ideas, Israel predictably opposed the plan as contrary to its interpretation of Resolution 242 and the Camp David agreements. The Reagan administration, which had not yet fully formulated its own policy toward the Arab–Israeli conflict beyond continuing the autonomy talks, did not wish to jeopardise its ties with Israel and pointedly discouraged further European pursuit of its initiative.[46]

Given the American and Israeli attitudes, further European action to follow-up the Venice Declaration seemed pointless.

During 1981, the focus shifted to the role Europe might play in the proposed Multinational Force and Observers (MFO) projected by the Egyptian–Israeli peace treaty to monitor Israeli withdrawal from the Sinai and assure compliance with restrictions on military deployments in the area. Under Egyptian–Israeli agreements, the United States had been accorded a key role in the organisation of the force. Israel had made clear that it would not complete its withdrawal, scheduled for April 1982, until the MFO was in place. Lord Carrington, Foreign Secretary of Great Britain, which held the EC presidency in the latter half of 1981, sought to link European participation in the Sinai force to wider acceptance of the role of the Palestinians in peace negotiations along the lines of the Venice Declaration. Carrington, as well as some British ambassadors in the Middle East, had already annoyed the Reagan administration and Israel by publicly expressing doubts about the prospects for Camp David and by indicating sympathy for a new plan advanced by Saudi Arabia calling for a complete Israeli withdrawal from the occupied territories and the establishment of an independent Palestinian state.[47] Reportedly, Secretary of State Alexander Haig admonished Carrington to stop promoting the Saudi plan so enthusiastically and to 'cool it'.[48]

In any case, Carrington's approach had little chance to succeed, again because of American opposition and because Israel refused to accept participation in the MFO by European governments based on the Venice (rather than the Camp David) formula. Yet if European governments decided not to supply contingents for the Sinai force, the European role in the only active Middle East peace process would be exposed as negative and impotent.

Faced with such constraints, as well as remonstrations from the Reagan administration, EC governments (now the Ten, reflecting Greece's accession in 1981) agreed in November on a statement that endorsed participation by Britain, France, Italy and the Netherlands in the multinational Sinai force.[49] The statement avoided mentioning the Venice Declaration, which had been included in an earlier draft, but it took note of the need for a comprehensive settlement in the Middle East including the right of Palestinian self-determination, though without mentioning the PLO. The carefully worded formula sought to avoid antagonising Israel while at the same time meeting the insistence of Greece, which had recently recognised the PLO, that it include affirmation of support for the Palestinians. Britain,

France, Italy and the Netherlands issued a separate statement, noting that 'participation by the four governments in the multinational force does not prejudice their well-known policy on other aspects of the region's problems',[50] an allusion to the Venice Declaration.

Except for the agreed four-nation participation in the MFO, which was not in any case a European inspired idea, any thought of reviving a European Middle East initiative along the lines of the Venice Declaration was virtually dead by the end of 1981. In addition to the reasons discussed above, the basis for a collective European effort was further undermined by an important shift in French policy during 1981 under the newly elected government of François Mitterrand. The new French approach reflected scepticism of the value of continued European initiatives in existing circumstances and a determination to pursue a more balanced Middle East policy primarily at the national level. Moreover, the re-election of Prime Minister Begin in Israel, signalling continued strong Israeli opposition to the Venice formula, and the uncertainties stemming from the assassination of President Sadat in October, further discouraged revival of a European initiative. Underlying the new 'realism' in French thinking was the recognition that the Venice approach, perceived by the US and Israel as harmful to the Camp David process, had damaged rather than advanced any prospects for a significant European role in Middle East peace diplomacy. Furthermore, it was recognised that any useful mediation role in the Middle East conflict required acceptance by both sides, a condition virtually ruled out by the EC's collective stance at Venice.

In seeking a new balance to its Middle East policy, the Mitterrand government set out tto distance itself from the Venice initiative, thus pleasing Israel while preserving France's credentials with the Arabs by going beyond the Venice Declaration to call for the establishment of a Palestinian state.[51] Reflecting the turnabout in French policy, Foreign Minister Claude Cheysson, while in Israel to prepare for a planned visit by President Mitterrand, decried that the EC's Venice Declaration had acquired anti-Camp David characteristics and therefore was 'wrong and absurd' since European governments had 'no direct involvement in the settlement'.[52] Drawing a distinction between the Venice Declaration, which he did not renounce, and an initiative on its behalf which he felt was useless, Cheysson declared: 'There is no French plan [on the Middle East] and, as long as we are in government, there will be no European plan or European initiative'.[53] Despite Cheysson's later softening of his critical remarks about Venice, it was nonetheless clear that France chose to dissociate from the Venice Declaration at least with respect to further European diplomatic initiatives on its behalf.

Moreover, European attempts to play a role in the Middle East consistent with their own collective positions received a further setback when Israel, backed by a US–Israeli declaration that tied the MFO solely to the Egyptian–Israeli agreements (without conditions such as Venice),[54] resisted inclusion of British, Dutch, French and Italian units in the Sinai force because the Four had alluded to the Venice Declaration in their statement of acceptance. Forced to retreat on the issue, or face exclusion from the MFO and further erosion of a European role in the Middle East, the Four issued a clarification that they were joining the force on the basis of the peace accords and without further political conditions.[55] As Panayiotis Ifestos observed: 'the participation of the European countries in the [MFO] seemed to be a surrender of the European approach to the American-sponsored Camp David framework, and a clear illustration of the Community's inability to implement its own independent policy based on the Venice Declaration of June 1980'.[56]

The Ten's virtual abandonment of the effort to launch a collective Middle East initiative, combined with their endorsement of European participation in the MFO, amounted to an acquiescence to the Camp David framework and continued American leadership in the peace process. The year after Venice had demonstrated what should have been apparent before, that a Middle East initiative not supported by the United States and totally rejected by Israel had no prospect as a basis for negotiations. However if Venice is looked at as part of a long-term political process of accommodating Arab–Israeli differences, rather than as a failed initiative at the time, a more positive assessment emerges. Seen in this light, the Venice Declaration was part of a growing trend of international opinion that viewed some form of Palestinian self-determination, going beyond the Camp David concept of autonomy, as essential to peace in the Middle East. While such opinion could not be decisive in affecting the modalities of the peace process, its influence on the United States as a main protagonist was not insignificant. Despite its support *for* Israel, the United States was uncomfortable at being isolated *with* Israel in opposing an approach to the Palestinian question that could offer a realistic prospect for negotiations.

Moreover, the continued Israeli settlements policy in the early 1980s, publicly discouraged by the United States and condemned by the EC, the Israeli annexation of the Golan Heights in 1981, the invasion of Lebanon in 1982 and the growth of Palestinian inspired terrorism, resulted in mounting criticism of Israeli policies and sharpened attention to the Palestinian problem. Indeed, such considerations spurred the Reagan administration to launch its own peace initiative in 1982 which, though in the framework of the Camp David process, nonetheless reflected some movement toward European positions. While the Reagan peace plan itself did not move negotiations forward, the subsequent European tendency was to acquiesce to US leadership in Middle East diplomacy related to the Arab–Israeli conflict or at least to avoid measures that could undermine it. Thus Alfred Pijpers' observation in 1984 generally held true for the decade: 'Looking back the Venice Declaration should probably not be regarded as a starting point for European Middle East policies in the eighties, [but] more as a culmination of the policies of the seventies. The MFO episode marked a kind of transition between the high aspirations of the Venice Declaration and the Ten's more limited perspective since 1982'.[57] Nevertheless, the Venice Declaration continued to represent the basic statement of European principles which should guide the Middle East peace process, later reaffirmed by the foreign ministers of the Twelve in 1987.[58]

9 European Pillars in the 1980s

POLITICAL COOPERATION

As discussed in the preceding chapters, by the 1980s the EC's mechanisms for political cooperation had helped to achieve some notable successes in articulating independent European positions on specific issues, often either at variance with or in direct conflict with those of the United States. Beginning with the 1973/74 Atlantic crisis, Europeans started utilising the newly established procedures for political cooperation as a framework for concerting and articulating what they regarded as distinctively European interests on the issues at hand. However, the effectiveness of European Political Cooperation was often impaired by internal disagreements among EC governments, the inefficient machinery of political cooperation, and by strategic dependence on the United States which discouraged the pursuit of initiatives to the point of risking a damaging break with Washington.

Nevertheless, some progress was achieved in strengthening the practical working arrangements of EPC and in modestly extending its scope. The decision in 1975 to establish the European Council (of heads of state or government) provided a forum for EC leaders to discuss both economic and political cooperation issues, thus partly bridging the institutional distinction between the two while augmenting the significance and visibility of European actions in the political field. This in turn led to abandonment of the strict practice of foreign ministers meeting in separate sessions to deal with EC and EPC business. While EPC remained grounded in intergovernmental consultations, in contrast to the EC's more supranational decision-making method, the fact that the two sets of issues could be dealt with by the same body and often in a linked context tended to blur the distinction between them. This development was reinforced by the growing involvement of the EC Commission in EPC deliberations on matters relating to the competence of the Community.

The growing coordination between EPC and the EC was the natural outgrowth of the EC's unique authority over trade policy, and the effort of governments through EPC to develop common policies which could involve the use of trade or other economic measures. Indeed, beyond declaratory statements and sporadic and generally unsuccessful attempts at operational diplomacy, economic measures were one of the few means available to the EC to give practical expression to common positions. This virtually compelled a closer liaison between EPC and the EC to meet the need for more coherent policy coordination as well as to impart tangible substance to Community actions. In this manner, an EC presence could be manifested in the area of so-called 'high politics', traditionally the preserve of national governments.[1] Moreover, the Commission proved useful in bridging the quite different policy coordination mechanisms of EPC and the EC. The Political Committee, the chief coordinating body for political cooperation, and the Committee of Permanent Representatives, responsible to the Council of Ministers on EC policy, generally worked independently of one another though sometimes focusing on the same policy issue. The Commission, through its voice in both EPC and EC proceedings, was able to improve communications between the two structures and hence facilitate the development of more fully orchestrated Community policies (a role that became more formalised in the Single European Act).

Efforts to improve the efficiency and adaptiveness of the political cooperation machinery, clearly called for by the crises of the early 1980s, led to adoption of the so-called London Report by the foreign ministers of the Ten in October 1981. Yet despite growing external pressures for a European response, highlighted by the Iran hostage and Afghanistan crises, the London Report represented only a modest advance beyond the provisions outlined in the Luxembourg and Copenhagen reports (see Chapter 4). As with the Copenhagen Report, in some respects it basically formalised arrangements that had been evolving pragmatically. Thus, largely in response to a shift in French policy under the new Mitterrand government, the EC Commission was accorded a more regularised and integral role in EPC deliberations for reasons discussed above. Whereas the 1973 Copenhagen Report had merely 'invited' the Commission to make known its views, the London Report acknowledged that it was important for the Commission to be 'fully associated with Political Co-operation at all levels'.[2] While this did not alter the intergovernmental character of EPC (for example, the Commission lacked the unique power of initiative it held in the EC), it did represent a practical accommodation to the functional interdependence between political cooperation and the competency of the EC.

Addressing the problem of continuity in EPC resulting from the six-month rotating presidency (during which each serves as coordinator and spokesman in political cooperation), the so-called *troika* principle was formalised providing for coordination among three successive presidencies. In particular, it was agreed that the president in office would be assisted by national officials from the preceding and succeeding presidencies and that the president could delegate tasks to his successor. Moreover, the *troika* principle could also apply to EPC meetings with representatives from non-member countries. Primarily inspired by the Nine's tardy response to the Soviet invasion of Afghanistan, a British proposal for crisis consultation was adopted whereby any three member states could call for a meeting within 48 hours at the level of the Political Committee or foreign minsters.

However, apart from such essentially procedural refinements, the London Report largely reaffirmed the status quo with respect to political cooperation. To be sure, for the first time in a formal EPC document the Ten gingerly introduced the security issue by noting that their 'flexible and pragmatic approach' had made it possible to discuss foreign policy questions 'bearing on the political aspects of security'. Yet this was less of an innovation than it appeared. Indeed, the 1970 Luxembourg Report had pledged governments to 'consult on all important questions of foreign policy', and the Six/Nine/Ten had been formulating positions on security-related topics for years toward the Conference on Security and Cooperation in Europe. Moreover, the Venice Declaration had included a pledge by the Nine to participate in a system of international guarantees within the framework of a comprehensive Middle East settlement. Furthermore, the language of the London Report made clear that endorsement of discussions relating to the political aspects of security represented a formalisation of existing practice rather than a new departure. Of course, the specification of the political aspects of security was intended to clarify that political cooperation would not include discussion of defence questions *per se*, in deference to neutral Ireland's sensitivities and because of reluctance to be seeming to intrude on NATO's established position in this area. Well-known American reservations toward any European bloc approach *vis-à-vis* NATO undoubtedly contributed to European caution in staking out a position in the security field.

It is noteworthy that despite significant European success by this time in developing collective positions *ad hoc* (the Iran hostage crisis,

Afghanistan, the Venice Declaration), the London Report did not manifest a significantly firmer commitment to the principle of concerted or common foreign policy action. Using somewhat stronger language, the report essentially reaffirmed the undertakings endorsed at Luxembourg and Copenhagen, particularly with respect to consultations before the adoption of final positions or launching national initiatives, and the pledge to take full account of other members' views while giving 'due weight to the desirability of achieving a common position'. Nevertheless, while noting that joint action '*should* be increasingly within the capacity of the Ten [emphasis added]', the report underscored the essence of EPC, which was that foreign policy continued to be a national responsibility. EC governments were still unwilling to go beyond the commitment to consultations and to seek joint positions, however often they were able to do so in concrete situations.

The aborted Genscher–Colombo initiative in 1981 and the Ten's Solemn Declaration on European Union adopted at Stuttgart in June 1983 further exemplified the European reticence toward EPC involvement in security issues. The Genscher–Colombo plan, formally proposed by the West German and Italian foreign minsters in the form of a draft European Act in November 1981, responded to a number of considerations in the early 1980s that seemed to warrant new steps toward consolidating and extending the European pillar. On the one hand, the EC itself was absorbed with interminable debates over reducing the common agricultural policy's costly surpluses and subsidies and by quarrels over Britain's contribution to the budget. General economic stagnation and high unemployment throughout Western Europe found expression in a revival of national protectionism and lowered interest in Community-level solutions. Thus with the EC in the doldrums, risking popular disaffection with the unity movement in general, it seemed timely to propose compensatory initiatives in the political field where fewer domestic restraints operated to impede progress. In addition, while EPC had achieved some success in formulating common foreign policy positions, the larger consideration was awareness of Europe's lack of significant influence on events directly affecting European interests. Moreover, West Germany, anxious to defuse growing domestic pacifist and anti-nuclear sentiment following the controversial 1979 decision to accept US intermediate-range nuclear missiles, viewed a new European initiative as a means for regaining domestic support for strengthening Germany's anchorage in the West. Furthermore, the recent successful experiences in shaping common and distinctively European positions had created some momentum upon which to build.

Finally, while the German–Italian plan contained no hint of separation from the US or the Atlantic Alliance, the recent tensions with Washington over the Middle East and crisis responses in the early 1980s had prompted a clearer awareness of European interests often different from those of the United States. The gathering diplomatic 'case law' in this area of Atlantic relations tended to reinforce the sense of a separate European identity (and interests), and the need for closer concert among the Ten on foreign policy and security questions. Relatedly, European dissatisfaction with specific aspects of American foreign policy leadership contributed to the same mood. West Germany's irritation over the Carter administration's handling of the neutron bomb episode, US–European differences over *détente* and relations with the Soviet Union, European apprehensions over the Reagan administration's emphasis on military strength at the expense of an active arms control policy, public speculation by Reagan himself about the possibility of a limited nuclear war in Europe, the security implications of the administration's Strategic Defence Initiative (which might protect the US but not Europe from Soviet missiles), concern over US global unilateralist tendencies, and emerging differences over Central America all contributed to a sense of unease in Europe over the direction and wisdom of American foreign policy and its leadership of the Alliance.

The Genscher–Colombo initiative (draft European Act)[3] sought to strengthen the political organisation and activity of the Ten in three ways. First, it was proposed to amalgamate the existing structures of the EC and EPC which would be brought together under the responsibility of the European Council. The expressly political character of the plan was signified by inclusion of the foreign ministers in the European Council which would deliberate on all matters relating to the EC and political cooperation and could take decisions and establish guidelines. While the practical meanings of 'amalgamate' and 'brought together' required elaboration, it was clarified that there was to be no derogation from the existing competencies of the EC and that Council actions in the sphere of political cooperation would not affect the powers of the Community. Hence, the existing distinction between EPC and EC decision-making procedures would be preserved, while enabling greater coordination and coherence between the two at the Council level. Actually, the responsibility envisaged for the Council was close to the role it was already playing in the areas of both EC and political cooperation activity. More controversially, it was proposed to create a Secretariat for political cooperation, an idea opposed by France at the time.

Second, building upon the recent London Report, the draft European Act called for 'the coordination of security policy and the adoption of common European positions in this sphere in order to safeguard Europe's independence, protect its vital interests and strengthen its security'. Taking account of special Irish sensitivities and French and Greek objections to including defence matters in the domain of the Ten, the plan provided that the Council 'may convene in a different composition [for example, defence ministers] if there is a need to deal with matters of common interest in more detail'. Thus despite the vague language, the intent was to enable defence issues to be discussed in the framework of political cooperation.

Third, the plan envisaged a significant tightening of EPC through the aim of 'a common foreign policy', going somewhat beyond the language of previous EPC reports. Proposed measures included the adoption of final foreign policy positions by member states 'only' after consultation with their partners, thereby dropping the important 'as a general rule' qualification contained in the Copenhagen Report. Moreover, the plan proposed that acceptance of statements by the Ten be treated 'as a binding common basis'. While the draft European Act was not proposed as a treaty or a legally binding document, a general review five years after its signing was envisaged with the purpose of incorporating the progress achieved in a Treaty on European Union.

It soon became apparent that the Genscher–Colombo proposal was overly ambitious and exceeded the level of consensus attainable among the Ten. The European Parliament refrained from providing any substantive opinion on the plan, insisting only that it be consulted as part of future deliberations. France and Denmark objected to the strengthened commitment to a common foreign policy, while France also continued to oppose establishment of an EPC Secretariat, an idea also viewed sceptically by several smaller European governments. Greece, particularly under the Papandreou government elected in 1981, was embarking upon a more independent course in foreign policy, which included objection to some EPC positions, and was clearly unwilling to commit to stronger foreign policy discipline at a European level.[4] The provision for coordination of security policy and the adoption of common European positions, which went beyond the London Report and clearly implied inclusion of defence matters (as

Genscher had earlier suggested), was resisted by France and Ireland on different national grounds, and by others (for example, the Netherlands) who feared it would be mistrusted by the United States and risk divisiveness in the Alliance. Moreover, a special problem would have arisen given that three European countries, Iceland, Norway and Turkey, were members of NATO though not of the EC/EPC.

The end result, as Elfriede Regelsberger concludes, was that the Genscher–Colombo initiative 'was tabled in an unfriendly if not hostile Community environment'.[5] It may have been particularly wounding that the European Council, initially inclined to 'welcome' the proposal, mainly at Danish insistence ended by merely recording in its communiqué that it had 'received the initiative . . . and took note of their proposals'.[6] However, it is certain that the West German and Italian governments were cognisant of their partners' views toward various aspects of the plan, and thus its generally negative reception could hardly have been a total surprise. Indeed, it is clear that the expectation was not prompt acceptance of the draft, but rather that the initiative would serve to encourage and focus debate on more progressive targets for strengthening and extending European political cohesion (much as had been the purpose of the broadly similar report on European union prepared by Belgian Prime Minister Leo Tindemans in 1975).[7] In fact this is the role it did play, as the European Council session in November 1981 instructed the foreign ministers to examine and clarify the proposals and report back at a future meeting of the Council.

Nevertheless, ensuing deliberations among the Ten did little to soften resistance to the Genscher–Colombo plan. In what may have been little more than a courtesy gesture in recognition of German and Italian efforts, in June 1983 the European Council session in Stuttgart endorsed a so-called Solemn Declaration on European Union,[8] which might also be described as a solemn burial of most of the innovative features of the draft European Act. Apparently motivated by the wish to pre-empt the European Parliament, which was considering its own more ambitious plan for European union,[9] the Solemn (Stuttgart) Declaration differed little in substance from the 1981 London Report that appears to have served as a benchmark for considering the German–Italian proposal. The declaration reaffirmed previous EPC statements endorsing the objectives of achieving joint positions and joint action, though avoiding commitment to a common foreign policy. Specifically restating the Luxembourg, Copenhagen and London Reports as the bases for political cooperation, the Ten shunned a pledge to adopt final positions only after consultations in favour of the traditional formula of 'taking full account' of their partners' views and giving 'due weight' to the adoption of common European positions 'when working out national positions and taking national actions'. It is clear that the state-centred locus of European foreign policy decision-making was to be left firmly intact.

Moreover, rather than accepting EPC statements 'as a binding common basis', the Ten only agreed that common positions would constitute 'a central point of reference' for the policies of member states. The scope of EPC deliberations was extended somewhat to include coordination of positions on 'the political and economic aspects of security' without, however, affecting the competencies of the EC in economic matters. The significance of the Solemn Declaration, clearly modest at best, was further diluted by reservations on various points recorded by Denmark, Greece and Ireland.[10] As a Belgian diplomat with wide experience in political cooperation wrote: 'A good rule of thumb in European matters is that the more solemn the declaration, the more empty it is of true content'.[11]

Notwithstanding the generally unexceptional substance of the Stuttgart Declaration, it served a useful purpose by formally articulating for the first time the growing importance of the role of the European Council in Community affairs. In this respect it was declared, *inter alia*, that the European Council

> provides a general political impulse to the construction of Europe; defines approaches to further the construction of Europe and issues general political guidelines for the European Communities and European Political Cooperation [including attention to maintaining consistency between them] . . . and solemnly expresses the common position in questions of external relations.[12]

A later development in the consolidation of a European political pillar linked to the EC was the adoption of the Single European Act (SEA) at the European Council meeting at Luxembourg in December 1985. Following signature and ratification by national parliaments, including Spain and Portugal which joined the EC in 1986, the SEA came into force in July 1987. The SEA encompassed four main objectives: (1) to enhance the effectiveness of EC decision-making by enabling the Council of Ministers to take many decisions based on a weighted majority vote (rather than unanimity), particularly on matters relating to the projected completion of the single internal market scheduled to be achieved by the end of 1992; (2) to strengthen the democratic character of Community institutions by assigning a larger role to the European Parliament in the adoption of EC legislation; (3) to formally extend EC authority into new areas such as environmental policy, technological research and development, monetary policy and social legislation where the Community was already engaged but which lacked an adequate statutory foundation in the existing treaties; (4) to provide for the first time a treaty basis for European Political Cooperation, previously based exclusively on summit and ministerial statements and evolved practices, while linking EPC to the EC, the two representing distinct though mutually reinforcing approaches to European unity.

With respect to political cooperation, the SEA essentially codified existing arrangements based on the Luxembourg, Copenhagen and London Reports, and the Solemn Declaration on European Union. The main exception was the establishment of a Secretariat for political cooperation in Brussels to assist the Presidency. However, the principal responsibility for initiative in political cooperation remained with the Presidency; thus the Secretariat was conceived as essentially an administrative organ in no way paralleling the role of the Commission in the EC. On the matter of consultations, the SEA did strengthen the language of the earlier reports and the Solemn Declaration by stipulating that 'consultations shall take place' *before* member states decide on their final position[13] (a formulation close to the Genscher–Colombo proposal).

However the key point remained, as before, that authority for foreign policy decision-making rested with national governments and that the effort to achieve common positions represented no more than 'a reference point' for those decisions. Moreover, pledges to seek common policies were laced with qualifiers such as 'endeavour', 'as effectively as possible', and 'as far as possible', which left the outcome of the obligatory consultations very much in doubt. Thus despite EPC's new treaty status, the only intentional and hence contingent nature of the obligations undertaken (except to consult), in reality created no new restraints on member states and no stronger assurances that common positions would emerge. Moreover, the formal obligation to consult was apparently intended to apply only to issues with which EPC was or had been engaged, not indiscriminately to all foreign policy questions.[14]

The Single European Act also formalised an umbrella relationship between the EC and EPC, including the Commission's association with the latter, which as we have seen had been developing in any case since the early 1980s. Nevertheless, the institutional and operational distinction between the two was maintained. Thus, Article 1 of the SEA affirmed that the EC and EPC constituted different yet complementary approaches to European unity. The EC would continue to be based on the existing Community treaties (as modified by the SEA), while EPC would continue on the foundations of the Luxembourg, Copenhagen, London and Stuttgart documents as extended and consolidated by the Single European Act. The linkage between the two was both political and functional, reflecting ideas advanced in the Tindemans report, the Genscher–Colombo proposal, and already partly incorporated in the Solemn Declaration and corresponding to evolved working practices during the 1980s. The European Council and the foreign ministers, acting according to the respective EPC and EC procedures, were to provide overall leadership and coordination and assure consistency between the external policies of the EC and policies agreed to in political cooperation (a principal responsibility of the presidency and the Commission).

In considering the progress of European Political Cooperation from the Luxembourg Report through the Single European Act and beyond, several conclusions emerge. On the institutional side, there has developed extensive expansion of EPC infrastructure, frequency of meetings and communications, increased visibility through involvement of the European Council, closer coordination with the EC (Council, Commission and Parliament) and establishment of a Secretariat. On the output side, while beyond the scope of this study,[15] there has been a steady proliferation of EPC positions on most significant international issues as they have arisen. Clearly EPC has moved well beyond an earlier characterisation that it amounted to 'procedure as substitute for policy'.[16] As Guy de Bassompierre observed: 'Thanks to the EPC, the Twelve have achieved common positions and a recognized status with regard to most, if not all, of the main international issues'.[17] Moreover, the rather arbitrary compartmentalisation of security-related issues has been difficult to maintain in practice. As former EC Commissioner Christopher Tugendhat observed: 'When the heads of government meet in the European Council, the line between security and other matters is sometimes completely forgotten in their intimate exchanges, and it can be blurred a good deal in Political Cooperation meetings as well'.[18]

Nevertheless, despite extension and improvement of the modalities of EPC, the type of commitment that states have been willing to accept in political cooperation has not substantially changed since the Luxembourg Report. The key operational commitment in EPC, as distinct from stated intentions, has always been to foreign policy consultations. This pledge was as explicit in the Luxembourg Report as it was in the Single European Act. The only difference between the two apart from the SEA's legal character, in any case unclear and problematic with regard to enforcement, relates to the timing of EPC consultations in connection with the determination of national positions. As we have seen, progressively from the Luxembourg Report to the Single European Act, both in practice and in formal pledges, it became increasingly explicit that consultations were to take place *before* the adoption of national positions. This was neither a commitment nor a consistent practice in EPC during much of the 1970s.

The clear intent of the required sequencing of consultations prior to national decisions was to enable EPC deliberations to constitute a significant albeit non-binding factor in the determination of national policies. To the extent that such consultations would exert influence on the shaping of national policies, the groundwork would be laid and developed for the progressive harmonisation of national policies at the European level. And as these policies came to be formulated and stated as European positions, they would henceforth serve as 'reference points' for future policies at both the national and European levels. Thus, the sequencing approach to consultations was designed to facilitate and encourage a progressive Europeanisation of national foreign policy processes, intended to yield a growing corpus of European positions which in turn would serve as benchmarks for further policy elaboration. The anticipated dynamic effects of consultations, that is, the influence on national decision-making of extensive and multi-level European deliberations, was seen as the only practical way of achieving progress. Hence, the operational commitment to European consultations before adoption of national positions was seen as at least facilitating attainment of common positions and joint action that governments were pledged to seek.

Of course national governments, while including EPC consultations in their own policy deliberations, retained final decisional authority. Moreover, member states continued to regard EPC primarily as an instrument for advancing national policies through reinforcement and solidarity at the European level. Yet the important point is that the often reaffirmed intentionality to seek common positions, the sequencing of EPC consultations and thus their potential influence prior to national decisions, and the cumulative socialisation effects of consultations on political and bureaucratic officials, have indeed moved EC governments toward closer foreign policy alignment than the mere pledge of consultations might lead one to expect. This phenomenon has been reinforced, as we have seen, by growing external expectations for a European response in specific situations, by a stronger European awareness of its own distinctive interests on particular issues, and by the availability of greater means of policy influence through coordinated action between EPC and the EC. Of course, it is not always clear to what extent the EPC process itself performs as an effective agent in promoting foreign policy harmonisation, as distinct from it essentially reflecting changes generated primarily at the national level.

Nevertheless, the growing convergence of European foreign policy outlooks, whether resulting from or simply reflected in EPC (or both), has not altered the mixed national and collective nature of European foreign policy. The resulting ambiguity, as Christopher Tugendhat has observed, creates the crucial problem of determining 'when the member states intend to operate as a group and wish to be seen as such and when they wish to be considered as individual countries. At one moment it seems to be the former and at the next the latter'.[19] Since the mixed-system character of foreign policy (with respect to both procedure and substance) is preferred by all EC governments, this situation is unlikely to change.

DEFENCE COOPERATION

Reactions to the Genscher–Colombo proposal and discussions leading to the Stuttgart Declaration made clear that some EC member states, notably Denmark, Greece and Ireland, were unwilling to include defence issues in the scope of European Political Cooperation.[20] Nevertheless other EPC countries, for reasons mentioned above, believed that it was important for the European members of the Alliance to concert more closely among themselves on defence matters. Apparent developments in US–Soviet relations and in West Germany stirred further anxieties. The 1986 Reykjavik summit between Gorbachev and Reagan, which seemed to put traditional American strategic deterrence policy on the auction block of US–Soviet arms control diplomacy, while reviving the spectre of decoupling, further reminded Europeans of their vulnerability to superpower actions beyond their control. The 1987 US–Soviet INF treaty banning intermediate-range nuclear missiles, but a few years after European governments had pleaded their necessity in the face of strong domestic opposition, was another reminder only partly disguised by public proclamations of support for the treaty. Earlier, France in particular had been concerned by anti-nuclear and pacifist tendencies in West Germany, sparked by the missile debate, which spurred the Mitterrand government to search for ways to strengthen the Federal Republic's ties to the West.

With EPC blocked as a forum for European defence consultations, efforts shifted toward other multilateral and bilateral approaches. The Independent European Programme Group (see Chapter 3) continued as the main consultative framework for collaboration in military procurement. Including all European Alliance members except Iceland, the IEPG had already inherited from the Eurogroup principal responsibility in this field. Initially operating at a level of defence procurement experts, it was elevated to ministerial status in 1984. In 1988, IEPG defence ministers took several initiatives aimed at creating a common market for armaments in parallel with the gradual establishment of the single internal market of the EC.[21]

By the mid-1980s, the IEPG had begun to establish its usefulness as a framework for exploring possibilities for collaborative weapons procurement and for coordinating specific joint projects by interested countries. However, IEPG proved to be only partly successful in resolving a fundamental dilemma of weapons collaboration which is to reconcile the aim of promoting more efficient use of resources and increased cost effectiveness with the interest of many states in preserving strong industrial sectors in the defence field. Experience has shown that collaborative co-production ventures can be more time-consuming and costly than single country programmes (or purchases of US-manufactured equipment) because of the need to involve different participants in various parts of the project – from the design phase through research and development, manufacture, testing, deployment and service – including coordinated project management throughout. Moreover, the inherent need to establish a common denominator with respect to performance characteristics of particular systems may require national defence ministries to compromise on their own requirements or forego participation in the project. Thus the trade-off between the interests of particular countries (for example industrial, employment, military needs, export markets) and the aims and putative benefits of collaboration often results in only partial satisfactions in both areas.

The American perspective on European procurement collaboration has been mixed, as with other areas of European cooperative activity. While welcoming European collaboration in the name of promoting a sound European defence industrial base, enhancing standardisation and/or inter-operability of weapons systems, and achieving a more efficient use of defence funds in a stagnant to shrinking budget environment, the US expressed concern that the expense of collaboration, often resulting in higher than necessary unit costs, could deflect European countries from maintaining a balanced modernisation of their conventional forces.[22] Moreover, to the extent that European cooperation results in greater internal procurement rather than from the United States, American defence industries are adversely affected. Relatedly, while the ratio of American–European mutual arms sales remained heavily in favour of the US, the gap narrowed considerably from 7:1 to less than 3:1 during the 1980s.[23]

In any case, it is clear that the political objective of maintaining a competitive defence industrial base through national and multilateral means constituted an increasingly important dimension of the European pillar in the 1980s. Beyond the IEPG itself, and numerous *ad hoc* bilateral and multilateral projects, the Single European Act innovatively associated the EC with defence activity through the stated determination of member states 'to maintain the technological and industrial conditions necessary for their security'. Pursuant to this proviso (and pressure from France), the EC Commission has considered the establishment of a common external tariff for many arms imports (currently excluded from the single market through Article 223 of the Rome Treaty), a move strongly resisted by the United States since it would add another dimension of European preference in the arms procurement field.[24]

The most significant development in bilateral relations was the invigoration of Franco-German defence cooperation through revival of their 1963 Treaty of Friendship and Cooperation (see Chapter 2). For nearly two decades, the treaty had been largely of symbolic value, providing a framework for cooperation but imparting little political substance to it. In 1981, early in the Mitterrand Presidency, France initiated talks to reactivate joint Franco-German military discussions as provided by the treaty.[25] However, the developing Franco-German defence cooperation in the 1980s had to be fitted to the different security perspectives and postures of the two countries. As then

West German Defence Minister Manfred Wörner described it in 1987, conveying the assumptions of collaboration while highlighting the different positions, Franco-German defence cooperation reflected agreement on five points:

> the aim of strengthening NATO; agreement that France cannot assume America's role in European security; agreement that Bonn and Paris do not want to form an "axis" and do not seek an exclusive relationship; that no attempt will be made to return France to NATO's integrated military command, and that Bonn will not attempt to induce France to abandon its autonomous nuclear policy.[26]

Thus cooperation had to be based on compatible though not identical security orientations.

Nevertheless, a closer relationship in defence suited the needs of both countries. France sought to anchor the Federal Republic more firmly in the West and also wanted a European framework for its defence policy that would not entail reintegration with NATO. The Federal Republic found it useful to associate France more directly with West European defence, in parallel with France's warmer relations with NATO, with both sides maintaining their different positions *vis-à-vis* the Alliance. Moreover, Bonn saw in Franco-German cooperation a means of reaffirming its ties with the West partly to assuage concerns about an eastern drift in German policy. As a senior West German official put it candidly: 'We don't want any distrust in America that we are changing our position. . . . Getting rid of this distrust is essential to get room for maneuver in our relations with the East. The backing [of France] makes that easier'.[27] Mindful of earlier US and European misgivings about the Franco-German treaty, both parties stressed the compatibility and value of their relationship as strengthening the Alliance and that it could serve as a basis for a more inclusive European defence cooperation.

Given the need to reconcile Franco-German cooperation with their different defence policies, and to minimise negative reactions elsewhere, most of the practical steps taken, though significant, were largely of a symbolic character. In 1983, France undertook an army reorganisation programme that led to the creation of a rapid deployment force to be used for defence in West Germany, among other possible contingencies. A large-scale joint military exercise was held on German soil in 1987 to demonstrate French deployment capabilities and to give visibility to Franco-German defence cooperation. In deference to France's position outside the NATO-integrated command, top NATO officials were not invited to observe the manoeuvres.[28] Also in 1987, agreement was reached on the formation of a joint military brigade to be stationed in West Germany under alternating French and German leadership. To avoid domestic charges that France was re-entering NATO via the back door of cooperation with Germany, and so as not to reduce the Federal Republic's contribution to NATO, the West German units assigned to the brigade were to be drawn from its territorial defence forces. Moreover France, while retaining final authority over any decision to use its nuclear weapons, began to move closer toward a position of unequivocal defence support for West Germany, in contrast to earlier French positions which stressed defence of its national frontiers. In addition, France agreed to consult with West Germany in some circumstances regarding the possible use of its pre-strategic weapons and announced an extended range for its new Hades missile, thereby easing German concerns that it would only be used in defence on West German territory. In any event, Mitterrand accepted a significant limitation on French freedom of action by affirming that in the event of war France's first nuclear strike would 'not be delivered on German soil'.[29]

Finally, in conjunction with the twenty-fifth anniversary commemoration of the Franco-German Treaty in January 1988, agreement was formalised through a protocol to the treaty on the creation of a Franco-German Defence and Security Council composed of the heads of government or state and the foreign and defence ministers. Meeting for the first time in April 1989, the Council was to focus on specific measures of bilateral defence cooperation, with a still broader mandate to develop mutual defence and security concepts and to effect 'increasing coordination between the two countries in all questions relating to European security, including arms control and disarmament'.[30] Stressing the European dimension of Franco-German cooperation, the preamble to the agreement noted that they were 'certain that the work of European unity will remain incomplete as long as it does not include defence and security'. Suggesting that the Franco-German brigade could serve as a laboratory for much broader defence cooperation, Chancellor Kohl and Defence Minister Wörner spoke ambitiously about the possibility of a European army as a long-term prospect.[31]

Despite efforts to portray Franco-German defence cooperation as a contribution to European unity and to the European pillar of the Alliance, the scope and seeming momentum of the activity in 1987 and early 1988 provoked visible irritation and mistrust elsewhere, particularly in Britain, Italy and the Netherlands.[32] Prime Minister Thatcher questioned the use and need for the Franco-German brigade, characterising such forms of cooperation as 'initiatives for the gallery'.[33] Partly to mollify Thatcher and to overcome suspicions of Franco-German exclusivity, France (and later West Germany) made overtures to Britain suggesting discussions on bilateral defence cooperation. While relatively minor agreements were reached to explore the use of French facilities to move British forces inland in the event of war, and to exchange nuclear submarine visits at each other's ports, a more ambitious idea for joint development of an air-launched, nuclear-armed cruise missile remained at a stage of technical discussions.[34] Whereas Thatcher was not opposed to bilateral defence cooperation *per se*, she remained adamant that any such activity conducted outside of NATO, such as was the case with France and Germany, would risk undermining the Alliance. Given its more divisive than unifying effects in Europe (resembling earlier reactions to the 1963 treaty) and the sharp improvement in East–West relations beginning in 1989, it appeared that Franco-German defence cooperation had reached a plateau beyond which it was unlikely to advance.

The most important multilateral effort to establish a European pillar in defence was the revival of the Western European Union (see Chapter 1) beginning in 1983/84, largely at French initiative with support from Belgium. Motivated by similar considerations that were reopening the Franco-German defence dialogue, the two roughly parallel initiatives were politically connected. By providing a wider European framework for defence consultations, WEU could compensate for the narrowness of the Franco-German partnership, accord it a certain 'European' legitimacy, and assuage recurring concerns about a Franco-German axis. Given its status as the only multilateral European organisation with a mandate in defence, and its already established organisation and charter (including a tighter mutual defence commitment than that of the North Atlantic Treaty), WEU had obvious advantages. Moreover, at the time WEU included all members of the EC except the three (Denmark, Greece and Ireland) which were unwilling to include defence issues in EPC. As one inside observer said, 'To put it bluntly, the WEU coincided with the EPC minus the "difficult" countries'.[35] In short, a major motivation for the WEU's revival was the blockage of attempts to extend the EC's role to defence matters. Indeed, the political cooperation section of the Single European Act gave a green light to closer security cooperation within the framework of WEU or the Atlantic Alliance.

Some countries, notably Britain and the Netherlands, were initially sceptical about the revival of WEU on grounds that it could be interpreted by Washington as an unfriendly gesture and introduce a divisive factor in the Alliance. And as earlier in the case of Eurogroup (see Chapter 3), there was concern that a new European defence initiative could promote decoupling and a lessened US involvement in European defence. West Germany also had hesitations. It will be recalled (see Chapter 1) that the Paris Agreements of 1954 establishing the WEU contained arms control restrictions applicable to the Federal Republic, including prohibitions on the manufacture of specified types of offensive armaments. These provisions, together with other aspects of the accords that suggested continued mistrust of Germany, meant that the WEU was an uncomfortable reminder of Germany's past and subjection to controls and thus could not, in its existing form, be a suitable vehicle for European defence cooperation in the quite different circumstances of the 1980s. Hence, West Germany insisted that the remaining restraints on its production of conventional arms be lifted, which was agreed to by the WEU in 1984.[36] Indeed, restrictions on West German production of conventional arms had been progressively relaxed through several little noticed WEU decisions beginning in 1973.

Nevertheless, the initial interest in reviving WEU shifted somewhat toward the end of 1984. The anti-nuclear protest movement in Germany had subsided, having failed to block deployment of US missiles begun the previous year, thereby easing French concerns over the German 'drift' problem. Of undoubtedly greater importance, however, was the close Senate vote in June on a proposal by Senator Sam Nunn, known as a strong supporter of NATO, which would have reduced US troops in Europe by 90 000 over a three-year period if European NATO members failed to meet the agreed goal of increasing defence expenditures by 3 per cent a year.[37] While the measure was defeated 55–41, following intensive lobbying by the Reagan administration, it nevertheless sent a strong message to Europe about Senate attitudes toward European support of NATO. Hence the earlier more assertive interest in greater Europeanisation on defence questions, which had sparked the revival of WEU, yielded to a reluctance to contour WEU in a manner that could antagonise American attitudes toward the European allies and alienate US support for its NATO commitments.

The new mood was reflected in the WEU Council session in Rome in October, the first to include foreign and defence ministers, meeting to mark the thirty-year anniversary of the founding of the organisation. The tone of ministerial speeches and briefings emphasised the central and irreplaceable role of the Atlantic Alliance as the foundation of Europe's security, and that the role of WEU was to strengthen the European pillar of the Alliance. According to the Rome declaration, WEU consultations were to embrace defence questions, arms control and disarmament, East–West relations and European security, Alliance defence burden-sharing and European armaments cooperation. With respect to the latter, which was accorded major emphasis, the aim was to develop an effective and competitive European armaments industry, working principally through existing organisations such as the IEPG. It was decided that henceforward the WEU Council would meet twice yearly including foreign and defence ministers.

Despite affirmations that WEU activity would be fully in accord with the Alliance and that other NATO members would be kept informed, the broad scope of the Council's mandate and the fact that it could not only deliberate but also take decisions, provoked sharp concerns in Washington over the implications of a possible European caucus in NATO (see Chapter 7). This was particularly the case given the later interpretation of the Rome meeting by some participants, notably West Germany. In a policy statement to the Bundestag on European cooperation in November, Foreign Minister Genscher noted that a stronger WEU will enable Europe to 'gain greater political weight within the alliance and can thus make a more effective contribution to the stabilization of East–West relations'.[38] In plainer language, it appeared to mean that Bonn intended to utilise the WEU as a vehicle for attempting to moderate the Reagan administration's confrontational posture toward the Soviet Union. The European caucus idea was conveyed in Genscher's observation that the WEU members 'will seek to harmonize their views on all important security and defense issues on which a common European position within the alliance seems appropriate' (including specifically the areas mentioned in the preceding paragraph). In all likelihood, it was this perspective on WEU and its relation to NATO that prompted the Reagan administration's reportedly 'blunt and direct' discouragement of the revitalisation of WEU and its pointed advice that 'any larger European role in defence should take place within NATO'.[39]

In April 1985, US concerns that WEU could become a rival of NATO[40] combined with state-level interests in Europe to block a coordinated response to President Reagan's Strategic Defence Initiative (SDI). WEU members were unable to agree on a collective response to the Reagan administration's offer of European research participation in the project, which was mainly a US tactic for mobilising European support for SDI. While WEU ministers agreed 'to try to achieve as far as possible' a coordinated reaction to the US proposal, advocated particularly by France and Germany, British reservations for the most part prevented agreement. In a revealing commentary on Britain's priorities, Defence Secretary Michael Heseltine noted: 'Once we have explored bilateral opportunities, the [WEU] countries here will want to see how far European coordination will be possible'.[41] This, of course, was precisely the approach preferred by the Reagan administration. While the sensitive nature of the SDI research programme necessarily required government to government agreements, nevertheless it could have been advantageous to Europe for the WEU to establish guidelines to strengthen the leverage of individual countries in negotiating collaboration with Washington. By the time WEU ministers convened again in November, negotiations were well advanced between the US, Britain and West Germany toward the conclusion of bilateral cooperation accords.

In any case, the possibility of a common European approach was further damaged in May when the Mitterrand government announced that it would not participate in the SDI research programme[42] (though later allowing private contractors to do so), and subsequently blocked a US attempt to gain formal NATO endorsement of the plan.[43] NATO's Nuclear Planning Group, of which France was not a member, did provide a somewhat qualified statement of support in March. France, sceptical of SDI on strategic grounds, also resented American expectations that Europe would play the role of 'subcontractors' in the programme, a term used by Reagan, which jarred traditional French sensitivities about equality. Instead, France sought support from its European allies for its Eureka programme of civilian-oriented research and development of space-related technologies. Rather than presenting a common front to Washington, it seemed for a time that European governments would be faced with the familiar dilemma of reconciling different and competing US and French initiatives. It is clear that WEU was ineffective in developing a coordinated European response to SDI, despite the fact that issues of space-based defence – including their relation to deterrence, strategic arms negotiations and the anti-ballistic missile treaty – had direct implications for European security and fell within the scope of the WEU's recent Rome declaration. It is interesting that Ivo Daalder's thorough analysis of European reactions to SDI does not even mention the WEU.[44]

As previously indicated, WEU's slow revival, begun in 1984, received a boost as a result of the Reykjavik summit in October 1986, followed by quickened progress in the US–Soviet negotiations leading to the INF treaty. Despite Reykjavik's failure to resolve the deadlock over linking substantial cuts in strategic forces to limits on space-based defences, US–Soviet agreement in principle to reduce strategic forces by 50 per cent, and the US proposal to eliminate all ballistic missiles over a ten year period, provoked concerns in Europe that nuclear deterrence could be gradually undermined. As one French official put it caustically: 'It was Yalta II. . . . The two superpowers got together and in two days, without any consideration, without any consultation with us, sold out Europe again'.[45]

Moreover, the rapid post-Reykjavik progress toward the INF treaty, concluded less than fifteen months later, when coupled with prospective major cuts in strategic forces, increased the risk of a weakened NATO deterrence posture when the Warsaw Pact was believed to hold substantial advantages in conventional and chemical forces as well as short-range nuclear systems. More broadly, Gorbachev's call for the elimination of all nuclear weapons by the year 2000, and Reagan's SDI-projected shift from offensive to defensive deterrence (of attacks against the US), posed the spectre of European vulnerability in a de-nuclearising world. Notwithstanding satisfaction over the warming trend in superpower relations, in view of the scope and pace of the US–Soviet dialogue on such matters, Europeans were made to feel all the more powerless to influence decisions bearing directly on their own security.

Given such factors, there was renewed interest in WEU as a forum for considering Europe's position in light of the accelerated momentum in superpower arms control diplomacy. The previously sceptical British, who also held serious reservations about Reykjavik and the INF negotiations, moved toward clearer support of WEU. In an important speech in Brussels in March 1987, Foreign Secretary Geoffrey Howe cited America's stronger orientation toward the Pacific, pressures in Washington for deficit reduction and greater Alliance burden-sharing, a protectionist trade atmosphere, and the new interest in strategic defence as 'trends in American thinking which might diminish our security'.[46] While noting that NATO must remain the decision-making forum on defence matters, Howe emphasised 'the need for the European countries to consult more closely among themselves about their defense interests . . . and come wherever possible to a common view . . . if we want our particular European concerns to be clearly perceived and taken into account' in superpower negotiations. In the same vein, as discussed previously, Franco-German defence cooperation intensified in 1987 with plans to create a joint brigade, a defence and security council, and the holding of joint military manoeuvres on West German territory in September.

The new European defence awakening led to adoption of a Platform on European Security Interests by the WEU Council at The Hague in October.[47] Originally proposed by France as a 'European defense charter', a term later dropped because it was deemed potentially objectionable by the United States,[48] WEU members reiterated the importance of security and defence as elements of European unity and pledged to develop a more cohesive European defence identity. Substantively, however, the platform broke little new ground and essentially reaffirmed commitments to intensified cooperation in areas which had been previously enumerated in the Rome declaration. Pledges were renewed 'to defend any member country at its borders', thus strengthening France's commitment to a forward defence of West German territory. The nuclear-sensitive Federal Republic agreed to the reaffirmation that deterrence and defence 'must continue to be based on an adequate mix of appropriate nuclear and conventional forces', noting that only the nuclear element can confront a potential aggressor with an unacceptable risk. Beyond specific aspects of defence cooperation in both a European and Atlantic context, the platform emphasised the importance of arms control and disarmament and of furthering East–West dialogue and cooperation, particularly along the lines of the Helsinki Final Act and the CSCE process.

However, the platform made clear that there was no European defence revolution underway *vis-à-vis* the United States and NATO. On the contrary, the platform stressed traditional Atlanticist views that the security of the Alliance is indivisible, that Europe's security can only be ensured in close association with the North American allies, and that 'the substantial presence of US conventional and nuclear forces plays an irreplaceable part' in the defence of Europe. In this context, the role of European defence cooperation and other elements of European unity was to enable 'a balanced partnership across the Atlantic' and 'to strengthen the European pillar of the Alliance'. Interestingly, though the contribution of the independent British and French nuclear forces to European security was noted twice in the platform, there was no direct mention of the recently intensified Franco-German defence cooperation. While the reason for this omission is not altogether clear, it probably reflected a reluctance by other countries, as discussed above, to encourage this type of activity particularly outside the framework of NATO. In any case, it was apparent that the 'ideology' of the WEU's security platform on European defence cooperation and relations with the Alliance differed little from that of the Eurogroup when it was created nearly 20 years earlier.

Plainly, later US statements of support for European defence cooperation, intended largely to encourage increased European sharing of Alliance defence costs, reflected diminished apprehensions that a European defence entity would pose a challenge to American leadership in NATO or risk a European separatist drift from the Alliance. President Reagan's speeches in 1987 welcoming a European identity in defence closely followed WEU's adoption of its platform on security interests. While proclaiming the need for a more cohesive European defence identity, the platform backed away from the more ambitious formulations of the Rome declaration that had implied a European caucus 'to gain greater political weight within the alliance'. Acutely aware of recurring pressures in the US Congress for larger European defence contributions and for American force reductions, complaints about EC trade policies, and perceptions of lack of European support on the issues discussed in Chapters 7 and 8, European governments did not wish to further exacerbate Atlantic tensions by moves that could be construed as challenging American leadership of the Alliance. Nor did they wish to begin a process that could be perceived in Washington as movement toward European self-reliance in defence, thus providing a pretext and rationale for reduced US commitments to European security. Moreover, in light of the security uncertainties associated with US strategic policy and the superpower arms control dialogue, and Europe's dependence and limited internal cohesion on security matters, political instincts argued against significant change in the status quo. Reflecting the new mood, British Foreign Secretary Geoffrey Howe later characterised WEU in modest terms as 'not an operational forum nor . . . a framework for developing a consensus in particular negotiations'.[49] Indeed, the notion of a European caucus appeared dead. While WEU sought to achieve 'the closest possible identity of view on security issues', Howe observed, this was so that its members could 'individually' make a stronger contribution to the Alliance. Thus while Spain and Portugal joined WEU in 1988, it appeared that by this time both WEU and Franco-German defence cooperation, though for somewhat different reasons, had reached a development plateau.

Moreover, it was clear, as Ian Gambles observes, that any enlargement of the role of WEU 'is impeded by a conceptual division among its members as to the long-term goals of the organization and its place on the institutional map of Europe'.[50] This was revealed by a dispute during 1988/89 between France and Britain over the issue of establishing a common location for the WEU Secretariat in London and its agencies in Paris. Britain promoted WEU's relocation to Brussels, which would create the possibility of establishing closer ties with NATO headquarters nearby. However because of the substantial differences in size, activity and prominence between the two organisations, the natural links between the two would risk a WEU junior partner image *vis-à-vis* NATO, precisely the kind of identification that led France to remain out of Eurogroup. Closely linking the various aspects of European defence cooperation to NATO had of course always been a central British interest (and condition) in the revival of WEU. France, on the other hand, rejected a WEU move to Brussels chiefly for the very reasons Britain advocated it. Moreover, a WEU headquarters located in Paris, in addition to enhancing France's status as a European 'capital', would also position the organisation for a more independent role while promoting France's interest in a more distinctively European approach to security policy. While a compromise to create a small European defence institute in Paris and keep the WEU Secretariat in London at least temporarily eased the dispute, it did not resolve the basic differences between London and Paris as to WEU's relationship to NATO.[51]

To be sure, the WEU played a useful though secondary role in the participation by member states during 1987/88 in mine-clearing operations in the Persian Gulf region in the context of the Iran–Iraq war. At the seven-nation summit of industrialised democracies in June 1987, the United States was unable to obtain endorsement for its own efforts to safeguard shipping traffic in the Gulf or commitments from the major European countries to provide assistance. A new situation arose in August when a US-operated oil tanker struck a mine in the Gulf of Oman, south-east of the Persian Gulf, though in an area where British and French naval vessels had been operating. Reacting to this first such incident outside the Persian Gulf, which suggested a widening zone of danger to shipping, Britain and France announced separately though almost simultaneously that they would send mine-sweepers to the Gulf of Oman, tasked to protect their own flagged vessels, as reinforcements for their existing naval forces in the region.

Given recent US pressures for active European involvement in the protection of Gulf shipping, a waterway more important to Europe for oil supplies than to the United States, the British and French actions increased pressure on other European governments to take positive measures of their own.[52] The recently revitalised WEU was the obvious forum for attempting to coordinate the effort, all the more so because it enabled acceptance of a military commitment in the name of a European policy, thereby facilitating the policy reversal of governments that had previously resisted US pressures for action. The soon to be concluded Platform on European Security Interests also played a part, since a WEU role in coordinating Gulf mine-clearing operations would give some tangible substance to the intent to develop a more cohesive European defence identity. Britain, France, Belgium, Italy and the Netherlands provided ships for the operation while West Germany, which claimed that its constitution prohibited use of its military forces outside the Alliance area, for the first time assigned ships to a NATO standby force in the Mediterranean (to release other allied ships for the Gulf) as a gesture of solidarity for the Gulf operation.[53] Luxembourg provided a small financial contribution, thus symbolically completing some form of involvement by all WEU members.[54]

Nevertheless, the role of WEU was to provide a framework for the political and military coordination of member state actions, rather than constituting a collective operational presence itself.[55] Indeed Britain, France and Italy later denied reports that there had been agreement among the three to establish a multi-nation task force to conduct mine-clearing operations under rotating command.[56] Moreover, the initial unilateral actions by Britain and France, which virtually forced the hands of other WEU members, underscored that matters of defence policy remained very much a national prerogative. On the other hand, it is noteworthy that at least in this instance actions taken by one or more members individually exerted pressures on others to take complementary measures in the name of European solidarity and to avoid the impression of a divided Europe at a time when they were seeking to emphasise their unity.

10 The United States and the European Pillar in the 1970s and 1980s: Concluding Assessment

During the 1970s and 1980s, the United States did little to encourage strengthening European Political Cooperation as a pillar in the transatlantic relationship and often projected attitudes and conducted policies that indirectly discouraged it. As the case studies have shown, earlier American complaints that it did not have a European partner with whom to negotiate were gradually replaced by a pattern of irritation over European responses when it was able to speak with one voice. Moreover, having only indirect access to EPC deliberations (via Gymnich-type consultations), the United States became wary of the growing political weight of a collective European body with which it had but limited influence. Regular US–EPC consultations did develop as an adjunct to the traditional bilateral and multilateral patterns of Atlantic diplomacy. Yet the American interest in these consultations was primarily to influence the character of the European position that would eventually emerge, rather than to reinforce the EPC structure itself as a collective body speaking and acting for Europe. Hence, the American tendency was to emphasise bilateral contacts with individual European governments and multilateral consultations in the Alliance – both of which provided larger and more differentiated scope for US influence on European policies. As discussed below, both patterns conformed to a generally hierarchical pattern of US–European relations of advantage to the United States, as compared to the more equal twin-pillar model of a US–EPC configuration. This pluralistic US diplomatic style was often exercised to encourage or discourage particular EPC positions indirectly through influence brought to bear on key European governments. Indeed, the United States found it advantageous to exploit an essential characteristic and weakness of EPC – that member states retain control of their own foreign policies and are politically more accessible to outside countries through bilateral contacts than through the machinery of political cooperation.

As reflected in the earlier case studies, an assessment of mutual US–EPC influences yields a mixed picture. Clearly in the Iran hostage crisis, the Afghanistan and Polish crises, and the Libyan crisis, all involving economic and diplomatic pressures advocated by the United States, such measures as the Europeans were prepared to adopt were responsive to strong American urgings. In the case of the Iranian and Libyan crises, European actions were taken in the hope that they would forestall more extreme US measures and to attain some influence on American policy decisions. With respect to the Middle East, US opposition to any European initiative that might jeopardise the Camp David process clearly influenced the more moderate European stance reflected in the Venice Declaration as well as its less assertive posture thereafter, in combination with the other factors discussed. On the other hand, US influence on the relatively low-keyed European policy toward Central America appears to have been modest at best, and on the Soviet gas pipeline dispute none at all. In any event, beginning with the 1973/74 Atlantic crisis, all of these episodes contributed to the growing American ambivalence and reserve toward the idea of European political unity, and resentment and even hostility toward some of its expressions through EPC. Indeed, as David Allen and Michael Smith observed:

> The near paranoid perception of Europe that had led both Nixon and Kissinger to complain that European unity was being built around hostility to the United States had in fact more substance during the Carter and Reagan periods. In their reactions to Camp David, to the Iranian revolution, to the Soviet invasion of Afghanistan, to the events in Poland and to the question of economic sanctions the Europeans did indeed begin to build common postures . . . around their mutual differences with the United States.[1]

The most obvious example of European influence on American policy was the Soviet gas pipeline dispute where strong and united European opposition to the extension of US sanctions, coupled with congressional resistance, was a major factor in the Reagan administration's decision to abandon them. Not surprisingly this episode, and also the case of Central America, suggest that European influence on American policy was most effective when combined with substantial US congressional dissent from administration positions.

Otherwise, given the multiple causality usually characteristic of foreign policy decision-making, it is difficult to attribute or weigh specific collective European influences on American policy in the cases considered. (This of course was also often true for US influence on European positions). However, the limited and often symbolic nature of European responses did impair the potential effectiveness of US initiatives. In some cases (for example, the pipeline dispute and the Libyan crisis), Europe's partial measures were a factor in the Reagan administration's decision to escalate its own pressures. On other issues, particularly in the area of European and even US–Soviet arms negotiations, European influence on American policy initiatives was more palpable,[2] though it was exerted primarily through bilateral and Alliance channels rather than from Europe as a collectivity.

Thus it is virtually certain, given US efforts to preserve as much Alliance unity as possible, that European positions, in whatever form advanced, did sometimes have a moderating influence on American policy both with respect to the timing and substance of particular actions. Moreover, the ending of US military support for the Nicaraguan Contras by the late 1980s, coupled with greater reliance on regional efforts at political accommodation in Central America, moved the United States closer to traditional European positions in this area. The establishment of the freely elected government in Nicaragua in April 1990 effectively ended what had been the most serious source of US–European discord over Central America. Somewhat similarly, the outbreak of the Palestinian resistance movement in the late 1980s spurred the United States to revive its Middle East diplomacy, for the first time including dialogue with the PLO, which narrowed US–European differences in this area of policy. Finally, the ending of the cold war during the late 1980s and 1990 (see Chapter 11), coupled with a renewed transatlantic consensus for *détente*, reduced US–West European policy differences on East–West relations which had been the principal source of US–European friction during the 1980s.

All of the cases studied were marked by a general though not uniform tendency by US and European decision-makers to seek to prevent differences over particular issues from affecting other aspects of Atlantic relations, in particular NATO and US–EC trade relations. Nevertheless on occasion, particularly during the 1973/74 Atlantic crisis and more indirectly later, the United States did invoke linkage between European support for American policies and US security protection for Europe. Of course, such linkage did not have to be expressly invoked for it to constitute a major factor in European thinking as to how far to press its views with Washington. Europeans, too, on occasion invoked a form of linkage by hinting that US actions on particular issues could undermine European domestic support for maintaining policies in other areas closely identified with the United States. Typically, as a matter of diplomatic form and to preserve their own flexibility, the US and European governments cited domestic public and/or parliamentary attitudes that could compel a shift in policy.

Moreover, the continued disciplining effects of the East–West confrontation and military bipolarity through much of the 1980s operated to somewhat insulate Atlantic Alliance relations *per se* from US–European differences on other issues. Indeed, the formidable and controversial nature of the Atlantic security agenda – the intermediate-range nuclear missile issue, conventional and short-range nuclear forces modernisation, burden-sharing, SDI, and arms control – to name but a few, discouraged overloading the Alliance with other issues. Relatedly, European governments generally preferred a more literal and restrictive view of the importance of Alliance solidarity with respect to scope (the North Atlantic area) and to purpose (deterrence, defence and arms control). With the adoption of the Harmel Report in 1967, the pursuit of *détente* was endorsed as a complementary Alliance objective, though this tended to serve as an overall legitimation (cited particularly by West Germany) for the often quite different policies of Alliance members on specific issues of East–West relations. The more narrow European interpretation of the Alliance reflected in part the desire of European governments to preserve freedom of manoeuvre in other areas and to limit the range of issues subject to predominant American influence. Not coincidentally, moreover, it was on such 'non-Alliance' issues (restrictive interpretation), that European Political Cooperation chose to carve its niche and where it was most successful in developing positions independent of the United States. This generally applied to so-called out-of-area issues, as well as to some non-defence aspects of security. Also, not surprisingly, US–European differences occurred most often on such issues where US influence and leverage on Europe to support American policies was limited, in comparison to paramount US influence on matters of Alliance defence.

The general American preference for a more expansive view of the Alliance as a forum for Western consultations and coordination of responses has long been evident. Whether or not formal

Alliance consultations as such were used for these purposes, the United States often invoked the need for Alliance solidarity to mobilise European support for American policies and to pre-empt or counter European initiatives considered harmful to them. As the case studies have shown, the United States has sought to extend the range of its unique predominance on Alliance security matters to other issues deemed to be essential or complementary to the purposes of the Alliance. Given the centrality of the US role in European deterrence and defence, American leverage within the Alliance on such issues has often been decisive, at least in eliciting a level of European support that otherwise might not have been forthcoming.

Moreover, the multilateral character of alliance diplomacy inevitably plays to the advantage of the senior coalition member. Thus, given the usual behavioural dynamics of hierarchical multilateral security organisations, including a propensity for following the leader by those who are dependent, any formal extension of the political scope of the Alliance would likewise imply enlargement of overall American leadership in the orchestration of Western policies on global issues. This would be so because of the practical difficulty of isolating within the same organisational context issues such as defence, in which American views would ordinarily be given preponderant weight, and other issues which would be subject to different and non (or less) dependent European calculations of interest. Or put another way, if the Alliance were to become more central as a coordinating body for Western positions on global issues, as occurred at the beginning of the 1990 Persian Gulf crisis, the hierarchical US–European relationship deeply embedded (though by no means automatic) in the NATO defence tradition would tend to spill over into other issue areas as well. The corollary, of course, would imply a more limited scope for European influence on such matters than would be possible through a forum largely independent of the Alliance. This partly explains the traditional European reluctance to utilise the Alliance as more than a consultative body on out-of-area questions, and its preference instead to use its own political cooperation mechanisms where European positions can be deliberated apart from the inevitable American shadow in NATO.

Hence, despite periodic NATO consultations on out-of-area issues, and occasional understandings on 'compensation' for a member's external commitments, the Alliance as such played but a limited role in these matters through the 1980s. Moreover, despite the more expansive American view of the need for Western solidarity on particular issues, the United States sometimes preferred not to use the Alliance for this purpose in cases where known European views would have risked a public airing of allied differences. Such American reservations would be reinforced to the extent that European members might seek to advance their own concerted positions within the Alliance. In any event, the United States has generally preferred not to overload the Alliance *per se* with unrealistic expectations of solidarity on issues not clearly within its purview, while at the same time seeking to promote consensus and narrow the range of US–European divergence in particular cases.

Equally important, and closely related, the differing US and European views on the importance of Alliance out-of-area solidarity has been a function of their different roles, perspectives and responsibilities with regard to the East–West confrontation and other issues. An interesting US–European role-reversal occurred in this respect. Since the East–West conflict always had global dimensions and ramifications, NATO countries often tried to invoke the need for Alliance solidarity as a means of gaining support for their own out-of-area problems, hence placing them in the context of the global East–West struggle. Thus in the late 1940s and 1950s, some European NATO countries, trying to cope with the pains of decolonisation, sought Alliance solidarity or non-interference in their Third World policies (France in Indochina and later Algiers, the Netherlands in Indonesia/West Irian, Belgium in the Congo, and Britain at Suez), often citing the risks of communist or other radical influence or domination in nationalist movements. Notwithstanding strong US military support for France in Indochina, the general American opposition to colonialism and its ideological affinity for national self-determination resulted in a pattern of US–European tensions over such issues. Of course, the consistency and credibility of US policy was often marred or diluted by the political need to show a measure of solidarity for its European allies. However, the general American tendency was to resist treatment of European decolonisation issues as matters for the Alliance. Moreover, to the extent that Third World issues involved matters of military security, the United States regarded other regional and bilateral alliances as the appropriate fora for consultations. As discussed in Chapter 2, this perspective was a central element in the US rejection of de Gaulle's proposal to broaden the scope of the Atlantic Alliance to include coordination on global issues.

By the 1970s and 1980s, in contrast, the US–European roles were reversed – with the West Europeans geographically more retrenched on the Continent and the United States still globally committed and prone to invoke the need for Alliance solidarity on out-of-area issues. Indeed, Henry Kissinger's condescending reference in 1973 to America's global interests and responsibilities, in comparison to Europe's more regional concerns, was resented less because it was inaccurate than because its essential (if oversimplified) accuracy was demeaning and drew attention to basic disparities in the two global positions at a time when EC governments were trying to re-extend their collective political outreach in the post-colonial era. Closely resembling the early post-war US resistance to identification with colonialism as a structure of European global influence, Europeans later resisted co-optation into an essentially bipolar conceptualisation of global relations characterised by American predominance in the Western pole. Nevertheless, during both periods the general US and European tendency was to distinguish Alliance from non-Alliance matters with respect to expected common responses, and to attempt to insulate the Alliance *per se* from negative spill-back influences arising from differences on outside issues. The 'acceptable' range of divergence of course varied widely, depending upon the exploitable leverage available to an Alliance member (most often the US), the importance of the issue, and hence the value ascribed to obtaining allied support.

The United States, then, as leader of a global network of alliances and supportive relationships aimed at opposing Soviet and communist expansion during the cold war era, tended to view East–West and regional issues primarily in terms of their perceived significance for the wider global confrontation. However, the European effort to mold a separate foreign policy identity was not motivated primarily by East–West considerations, however much events often compelled a European response in specific cases. Rather, as discussed previously, the impulse came from the long standing aim of constructing a political Europe – a goal rendered more important and feasible by the external role and competencies of the EC, and by the growing sense of need to seek independent European positions on global issues, often prompted by dissatisfaction with US policies and an awareness of distinctive European interests that might differ from those of the United States. Given the deeply etched character of traditional American influence on European foreign policies, the notion of independence easily translated into independence from the United States. Of course 'independence' did not necessarily imply 'different from', though it did call for a uniquely European consideration of particular issues which might or might not yield alignment with American positions. Less preoccupied than Washington by an East–West view of regional conflicts, Europeans tended to focus more on their indigenous causes and to propose solutions that would encourage insulating such disputes from the East–West confrontation, while creating expanded possibilities for European influence in resolving or containing them.

Given these different views of regional conflicts, the strategies for dealing with them also differed. In contrast to the United States, West European governments generally did not recognise the propriety or utility of military measures as instruments of foreign policy, though French support for Chad against Libyan-backed incursions in the 1980s and action to put down a coup attempt in Togo in 1986 were notable exceptions. For the most part, however, the general European preference for 'civilian power' types of global influence, together with the EC's extensive involvement with North–South relations through the Lomé Conventions and ties with regional groups such as in Central America and Southeast Asia, further delineated a European role apart from the Alliance and East–West issues. Thus European efforts toward a redeployment of global influence since the early 1970s have been advanced more through EPC, the EC, and to a limited extent the WEU, than through the Atlantic Alliance. Europe's comparative advantage in such a role was further enhanced by the frequent preference of some Third World countries to expand ties with the West outside the context of the East–West confrontation and to avoid over-identification with the policies of the superpowers. In a sense, then, efforts at collective European foreign policy making have sought to establish positions and influence in the gaps or at the margins of superpower rivalry and in areas not staked out by NATO in the defence field. Moreover, as the case studies have shown, European positions often sought something of a middle ground between the extreme positions of conflicting protagonists.

Reinforcing the above consideration has been the strong American penchant, much more marked than in Europe, for viewing East–West issues through the lens of ideological confrontation. Lacking a tradition of global foreign policy involvement rooted in strategic or balance-of-power calculations, in 1947 the Truman administration based its appeal for public support for the containment policy heavily on a threat assessment derived from the ideological dichotomy between

free peoples and totalitarian (communist) regimes. While the ideological element of foreign policy thought in post-war US administrations has varied, with few exceptions until the late 1980s it was a major
factor in explaining and mobilising popular backing for US policies
aimed at stopping communism. Europeans, on the other hand, conditioned by a long experience of coexistence with the Soviet Union and
the Russian Empire before it, and moreover accustomed to domestic
communist parties in their midst, have generally not viewed global or
European issues in such ideologically polarising terms. Relatedly, the
European foreign policy mentality has been shaped by centuries of
experience in addressing national security issues through calculations
of equilibrium and balance of power and has tended to downplay
the significance of ideology as a foreign policy determinant. Hence,
differing underlying views of the ideological factor as an element of
East–West relations further limited US–European common ground in
the Alliance on issues extending beyond military security in Europe.

The general US and European preference for a somewhat compart-
mentalised management of transatlantic issues has been even more
marked with respect to US–EC trade relations. Both sides of the
Atlantic have generally sought to confine recurring trade disputes
to their issue-specific boundaries, to resolve them within their own
terms of reference, and to limit their potential for adversely affecting
other aspects of transatlantic relations (with the partial exception of
the policies of the Kennedy and Nixon administrations in the early
1960s and early 1970s, as discussed previously). The possibilities for
doing so exist because of the often discrete nature of the issues (for
example, hormone-treated beef, banking laws, agricultural subsidies,
telecommunications, local content rules) which lend themselves to
sectoral management, by the specialised international norms and
mechanisms through which they are handled, and by the different
government and parliamentary bodies involved. Nevertheless, to the
extent that such issues are viewed as a cumulative pattern of adverse
behaviour (for example, US perceptions of protectionist EC trade
policies or unfair use of export subsidies), there is an inescapable tendency for trade disputes to produce attitudinal spill-over effects into
other areas of transatlantic relations. Hence, allegedly discriminatory
EC trade practices have often been linked in the US public mind
to complaints of inadequate European defence burden-sharing and
weak European support for American global policies. This has been
particularly evident in some attitudes in Congress which are traditionally most sensitive to the real or alleged impact of EC trade policies

within their constituencies. The relative decline of America's global economic position and a recent history of US trade deficits with the EC have inevitably sharpened bilateral friction over particular trade issues. Nevertheless, such disputes tend to be managed and resolved more or less episodically, with limited internal linkage even within the trade sector (because of their often highly individualised nature), and even less with respect to other areas of transatlantic relations. Thus, while such issues undoubtedly have influenced US attitudes toward the EC, most have been sectorally contained and have not significantly affected US policy toward Europe in other areas or vice versa.

The instances of US–European discord surveyed in previous chapters generally shared a number of common or similar characteristics which are partly unique to the circumstances in which they took place. First, most of the tensions occurred in the context of an upswing phase of US foreign policy assertiveness and expectations of European support on specific issues that was characteristic of the Nixon administration's diplomacy toward Europe in 1973/74, the latter part of the Carter presidency and most of the Reagan administration. US appeals for allied backing placed strains on European governments and their political cooperation machinery and pressure to adopt responses that would show some solidarity with Washington, while at the same time projecting uniquely European assessments of issues and determinations of policy. The often divergent views of European governments among themselves, compounded by different values placed on the importance of supporting the US in particular cases, frequently yielded responses at a low common denominator of European consensus. Nevertheless, it is clear that the frequency and political visibility of American pressures for European support furnished a major part of the EPC action agenda in the 1970s and 1980s. Indeed, much of the substance of Atlantic relations, entailing European responses to American initiatives, reinforced the growing European tendency through EPC to forge independent positions *vis-à-vis* the United States. The dynamic interplay of these forces tended to accentuate the appearance of US–European differences, however much they were contained by a joint desire to avoid serious damage to the Atlantic Alliance.

Second, all of the crises and Atlantic differences on other regional issues occurred during the early articulation period and later consolidation phase of European Political Cooperation characterised by efforts to define and advance independently determined European positions. The attempt to do so, while often marred by internal differences and constrained by strategic dependence, was frequently successful. Thus, US pressure for supportive European policies on particular issues inevitably prompted closer European consultations to seek common positions, a process that was often used as a shield from bilateral US appeals exerted with individual European governments. Furthermore, the issues themselves provided a more or less continuous laboratory for the evolution of distinctively European approaches which were often in response to US initiatives. Thus, while EC governments were frequently in a reactive posture *vis-à-vis* the United States, the EPC process itself often yielded Europe's own assertiveness or resistance to American policies. Hence, the combination of American demands for European support with a maturing joint foreign policy determination process in Europe tended to produce a structural and attitudinal dichotomy in Atlantic relations on some issues. Indeed, the commitment to seek distinctively European common positions, facilitated by a policy 'coordination reflex', a developed EPC consultative infrastructure, and the EC's authority in economic policy, often resulted in an underscoring of US–European differences. This was because, to a considerable extent, the case for independent European foreign policy determinations rested implicitly on the assumption of distinct US and European interests and outlooks which the EPC process itself served to clarify and manifest. Moreover, EPC tended to cater to the disposition of some governments to resist alignment with Washington and to seek common positions as a way of affirming Europe's unique identity and interests. Finally, the collective nature of EPC actions at ministerial and summit levels served to heighten the visibility of European positions while sometimes sharpening the appearance of differences with the United States. Nevertheless, while cases of transatlantic discord typically attracted the most attention, it should not be overlooked that on most foreign policy issues US and European views as expressed through EPC closely corresponded. Moreover, this correspondence increased in the late 1980s, as differences narrowed over the Middle East, Central America and attitudes toward the Soviet Union.

In contrast to EPC as an independent European voice, the political culture of the WEU has been notably different, though the motivations that prompted its revival in the 1980s in some ways comported with those of EPC, and the foreign ministers have been regularly involved with both activities since 1984. Yet the ethos of WEU committed it unreservedly to the promotion of Atlantic solidarity in security matters, and its role in strengthening the European pillar in defence, implicitly a secondary role, was viewed essentially in that light. Hence, WEU member governments quickly retreated in the mid-1980s when the Reagan administration voiced reservations about signs of WEU deliberations and positioning activity on Alliance issues. The seemingly ambitious plans for WEU to seek common European positions within the Alliance, as implied by the Rome declaration in 1984, received less attention thereafter. While proclaiming the need for closer European defence cooperation, WEU governments seemed intent on avoiding initiatives or appearances that would articulate distinctively European defence interests apart from the Alliance itself. This was partly because any serious effort to develop a common European defence policy apart from the Alliance would have exposed and magnified divergences among the Europeans themselves – deriving from differences in geographical exposure, nuclear weapons status, views on tactical escalation, arms control, and positions toward NATO – while risking movement toward Atlantic security decoupling and a greater European responsibility and cost for its own defence. As a European parliamentarian put it, there is 'a widespread feeling that the WEU remains an excuse for not having a common defence policy rather than a means of producing one'.[3]

In a sense, then (and oversimplified), Western Europe as a collectivity has been characterised by a bicephalous institutional and attitudinal culture in its relations with the US, a phenomenon embedded in its post-war organisational evolution and its strategic circumstances. From the days of the Organisation for European Economic Cooperation (1948) and the European Coal and Steel Community (1952), a pattern of pronounced Europeanisation has prevailed in the economic sphere including institutional, programmatic and attitudinal manifestations. On trade matters, the EC has grown in confidence, assertiveness, determination to protect and advance its interests, and external respect as a formidable economic power. European Political Cooperation, as the EC's foreign policy offspring, has partly inherited these characteristics, however limited by EPC's weaker capability for collective action, national primacy in the control of foreign policy, and EPC's only partial involvement in security issues. Nevertheless, as the previous chapters have shown, to a significant extent EPC has evolved to constitute a foreign policy community with a distinctively European acculturation and disposition to seek concerted positions, particularly on issues outside the scope of collective Alliance action.

In contrast, during the 40 year period following conclusion of the Brussels Pact (1948) and the North Atlantic Treaty (1949), defence issues never acquired a pronounced degree of European individualisation apart from or even within the Alliance. De Gaulle's aborted attempt to do so through the Fouchet Plan was never successfully revived. As the logic of economic interdependence and incentives had yielded European solutions, the combined logic of Western Europe's political fragmentation, a potential Soviet threat, Soviet–West European military imbalance, and American security interests produced Atlantic solutions manifested through European strategic dependence on the United States. As long as these conditions prevailed, distinctively European approaches to defence remained limited in scope, purpose and significance – and as the revival of the WEU has shown, were committed to strengthening the Alliance in essentially its existing form.

The coexistence of a Europeanised economic and political entity with an Atlanticised approach to defence inevitably limited the potential effectiveness of a European pillar as a factor of influence in world politics and in Europe's relations with the United States. The pattern has helped preserve something of a division between the two sets of issues, however often blurred in practice, and an institutional dichotomy in dealing with them. Moreover, the interpenetration between the two has been uneven. Except in the case of the IEPG, which has pushed with some success for increased Europeanisation in military procurement, European defence cooperation has not sought to displace or challenge prevailing Alliance multilateralism with a concerted European entity as part of a dual core of an Alliance twinning the United States and Western Europe. Such tendencies have been discouraged from within as entailing a risk of decoupling, and from without by the US desire to avoid erosion of its paramount influence in the Alliance. On the other hand, as we have seen, Europe's strategic dependence on the United States has had a pronounced effect on the evolution and character of European Political Cooperation, first by discouraging EPC from pursuing a role in defence (reinforced by some national particularities as previously cited) and second, by encouraging EPC responses in specific cases to adapt to the need of avoiding or minimising differences with the US in the wider and conditioning interest of maintaining Alliance cohesion. This mixed Euro-Atlantic system has worked because it reflected and responded to Europe's different capabilities and willingness for combined action in the economic and to an extent the political sphere on the one hand,

and the defence sphere on the other. Yet it has perpetuated the ultimately anomalous though traditionally acceptable situation of a Europe organised and disposed to act more independently in some areas and more dependently in others.

Third, the cold war era furnished the global context which prompted and rationalised American calls for Western solidarity in responding to direct Soviet initiatives and instances of Soviet support for its allied or friendly states, a circumstance common in varying degrees to most of the issues studied. Yet the cold war environment produced somewhat countervailing effects on transatlantic relations. It tended to substantiate and legitimise the American case and pressures for coherent Western responses, while reinforcing US influence in defining the issues and orchestrating allied initiatives. Furthermore, it positioned the Atlantic Alliance as the centrepiece of the US–European relationship which functioned to set boundaries in individual cases beyond which European governments were reluctant to go in challenging American leadership, whether on Alliance or on out-of-area issues (though in the latter cases the boundaries were more permissive).

With respect to NATO, the potential Soviet military threat to Western Europe, and the capability for coercion, intimidation or political suasion deriving from it, were generally conducive to European acceptance of American leadership on the major defence issues affecting the Alliance. Moreover, European governments were often divided among themselves and unable to develop common views, a situation that further encouraged European alignment with American positions.

This was the case, for example, with regard to the closely linked issues of modernising NATO's short-range nuclear forces (SNF), the question of negotiating East–West reductions of such forces, and the negotiations on conventional force reductions which were prominent on the NATO agenda during 1988/90. The US–Soviet Intermediate-range Nuclear Forces (INF) treaty signed in December 1987, which banned missiles in both short and long range INF categories (the so-called 'double zero' solution), underscored the special position of West Germany with respect to the missiles of less than 300 miles range that would remain. Thus the treaty appeared to 'singularise' Germany since such missiles, if used, would have uniquely destructive effects on German soil. Not surprisingly, then, the treaty activated growing support in West Germany for an early opening of negotiations to reduce short-range nuclear missiles as well, a category of weapons in which the Soviet Union possessed a substantial advantage. Indeed, the INF treaty itself, despite official support for it by all West European governments, had produced concerns that the elimination of one category of missiles could generate momentum to reduce or even eliminate short-range systems as well, thus advancing the prospect of a denuclearised Europe as advocated by the Soviet Union.

Moreover, the issue posed the question of the continued implementation of the NATO decision taken at Montebello in 1983 to modernise the Alliance's short-range nuclear forces, particularly with respect to artillery, a new air-to-ground tactical missile, and the Lance ground-based missile. Urging prompt attention to East–West negotiations to reduce such forces, West Germany became increasingly reluctant to proceed with the modernisation programme (particularly the Lance replacement component), out of concern that it could jeopardise prospects for negotiations and reignite the anti-nuclear protests that had followed the 1979 decision to accept US intermediate-range missiles.

The problem was that movement beyond the INF treaty toward a further reduction of nuclear weapons, as long as a plausible Soviet military threat remained, could critically undermine the NATO deterrence and defence strategy of flexible response. This strategy, based on a combination of NATO conventional and nuclear forces to be employed according to the level and nature of an attack, included a threat of possible first nuclear use by NATO forces if faced with an overwhelming conventional offensive. While this strategy and force posture were intended primarily as a deterrent, by increasing the risks of aggression through the threat of escalation, nevertheless the consequences of implementing the strategy if deterrence failed were particularly unsettling to West Germans.

The West German interest in early SNF negotiations and deferring NATO nuclear modernisation programmes exposed divisions in the Alliance over both issues. Most other NATO governments, particularly the US and Britain, opposed further reductions in nuclear forces as long as a substantial Soviet conventional forces threat to Europe remained intact. France, while supporting the West German position on the Lance modernisation question, nonetheless sided with the US and Britain on the issue of reducing SNF. To further vitiate NATO's capability to threaten nuclear escalation as a deterrent to conventional attack, it was argued, would weaken the Alliance's defence posture and enhance the significance of Soviet advantages in conventional forces and of its geographical position. Similarly, as long as NATO's strategy remained based on a mix of conventional and nuclear weapons, it followed that such forces had to be maintained at momentary readiness. Typically, NATO communiqués during this period reflected consensus on this point, though fudging the particulars, as, for example, by noting that conventional and nuclear forces would be kept up to date 'where necessary'.

The opening of East–West negotiations in March 1989 on reducing conventional forces in Europe (CFE) prompted NATO governments to resolve their simmering differences over nuclear forces in the context of prospective East–West conventional force reductions. The CFE negotiations aimed at achieving reductions to parity in designated offensively capable conventional weapons (tanks, troop carriers, artillery) throughout Europe, thus enhancing security by reducing the risk of surprise attack and the capability for launching offensive military operations. The West German preference for a degree of parallelism between the CFE negotiations and talks on reducing nuclear forces contrasted with the prevailing Alliance view that a sequential approach should be adopted whereby further nuclear cuts would be considered only following a CFE agreement that would substantially reduce the Soviet conventional forces threat to Western Europe.

The eventual accord, announced at the May 1989 NATO summit, provided that negotiations on reducing short-range nuclear missiles would not begin until a CFE agreement had been achieved and the reductions were underway, and that any reductions in such missiles would not occur until the conventional force cuts had been fully implemented. Further decisions regarding nuclear force modernisation were deferred until 1992, by which time the need for such modernisation would in any case be reassessed in light of the CFE negotiations and the overall course of East–West relations. The latter provision was of course crucial to West German acceptance of the package, since it continued to finesse the Lance modernisation question while reducing Chancellor Kohl's domestic vulnerability on the issue in the context of the 1990 German elections. (In any case, as discussed in Chapter 11, the Lance modernisation programme was later abandoned in response to the political changes in Eastern Europe during 1989/90. In view of the planned withdrawal of Soviet forces from Czechoslovakia and Hungary, the momentum toward German unification and the democratic evolution in Eastern Europe, it made little sense to develop a missile designed for possible use in those areas). Moreover, President Bush's proposal for a reduction of US and Soviet forces in Europe, aimed at stimulating progress in the CFE talks, encouraged West German hopes that negotiations on short-range nuclear forces would not be indefinitely delayed.

Clearly, differences among the major West European governments themselves over these issues (tending toward the isolation of West Germany on the question of further nuclear reductions) obstructed the shaping of a unified West European position and reinforced the long-established practice of managing defence issues through traditional bilateral and multilateral (Alliance) channels, mechanisms which typically favour the senior coalition member. Indeed, given EPC's self-exclusion from a defence role, and WEU's pronounced deference to the Alliance, this was the inevitable result. Moreover, one is struck by the fact that despite WEU's much vaunted revival in the 1980s, including declarations of intent to harmonise views and develop a more cohesive European defence identity, the WEU played an insignificant and in any case unnecessary role in the resolution of these issues.

The absence of a strong European institutional base in defence, including the use of the WEU as little more than a forum for consultations (not to orchestrate common negotiating positions), thus encouraged bilateralism and Alliance multilateralism both by default and by mutual preference. The United States, for its part, has clearly benefited from this pattern, and has shown little interest in encouraging a strong collective European defence entity which could become a troublesome counterweight to US predominance in the Alliance.

With regard to out-of-area issues, as several of the case studies have shown, the general cold war milieu through the mid-1980s facilitated US invocation of the need for allied solidarity which often yielded some complementarity, if not uniformity, in US–European reactions, while tethering occasional European inclinations toward more independent positions. Despite their misgivings and even opposition to some American policies, European governments generally did not wish to be labeled 'uncooperative' in the American public eye and risk undermining US domestic support for the Alliance. At the same time, the absence of full allied solidarity limited the effectiveness of US policies and in some cases contributed to a moderating of American positions.

In addition, the return to US–Soviet confrontation in the early 1980s tended to sharpen US–European differences over a range of issues involving the Soviet Union and East–West relations in general. This included European distancing from the Reagan administration's ideological perspective toward the Soviet system and its behaviour, a European tendency to view regional issues in their own terms more than as instances of bipolar confrontation, European efforts to preserve *détente* from 'cold war II' damage (especially in Europe) while promoting US–Soviet moderation through encouragement of arms control dialogue, and differing US–European perspectives on strategic export controls toward Soviet bloc countries. Moreover, the US tendency to use or consider military options in dealing with out-of-area problems furnished yet another arena of transatlantic differences. Indeed, most of the instances of US–European discord discussed in Chapters 6 to 8 involved issues of these types. Nevertheless, as long as a paradigm of East–West confrontation (however differently viewed) continued as a primary reference point for Western foreign and security policies, differences within the Alliance were managed within a tolerable range of divergence.

It is clear that the concept, institutionalisation and activity of the European pillar(s) through the 1980s evolved with a deeply ingrained Atlantic sensitivity and identification, most clearly represented by the WEU in the area of defence. Yet it was also true, albeit to a somewhat lesser extent, with respect to political cooperation, notwithstanding EPC's more distinctively European ethos, agenda and method of operation. As indicated in the foregoing analysis, the 'Atlanticisation' of the European political identity had two main dimensions. First, the exclusion of defence-related issues from the formal EPC mandate – a result of differing European national positions, the established role of NATO, and European concerns about Atlantic decoupling – limited the functional scope of EPC activity and its potential influence on European and global security issues. While Europe as a 'civilian power' influence partly compensated for this, and whereas military power in relations among advanced industrial states may be of declining practical importance, nonetheless the idea of a European economic and political entity without a parallel defence component resulted in a continued American hegemonic relationship (however benign) with Western Europe on security issues, and a scope for European influence necessarily limited by its dependence.

Second, as the case studies have shown, even on non-defence and out-of-area issues, European governments felt constrained from pressing their positions with Washington too far – both because of their limited ability to exert influence on an issue of primary American engagement, and because of the political need to show solidarity with the US to maintain American Alliance commitments in Europe. Thus, even within EPC's normal range of activity, its independence as a

European entity was both conditioned and circumscribed by the deeply infused Atlantic dimension of its identity and personality. On the latter point, Europeans did not wish to contribute to American retrenchment sentiments, fuelled by budget and trade deficits and complaints of inadequate European defence burden-sharing, by appearing to be non-supportive or only weakly supportive of American global policies. Moreover, Europe's limited institutional capacity for shaping common positions, primarily a function of the anchoring of decisional authority at the national level, enabled European governments with particularly strong Atlantic affinities to influence the character of collective European policies. Conversely, it facilitated US influence on collective European decision-making through bilateral relationships with individual European governments and through multilateral Alliance diplomacy.

Finally, some perspectives on European defence and political cooperation interpret it as a necessary response to declining American power – a kind of gap-filling exercise. While to an extent this has been so, perhaps the more telling point is that in the area of defence cooperation the dominant European impulse has been to keep American power engaged in Europe. The two perspectives reveal the ambiguous character of European defence cooperation ever since the Eurogroup initiative in 1969. Publicly, and manifested through an unqualified Alliance identification, European defence cooperation has sought to assure a continued US binding to Europe's security by addressing American expectations for a more effective and equitable European contribution. Yet at the same time, European defence cooperation has represented a hedge against the possibility of an eventual disengagement or sharp reduction of the US security role in Europe. These somewhat diverging purposes – the first explicit, the second largely implicit – have blurred the nature of European defence cooperation while limiting the practical scope of its activity. Thus European defence cooperation has developed within minimalist bounds, determined by the need to preserve Alliance consensus, and has rejected the image of an entity evolving toward independence from the United States. A somewhat different counter-argument applies in the area of political cooperation. Rather than attempting to supplant declining American power, a frequent European impulse has been to contest – or to attempt to moderate – assertions of American power that Europeans believed to be mistaken.

11 The United States and the New Europe in the 1990s

THE TRANSFORMED EUROPEAN SETTING

The stunning political changes in Eastern and Central Europe during 1989/90 fundamentally altered the familiar political context of European international relations that had evolved since World War II. These changes, each dramatic in itself, combined to produce a diplomatic environment of unparalleled complexity and challenge as governments sought to design and put in place a post-cold war political and security order in Europe. The main elements of the new situation included the following:

First, continuation of Soviet President Mikail Gorbachev's efforts toward economic and political restructuring (*perestroika*) aimed at revitalising the Soviet economy and quality of life through the encouragement of open debate (*glasnost*), the empowering of reformist societal elements, and the re-channelling of the political process from entrenched and change-resistant party and bureaucratic groups toward national and local legislative bodies guided by strong presidential leadership. Nevertheless by 1990, the still dismal performance of the Soviet economy five years after Gorbachev came to power, combined with rising domestic dissent and demands for secession or autonomy from the Soviet republics, had produced a situation of chronic instability and uncertainty in the Soviet Union. The pronounced internal preoccupation of Soviet political activity had its counterpart in retrenched and accommodating foreign and defence policies, intended to reduce international tensions to enable a shift of resources from military spending (representing a quarter of the government's budget[1]) to the civilian sector, and to encourage improved political relations with the West and move toward a new cooperative East–West security order.

Second, the collapse of communist party authority in Eastern Europe, including the spread of political pluralism, respect for human rights and the introduction of democratic processes and institutions.

Led in September 1989 by Poland's installation of its first freely elected government since World War II, democratically elected governments followed in Czechoslovakia, Hungary, Bulgaria and Romania in 1990. Reinforcing these trends, while being reinforced by them, was a shift toward greater privatisation of East European economies, particularly in Czechoslovakia, Hungary and Poland, tending in each case toward an individualised mix of public and private sectors, though increasingly oriented toward participation in the European and global economic and trading systems. Advances in democratic institutionalisation and human rights practices by the three most progressive East European states increased the likelihood of their membership in the Council of Europe as a major symbol of their political and societal transformations.

Third, a receding NATO–Warsaw Pact military confrontation prompted by the breakup of the Soviet European empire, the effective demise of the Warsaw Pact as a functioning military alliance, momentum toward sharp reductions in conventional and nuclear forces in Europe, and a developing regime of confidence and security-building measures. Unilateral moves to reduce military expenditures and deployments within both alliances paralleled progress in the Conventional Armed Forces in Europe (CFE) negotiations, concluded in November 1990, that codified East–West parity in key conventional weapons systems which would virtually end the threat of surprise attack in Europe. An exchange of non-aggression declarations between members of the two alliances, and an affirmation that 'they are no longer adversaries [and] will build new partnerships and extend to each other the hand of friendship', dramatised the end of the traditional cold war alliance confrontation in Europe. Further negotiations were planned to lower troop levels in Europe to complement reductions in conventional military equipment.

Finally, the collapse of communist authority in East Germany by late 1989 catapulted the issue of German unification to the forefront of the agenda for the two German states, Europe, the United States and the Soviet Union. In March 1990, a freely elected transitional government was formed in East Germany, followed in July by Soviet acquiescence to a united Germany's membership in NATO which accelerated the pace of unification. In September, a unification treaty was concluded providing for East Germany's accession to the Federal Republic on 3 October under a provision of the West German constitution. In rough parallel with inner-German planning for unification, the so-called 'Two plus Four' talks commenced between the two German states and the United States, the Soviet Union, Britain and France – the World War II allies victorious over Germany who retained occupation rights in Berlin and responsibilities for Germany as a whole including the formal delineation of boundaries. These negotiations ended on 12 September with the conclusion of a 'final settlement' treaty that terminated Four Power rights and responsibilities relating to Berlin and Germany, acknowledged a united Germany's full sovereignty and confirmed its borders, included understandings on planned reductions of Germany's armed forces, and reaffirmed the German renunciation of the manufacture, possession, or control over nuclear, biological and chemical weapons.

In all of this Gorbachev's policies – such as announcements in 1988/89 of planned unilateral cuts in the Soviet armed forces, tanks, defence spending and military procurement, and acceptance and even encouragement of systemic transformation in Eastern Europe – furnished both a catalyst and permissive cause for change. As many in the West watched incredulously, wondering where Gorbachev would draw the line, Soviet leaders reacted to developments in Eastern Europe with a detachment that confounded scepticism that the Soviet Union, particularly at a time of its own internal upheaval, could afford to 'let go' of its satellite empire. Yet it became increasingly apparent that communist parties in Eastern Europe would remain in power or fall on their own merits, and that the structure of Soviet political, military and economic support on which they had depended was being withdrawn. Clearly, the unpopular and economically costly communist regimes in Eastern Europe, absorbing $10 to $20 billion a year in Soviet subsidies,[2] together with Soviet military costs in the region accounting for some 42 per cent of total defence spending[3], had become a dead weight on the prospects for reform in the Soviet Union.

During a visit to Hungary in April 1989, Gorbachev disavowed any Soviet right to intervene in the affairs of Eastern Europe.[4] Regarding Poland, Soviet leaders reacted positively to the restoration of Solidarity's legal status and the scheduling of free elections, and voiced no criticism over the humiliating electoral defeat of the Communist Party and the installation in September of a Solidarity-led government. In a speech to the Council of Europe in July, Gorbachev in effect repudiated the so-called Brezhnev doctrine – Moscow's *post facto* justification for the invasion of Czechoslovakia in 1968 which asserted the necessity of preserving 'the socialist commonwealth of

nations' allegedly endangered by Prague's domestic reform movement. Outlining in broad terms his idea of a 'common European
home', Gorbachev asserted that it ruled out 'the very possibility of
the use of force or the threat of force – alliance against alliance, inside
the alliances, wherever', and that 'any interference in domestic affairs
and any attempts to restrict the sovereignty of states – friends, allies
or any others – are inadmissible'.[5] While similar statements had been
made before by Soviet leaders, the new element was the remarkable
consistency between the Soviet government's public pronouncements
and its actual behaviour.

ARCHITECTURE FOR THE NEW EUROPE: THE EUROPEAN COMMUNITY – GERMANY AND EASTERN EUROPE

The European Community, spirited by increased growth rates and
robust investment activity, exhibited strong momentum and capability
as the chief European focal point of the new post-cold war architecture. Spurred by the expected completion of the internal market by
the end of 1992, corporate merger activity flourished as companies
positioned themselves to take advantage of falling barriers to the
movement of people, goods, services and capital. Previous estimates
that the single market programme could boost the Community's
gross domestic product by some 7 per cent in the 1990s appeared
conservative in light of the EC's economic performance and outlook by
the early part of the decade.[6] Indeed, the psychological impact of the
'1992' programme's buoyant imagery glossed over some formidable
problems that remained, such as indirect tax harmonisation, which
touched sensitive nerves of national fiscal policy, and the ending
of internal border controls, which posed problems with respect to
national control of immigration, drug trafficking and terrorist movements. Nevertheless, the widespread expectation that most internal
barriers would be eliminated during the early 1990s helped to dramatically reverse the EC's sluggish performance in the 1970s and early
1980s when terms such as Euro-pessimism and Euro-sclerosis were in
descriptive vogue.

In June 1989, despite resistance from Britain's Prime Minister
Margaret Thatcher, the EC Council advanced the aim of economic and
monetary union (EMU) by agreeing to hold an intergovernmental conference to consider steps toward the further coordination of economic
and monetary policies and the eventual establishment of a European

central bank and a common currency. The continued movement toward democratisation in Eastern Europe, and growing instability in East Germany, generated wide support for accelerating progress toward EMU partly to signal that the EC's own development would not be interrupted by the rapid pace of change. A major concern was that the sudden prospect of German unification might distract the Federal Republic toward excessive national preoccupations at the expense of its commitment to the EC. Chancellor Kohl's detailed proposal for German unification, announced in late November without prior consultations with his allies, stirred apprehensions in this regard, as did Bonn's decision in December to postpone signing the Schengen Treaty eliminating border controls with its Western neighbours, because it did not include visa-free travel guarantees for East Germans. Nevertheless, Kohl wished to avoid any impression of wavering toward the EC and followed an established pattern of West German policy of balancing its eastern interests with western commitments by agreeing at the Strasbourg EC summit in December to the convening of the intergovernmental conference on EMU by the end of 1990. At the same time, of course, through this gesture of support toward deepening West European integration, Kohl expected solid support from his EC partners as the unification process gathered momentum.

The dramatic changes in Eastern Europe during 1989 led to a strengthened role for the EC in the overall coordination and direction of Western responses, while signalling a tilt toward greater European influence in the Atlantic relationship with respect to the burgeoning East–West agenda. The decision at the Paris economic summit in July 1989 to ask the EC Commission to coordinate aid programmes for Hungary and Poland, while partly designed to allay Soviet concerns by seeming to depoliticise Western involvement, nonetheless embarked the EC on a growing role in the process of economic reform in Eastern Europe. It also served to enhance the prestige of the Commission and to buttress its role of assuring coherence between EC and EPC policies and actions toward Eastern Europe, further blurring the distinction between the two. While American officials had proposed that the United States coordinate the enterprise, the Bush administration readily acquiesced to a leading role for the EC. It was an important psychological shift in the transatlantic relationship, however subtle, through the American acceptance of stronger European leadership in the coordination of responses to the changes in Europe.

The Commission wasted little time in exercising its mandate. Within two weeks of the Paris summit, it convened a meeting of the 24 members of the Organisation for Economic Cooperation and Development, a group composed mainly of developed Western and Asian countries, to begin the task of organising immediate food relief for Poland and longer term assistance for Poland and Hungary. The aid programme sought to foster economic reform in recipient countries by encouraging movement away from centralised planning and management structures toward a market orientation, a stronger role for the private sector, and an improved climate for domestic and foreign investment.

West European leaders took a further step in November aimed at focusing attention on the role of the EC in responding to the forces of change in the east. Immediately after the opening of the Berlin Wall on 9 November, which stirred concerns that pressures could mount for German unification, presiding EC Council President François Mitterrand called a special meeting of EC leaders in Paris. Moreover, the planned Bush–Gorbachev summit at Malta in early December, which included discussion of events in Europe, increased the importance of making a visible manifestation of a unified West European approach and role in the process of change – partly to offset the attention expected to focus on the US–Soviet summit and to avoid any impression of superpower pre-emption or dominance of the new European agenda. As Mitterrand's chief spokesman put it, the EC meeting would focus entirely on 'how to manage the new equilibrium' so as to assure that the European Community will become 'the pole of attraction of this new big Europe that is being born'.[7] At Paris, EC leaders proclaimed their support 'with all our means' for the economic and political reforms underway in Eastern Europe and emphasised that the Community's economic assistance for particular countries would be linked to their progress in consolidating democratic practices and institutions. It was agreed, in line with Mitterrand's proposal to the European Parliament in October, to consider the establishment of a European development bank to aid in the capitalisation of East European economic restructuring and modernisation projects. While the Paris meeting was mainly symbolic, together with other EC initiatives and progress toward completing the internal market it served to underscore the growing importance and visibility of the EC as the pivot of West European strength and stability and the central gravitation point for Eastern Europe.

In rough parallel with the organisation of aid for Hungary and Poland, negotiations proceeded toward the first ever trade and cooperation agreement between the EC and the Soviet Union, concluded in December 1989, providing for mutual most-favoured-nation trading status and the phasing out of the EC's quantitative restrictions on imports from the Soviet Union. Bilateral trade and cooperation agreements with East European countries, concluded or in negotiation, complemented the EC's growing network of commercial ties to the east. Both developments had been accelerated by the June 1988 formalisation of relations between the EC and the Council of Mutual Economic Assistance (CMEA, or Comecon), the Soviet–East European trade bloc, which facilitated bilateral trade agreements between the EC and individual CMEA countries.

In December 1989, the EC led the way in decisions by the group of 24 aid countries to increase assistance to Poland. Whereas previous actions by the group had been limited to Poland and Hungary, the rapid spread of democratisation elsewhere in Eastern Europe and East Germany led to a decision in principle to broaden the scope of assistance to include other countries, linked to their establishment of political and economic reforms. Relatedly, EC finance ministers approved a more than $1 billion loan facility from the European Investment Bank to finance projects in Hungary and Poland, representing the bank's first loan commitment to Eastern Europe.

At the Strasbourg EC summit in December, acting quickly on Mitterrand's earlier proposal, the EC Council endorsed the creation of a European Bank for Reconstruction and Development (EBRD) intended to promote productive and competitive investment in the states of Eastern and Central Europe and to assist their transition toward more market-oriented economies. As approved, the EC, its member states and the European Investment Bank were to have a majority holding in the EBRD, while other countries, in particular members of the group of 24, were invited to join.

Following protracted negotiations, a treaty providing for the establishment of the EBRD was signed in May 1990 by 40 countries including all European states (except Albania), the United States, the Soviet Union, Japan, Canada, Mexico and several others. Ranking as one of the most important international financial initiatives undertaken since World War II, and the first to include the Soviet Union, the bank's central purpose, as stated in its charter, was to 'promote private and entrepreneurial initiative' in East European countries that were 'committed to and applying the principles of multi-party democracy, pluralism and market economics'.[8] Initial US and British reluctance to allow the bank to fund public sector investments was overcome by a formula whereby at least 60 per cent of total lending would be to the private sector, with the balance of 40 per cent available to governments for competitive state-owned enterprises and for environmental and infrastructure projects that would be necessary to underpin expansion of private sector activity. Thus while the 60–40 formula favoured private investment growth, it also reflected the stronger West European tradition, as compared to the United States, of government ownership or control of major enterprises. This contributed to acceptance that a mix of public and private sector investment stimuli was the only realistic basis on which to proceed with Eastern Europe, particularly given entrenched government economic dominance in the region since World War II which could only change gradually.

Another contentious issue was the beneficiary role of the Soviet Union in the EBRD, strongly favoured by most West European governments though initially opposed by the United States on grounds that the Soviet Union had not made sufficient progress toward democracy and a market economy, and had continued high levels of military spending. After threatening to withdraw from the EBRD negotiations if Moscow were allowed to become a major borrower, the Bush administration eventually acquiesced to including the Soviet Union on the condition that for at least three years it would not be able to borrow in excess of its own contribution to the bank. While both of these issues yielded US and West European compromises to achieve agreement, shifts in the Bush administration's position reflected awareness that the bank would be established with or without American participation, and that the United States could ill afford to stand aside from a major activity supporting constructive change in Eastern Europe. While the US share of 10 per cent was to be the largest single country component of the bank's total $12 billion pledged capitalisation, the leading West European role was again underscored by the fact that the EC, the European Investment Bank and individual EC member countries were to collectively provide nearly 54 per cent of the bank's funds, including majority influence on the bank's investment decisions.

As developments in 1989 prompted a coherent and unified EC response to change in Eastern Europe, so too did the rapid unfolding of events in East Germany and the accelerated momentum toward German unification in 1990. Until the fall of 1989, it was widely assumed that East Germany would continue as a separate German state and would remain somewhat insulated from the movement for economic and political reform that was sweeping through Eastern Europe and to a lesser extent the Soviet Union itself. East German Communist Party leader Erich Honecker, who had proudly proclaimed that socialism was working in his country, showed open disdain for the relevance of Soviet *perestroika* reforms in East Germany. Nevertheless, it soon became apparent that East Germany could not remain immune from the agitation for reform, particularly in view of the Soviet decision not to prop up the Honecker government and actions which had the effect of encouraging its replacement. In September, the Hungarian decision to open its border with Austria, allowing thousands of East Germans in Hungary to emigrate to West Germany, preceded in May by the richly symbolic dismantling of fencing along the Austro-Hungarian border, dramatised the collapsing iron curtain mentality and the growing permeability between East and West in Europe. At the same time, it catalysed the rapid destabilisation of the German Democratic Republic as pressures mounted, and opportunities opened, for dissatisfied East Germans to emigrate to the West. Despite the ousting of Honecker, and subsequent moves toward liberalisation by communist authorities, mounting pressures for emigration and unprecedented mass public demonstrations for democracy advanced the disintegration of communist rule in East Germany. Then, on 9 November, in a desperate move to meet popular demands and shore up its own authority, the government opened the Berlin Wall allowing East Germans to travel or emigrate freely. The hope, of course, was that the freedom to leave would staunch the desire to do so, and that radical new economic and political reforms – including abolition of the Communist Party's constitutionally guaranteed right to govern and a pledge of free elections – would restore public support for the government. It didn't work. In January 1990, in the face of a continuing population exodus and a growing crisis in public services, a largely non-communist coalition government was formed to manage the country until elections in March which were widely viewed as a transitional step toward unification with West Germany.

The rapid destabilisation in East Germany prompted West German Chancellor Kohl to propose in late November a ten-point plan for eventual unification, a move that provoked criticism that he was moving too fast and had not consulted with his Western allies. Despite formal assurances by Western leaders of their support for unification, rooted in numerous public declarations over the past 40 years, apprehension quickly surfaced over the geopolitical and economic implications of a unified German state. Whereas support for unification had always been central to the political relationship between the Federal Republic and its Western allies, it had had little practical relevance until the events in East Germany forced the issue to the surface. With the long-professed goal now in sight, Western governments, whatever their misgivings, had little choice but to become partners in the process and to infuse it with a solid European and Atlantic underpinning as a basis for their support.

The December 1989 EC summit, while 'extremely contentious' according to one informed account, nevertheless played an important role in broadening and solidifying the base of West European support for German unification. Closely resembling an earlier endorsement by the NATO summit in Brussels, EC leaders proclaimed support for a 'state of peace in Europe in which the German people will regain its unity through free self-determination'.[9] Whereas this formulation was virtually identical to previous Western positions stated frequently since the establishment of the Federal Republic in 1949, it took on added significance as the issue moved from the abstract to the concrete. The summit declaration linked the process of unification to full respect for the relevant agreements and treaties, including the Helsinki Final Act (which defined post-war frontiers as inviolable and changeable only through peaceful means), and to a context of dialogue and East–West cooperation. Moreover, the statement emphasised that German unification 'has to be placed in the perspective of European integration'. While there apparently was no direct connection between the summit declaration on German unification and Bonn's acceptance of accelerated progress toward EMU, Mitterrand nonetheless acknowledged that 'an objective link' between the two issues existed during the talks. That link reflected the emerging consensus that the new prospects for German unification would be viewed and pursued in the context of a parallel strengthening of unity in the EC. Bonn's partners were concerned that the rapid momentum for unification could divert West Germany from its attachments to the EC and retard progress toward achieving the free internal market, economic and monetary union, and strengthened political unity. Relatedly, it was becoming widely accepted that these aims had become more urgent as a means of anchoring a unified Germany in a reinforced EC structure, and that positive West European support for unification would be linked to such progress in the EC.

The vague formulation of the connection between the two sets of issues (unification must be placed 'in the perspective of European integration'), reflected awareness that the process of German unification was acquiring an intra-German and East–West dynamic of its own that, at least in its early stages, was largely extraneous to the domain of the EC. Moreover, internal Community differences, most notably Britain's resistance to economic and monetary union and closer political unity, meant that substantive progress toward strengthening the EC would lag behind the process of German unification, further making impossible any precise linkage between the two. Nevertheless, formal recognition at the Strasbourg summit of a relationship between unification and integration suited both Bonn and the other EC members. For Kohl, it provided an opportunity to mollify concerns about West German haste and unilateralism in pursuing unification, while gaining an important expression of support from his EC partners. For other EC governments, the implied conditionality of their support for unification meant that Bonn would be expected to show no wavering in its support for unity in the EC. Hence, albeit somewhat indirectly, the summit inserted the EC into the political context of the unification process. President Bush's statement in Brussels, shortly before the Strasbourg summit, that unification 'should occur in the context of Germany's continued commitment to NATO and an increasingly integrated European Community',[10] reinforced and broadened the developing linkage between unification and the German role in Western institutional arrangements. None of this implied that West Germany was brought to make 'concessions' to its Western partners in exchange for their support for unification. Indeed the Kohl government, and others before it, had always maintained that continued commitment to the EC, NATO and the process of pan-European reconciliation were essential elements of its unification policy. Nevertheless, the Strasbourg summit served to re-establish a measure of confidence that Bonn would not pursue the unification goal at the expense of the EC. Taken together, then, by December 1989 the EC response to the events in East Germany and Eastern Europe had strengthened the Community's role, in the words of the Strasbourg declaration, as 'the cornerstone of a new European architecture and, in its will to openness, a mooring for a future European equilibrium'.

The explicit understanding at the Strasbourg summit, that the process of German unification should be linked to a stronger EC (despite the impossibility of synchronising the pace of the two), was advanced a step further by a joint Franco-German *démarche* announced on 19 April 1990.[11] The proposal anticipated a special EC summit meeting in Dublin on 28 April which had been scheduled to consider the implications of German unification for the Community as well as EC relations with Eastern Europe. The Kohl–Mitterrand initiative, citing the changes in Europe and the necessity 'to accelerate the political construction of the Europe of the 12', proposed that preparations begin for an intergovernmental conference on political union. According to the plan, the conference was to be launched in December 1990, coinciding with the beginning of the conference on economic and monetary union, and entry into force of agreements in both areas was anticipated in January 1993 – thus coinciding with the expected completion of most aspects of the internal market programme. In particular, the aim was to define and implement a common foreign and security policy, to ensure the unity and coherence of the union's economic, monetary and political action, and to enhance the efficiency of Community institutions. The call for a common European foreign and security policy was accompanied by assurances that the Atlantic Alliance would remain necessary.

The special EC summit in Dublin, as expected, affirmed the nexus between German unification and reinforcement of the EC. Declaring that it was 'imperative' to strengthen the EC, which had become 'a crucial element . . . in establishing a reliable framework for peace and security in Europe', EC leaders declared their satisfaction that German unification was taking place 'under a European roof',[12] that is, via the anticipated integration of East Germany into the Federal Republic and hence the EC. As Kohl put it: 'For us the question of German unity and the unification process of Europe are two sides of the same coin'.[13]

With respect to the EC, despite continued uncertainty as to the British role in planning for EMU, Thatcher accepted the objective of completing the work of the intergovernmental conference so as to enable ratification by member states before the end of 1992. Yet while the summit confirmed the longstanding commitment to political union, it was clear that little progress toward consensus had been achieved as to the concept's practical meaning. Significantly, the summit statement made no mention of the Kohl–Mitterrand proposal for the EC to define and implement a common foreign and security policy.

The regular June 1990 EC summit in Dublin played only a transitional role with regard to the issue of political union. EC leaders agreed to convene an intergovernmental conference on political union in December with the objective of ratification by member states of agreements reached by the end of 1992. However, the Dublin meeting did little to narrow differences over the meaning of a European political union in relation to the member states. The French and West German view that the negotiations should take place 'within a federal perspective' (intimating another striking French move away from Gaullism), contrasted with British Prime Minister Thatcher's unchanged insistence upon cooperation among '12 independent, sovereign states'.[14] Nonetheless such differences, however fundamental, did not bar possible progress in strengthening the Community's democratic legitimacy (through expanding the role of Parliament) and enhancing the effectiveness and efficiency of EC institutions, including those in the area of political cooperation. While proclaiming that 'the Community will act as a political entity on the international scene', EC leaders nevertheless hedged on the Franco-German proposal to move toward a common foreign and security policy, noting 'a number of questions' raised by the proposal that would have to be addressed by the intergovernmental conference.[15]

Whatever such internal differences, during 1989/90 the EC became the central focal point for defining the West European position in the emerging post-cold war European architecture. As discussed above, this was the case chiefly with respect to the Community's support for the consolidation of economic and political reform in Eastern Europe, its adaptation to the process of German unification, and measures to advance its own internal development. EC responses to these and other issues were accompanied by a plethora of conceptual ideas intended to impart coherence and direction to what was taking place.

The challenge was to outline a framework and vision that would reconcile the potentially conflicting aims of strengthening the EC Twelve while at the same time developing patterns of openness and cooperation with non-member European countries. While the issue was sometimes portrayed too simplistically as a debate between 'deepeners versus wideners',[16] nevertheless the new 'eastern question' prompted closer attention to the Community's own role and identity in the wider Europe that was emerging. In effect, EC governments opted for both deepening and widening, though with clear priority accorded to the former: thus the renewed emphasis on EMU (including the decision to establish a European Central Bank in 1994) and the parallel intergovernmental conferences dealing with EMU on the one

hand and with political union on the other; thus also the postponement of serious discussions over further EC enlargement until 1993
at the earliest, and the dampening of speculation about East European memberships in the Community for the foreseeable future.
The question of Austrian membership in the EC, even before its
formal application in July 1989, had already provoked debate over
the compatibility between its neutrality position (albeit of declining
practical importance) and the EC commitment to political union.

The most descriptive model of the emerging European configuration, identified with EC Commission President Jacques Delors and
others, envisaged a Europe of concentric circles with the EC at the
centre, the six members (Austria, Finland, Iceland, Norway, Sweden,
Switzerland) of the European Free Trade Association (EFTA) forming
the second ring, and the countries of Eastern Europe comprising a
third. The EFTA countries were already linked to the EC through
bilateral trade agreements, introduced in the 1970s and in place
by 1984, providing for tariff and quota-free trade in industrial and
some processed agricultural products – resulting in the world's largest
free-trade area comprising 18 countries and 350 million people. EFTA
as a group comprised the largest single market for EC exports, taking
over 31 per cent of the EC's total external exports (1987), compared
to approximately 25 per cent going to the United States.[17] Conversely,
the EC was by far the most important market for EFTA countries,
accounting for nearly 65 per cent of total EFTA external exports in
1987. Hence, given the high dependence of the EFTA countries on
exports as a component of gross domestic product (averaging 27 per
cent in 1987), their terms of trade access to the EC were a matter of
vital importance.

Building upon the free-trade area arrangements just established,
EC–EFTA discussions were begun in 1984 envisaging creation of a European Economic Space (EES), loosely defined as a common EC–EFTA
area within which goods, services, capital and people could circulate
freely, and with growing alignment and reduced discrimination as
to the conditions of commercial competition. Meanwhile, the EC's
own progress since the mid-1980s in establishing common industrial
standards, applicable to all products marketed in the EC, had already
prompted the EFTA countries to adapt their manufacturing practices
to EC norms in order to preserve their export positions toward the
Community.

Nevertheless the members of EFTA, despite their heavy export
dependence on the EC, had no direct role in the Community's

decision-making process relating to its completion of the internal market, and hence no voice in the adoption of standards to which their industries would need to conform. This concern helped revive the EES discussions during 1989/90 which centred in large part on how decisions on the creation of the economic area would be taken. The EFTA desire for institutionalised co-management of the EES contrasted with the EC's insistence on non-interference with its own established decision-making practices. Because of the close interrelation between Community internal market actions and matters relating to the EES, the EC regarded any formal joint decisional mechanism with EFTA as an infringement of its own institutional integrity and a possible impediment to the 1992 market programme. Moreover, the EC position was that creation of the EES must be on the basis of the relevant *acquis communautaire* (rights and obligations under EC treaties and laws) to be jointly identified, hence virtually mandating EFTA acceptance of much existing Community legislation, while excluding it from a formal role in the adoption of new EC laws that would inevitably shape the character of the EES. Reflecting the Community's prioritisation for internal development and institutional protectiveness, the 1989 Strasbourg summit communiqué reaffirmed support for a European economic area – based on the EC's *acquis* – that would ensure EFTA 'participation in certain Community activities . . . in full compliance with the independent decision making processes of each organization and a strict balance of rights and obligations'.[18] As Delors put it, the process of EC–EFTA 'osmosis', to ensure that EFTA interests are taken into account in major Community decisions, 'must stop short of joint decision-making'.[19] Given the common position of the EFTA governments that 'a basic prerequisite' for an agreement on EES was the creation of 'a genuine joint decision-making mechanism in substance and form',[20] the EC–EFTA negotiations begun in June 1990 promised to be difficult.

As previously discussed, beginning in 1988 the EC's East European 'third circle' policy was operationalised through bilateral trade and cooperation accords, the Community's leading role in the group of 24 aid programme and the European Bank for Reconstruction and Development, and the anticipation of more comprehensive association agreements with individual East European states. Moreover, the EC's active role in the Europe-wide Conference on Security and Cooperation in Europe (see below), provided another dimension of the Community's involvement with Eastern Europe. Relatedly, beginning in 1989 the Soviet Union and several East European states were represented in the Parliamentary Assembly of the Council of Europe by 'Special Guest' Delegations.[21] During 1990, discussions were begun anticipating membership by Czechoslovakia, Hungary and Poland in the Council of Europe in 1991[22] expected to include eventual acceptance of the Council-sponsored Convention on Human Rights and Fundamental Freedoms and the jurisdiction of the Commission and Court of Human Rights – thus prospectively widening the scope of European convergence with regard to domestic human rights guarantees.

In fact, the idea of the EC as the core of a unification process that should one day extend more widely had always appealed to Europeans dissatisfied with the Continent's division since World War II. As de Gaulle declared in 1966, presciently though prematurely, 'even if one day the economic group of the Six [founding members of the EC] is supplemented by their political concert, nothing either valid or sound would have been done regarding Europe, so long as its peoples of the West and its peoples of the East have not reached agreement'.[23] Indeed, de Gaulle's proposal for European political union embodied in the Fouchet Plan (see Chapter 2), firmly grounded in respect for state sovereignty, was intended partly to initiate a form of political cooperation in the West that would be suitable for eventual enlargement to embrace a pan-European association or confederation from the Atlantic to the Urals.

In 1990, facing circumstances and opportunities that de Gaulle could have only imagined, Mitterrand adumbrated a broad vision of a European-wide confederation aimed primarily at stabilising and compassing the economic, political and security orientation of the emerging East European democracies.[24] Given the profound changes underway in their domestic systems, simultaneous with the decay of Soviet-dominated regional economic and security structures, Mitterrand saw the risk of East European isolation from the West, domestic instability if the reform process faltered, and the danger of a return to divisive national rivalries fuelled by economic malaise and regional minority problems. However, in line with the Community's newly reaffirmed self-deepening ethos, Mitterrand's concept of pan-European outreach was rooted in the EC Twelve 'which absolutely must strengthen its structure', and which he credited with being a major factor inspiring East European demands for change by being 'a point of reference and magnet for them'. Nevertheless, Mitterrand's suggestion, while slim on details, sought to link the EC's immediate responses to the changes in Eastern Europe with the wider evolutionary aim of closer pan-European association. It was an attempt to promote a direction of European-wide inclusiveness and structure to avoid a vacuum of regional identity in Eastern Europe, encourage the new democracies in their Western reorientations, and to offset the effects of their probable long-term exclusion from membership in the EC.

Broadly speaking, French ideas corresponded with the longstanding West German view that the European Community will 'remain incomplete for as long as Europe remains divided into East and West'.[25] Kohl's frequent observation that the EC 'must not stop at the Elbe' was expanded in his June 1990 Harvard commencement address when he revived the vision of a federal United States of Europe which must not exclude any East or West European state that wanted to join – though he later acknowledged that a European Community of more than 20 members would be 'hardly imaginable'.[26] In any case, at the very least, open British hostility as well as traditional French aversion to the federal model for European construction assured that Kohl's vision represented but one of many ideas competing for attention in the burgeoning industry of post-cold war European architectural design. Indeed, the purpose of the Kohl and Mitterrand initiatives must be seen essentially as exercises in lodestar diplomacy – in both cases using familiar institutional nomenclature to articulate long-range aim points with little immediate relevance – but which could serve as ideational frames of reference for the EC's evolving outreach toward other European states.

As suggested by the foregoing discussion, several factors accounted for the relatively strong position of the EC as the principal pole of stability and attraction *vis-à-vis* the changes in Eastern and Central Europe. First, there was the longstanding West European interest in overcoming the Continent's division which provided an ethos for action when the opportunity arrived for concrete initiatives. While the United States had also long supported a 'Europe whole and free', the American interest had been primarily of a strategic and ideological nature in contrast to the deeper historical, socio-cultural and economic mainsprings of European motivation. After all, the cold war had divided Europe, not America, and the impulse to heal the division, and to assume responsibility for it, was bound to be felt more keenly in Europe than in the United States. Moreover, the United States had derived geopolitical advantage from the cold war in so far as its circumstances had perpetuated West European security dependence on the Atlantic Alliance as the foremost expression of the

American leadership system in Europe. Thus, for Western Europe, the natural interest in moving toward continental wholeness was reinforced by the prospect of reducing the constraints of dependency associated with the security-dominated East–West political climate during the cold war.

Second, given the severity of economic and environmental problems in the emerging East European democracies, and the centrality of economic restructuring in their reform movements, together with deficit-driven budgetary constraints in the United States, Western Europe represented the most viable source to meet East European needs for external assistance. In addition to the leading EC role in direct aid and lending programmes toward Eastern Europe, the Community's authority in common commercial policy automatically enhanced its position in expanding trade relations with the East. Moreover, the long-active role of EC governments in the CSCE process encouraged the East European transition toward free market economic principles. Relatedly, for reasons of geography, cultural affinity, favourable government policies and recent experience, West European businesses were strongly positioned to expand investment and joint-venture activity in Eastern Europe and generally moved more quickly and aggressively to do so than their American counterparts. Third, in addition to the positive image projected by the EC's economic performance, its stable and proven institutions, and the momentum and expectations of the single market programme, the very nature of the Community's main activity – economics – facilitated its broad acceptance as a natural vehicle to expand contacts between East and West. Though all its members except Ireland were also members of the Atlantic Alliance, the EC itself, partly because of its less-developed political and security side, more easily escaped identification as an institution of the cold war. Furthermore, as discussed previously, the EC represented the only viable European economic and political framework for integrating a united Germany within a wider continental structure.

Finally, the EC was the most visible and effective focal point for organising a European response to Iraq's invasion and subsequent annexation of Kuwait in August 1990. On 2 August, the day of the invasion, the Twelve condemned the move and called for Iraq to withdraw its forces – a promptness that stood in sharp contrast to the EC's three-week delay in reacting to the Soviet invasion of Afghanistan a decade earlier. On 4 August, EC governments announced an embargo on oil imports from Iraq and Kuwait, an embargo on military sales to

Iraq, and suspension of military, technical and scientific cooperation, two days before more sweeping sanctions, including a trade embargo, were adopted by the UN Security Council with the unanimous support of the Twelve. While the blatant nature of the Iraqi aggression and its nearly universal condemnation facilitated rapid Community action with little controversy, nevertheless the well-oiled EPC machinery combined with the EC's trade authority made possible a textbook example of Community foreign policy-making.

In contrast with the swift EC response to the Gulf crisis, the Western European Union did not formally meet until 21 August – nearly three weeks after the Iraqi invasion – by which time military measures to enforce the trade embargo or to help deter further Iraqi aggression had already been decided by several of its members. WEU foreign and defence ministers agreed to coordinate their military operations in the Gulf closely, though forces were to remain under national command. Thus, given NATO's out-of-area operational restrictions (not applicable to the WEU), and the absence of an EC/EPC role in defence, the WEU was the obvious forum for articulating a more cohesive European role in the crisis. Moreover, as had occurred in the 1987 Gulf crisis, some countries found it useful to associate their contributions with a collective European effort, rather than acting unilaterally or appearing simply to follow the American lead.

In a broad sense, both the EC/EPC and WEU responses to the Gulf crisis were motivated by the desire to manifest distinctive collective European attitudes and positions, notwithstanding their general conformity with the international consensus elsewhere. Moreover, given the leading US role in mobilising international measures to oppose Iraq, and massive American military deployments, governments felt it all the more necessary to demonstrate European resolve and commitment to balance the US engagement at least partly. Thus, as in the cases of East European change and German unification, the initial phase of the Gulf crisis elicited responses that helped to solidify the European identity and cohesion as a global actor, albeit in different magnitudes of importance for the EC/EPC compared to the WEU.

ARCHITECTURE FOR THE NEW EUROPE: THE ATLANTIC ALLIANCE

The logic of the EC's centrality in responding to developments in Europe during 1989/90 differed from that of NATO and in some obvious respects was more cogent. Well before the rapid acceleration of events in late 1989 signalled the ending of the cold war, the Alliance came under pressure to attune its stance to the warming trends in East–West relations, including Gorbachev's military de-escalation initiatives announced in his December 1988 UN speech. The widely publicised beginning of unilateral Soviet troop pullbacks from Eastern Europe, and later agreements to withdraw all Soviet forces from Hungary and Czechoslovakia in 1991, highlighted the ending of any plausible Soviet military threat to Western Europe. Progress in the Conventional Armed Forces in Europe negotiations, aimed at eliminating the capability for surprise attack or large-scale offensive operations, coupled with evidence of Soviet shifts to a defensive military doctrine, nurtured the climate of a fast-ebbing NATO–Warsaw Pact military confrontation.

The early unravelling of the carefully crafted May 1989 NATO summit accord on modernisation of short-range nuclear forces (see Chapter 10) reflected the East–West military and political thaw. Regarding the Alliance statement that ground-based nuclear missiles would be needed in Europe 'as far as can be foreseen', Kohl and Genscher speculated confidently to the West German parliament in June that in view of the fast-paced developments in Europe, 'foreseeable can mean a relatively limited period of time'.[27] It became increasingly obvious during the latter part of 1989, given the improving East–West military and political climate, the changes in East Germany and Eastern Europe, negative West German public attitudes toward nuclear weapons, and the approaching 1990 elections, that the Kohl government would oppose virtually any NATO nuclear enhancement measures.

Relatedly, it became clear that the Bush administration was moving closer to West Germany as its main European partner on defence, arms control and 'architectural' issues, in contrast to the Reagan administration's reliance on British support during the earlier more confrontational period of East–West relations. This factor, perhaps more than anything else, signalled the Bush administration's readiness by mid-1989 for flexibility on NATO issues and its awareness of the need to build alignment with West Germany, NATO's most eastern-oriented member, as the Alliance sought to adapt to radical change in Europe. It was potentially a shrewd combination, though not a predictable one, given the Bush administration's initial caution in devising a response to the fast-paced changes in Europe. A solid Bonn–Washington tie ('partners in leadership', as Bush put it) would bring together those major NATO countries which in recent years had tended toward the greatest divergence on defence issues – with other Alliance members, except for Britain, ranging in between. Moreover, if a close US–West German understanding could be sustained, it could not fail to encourage British movement toward the centre, to avoid an already troubling perception of isolation, while helping to shape French policy which needed to maintain its own special ties with Germany. Thus the prospect of closer US–West German alignment augured favourably for the chances of shaping Alliance-wide consensus on the issues that lay ahead. Furthermore, by taking the lead in supporting Bonn's drive toward unification, the United States expected to gain some leverage in influencing the German position on Alliance and East–West security questions. Finally, a main feature of the Bush administration's policy toward Europe, that a unified Germany should fully belong to NATO, required that the Alliance be adaptive to German concerns and interests in the new pan-European political and security environment.

While in an immediate sense the US edged more closely toward Bonn on some NATO issues than vice versa, this was because the rapid disintegration of the Warsaw Pact military threat outmoded some of the Bush administration's earlier positions, while vindicating those advanced by West Germany. Indeed, on the Lance modernisation question, as early as June 1989 Secretary of State Baker interpreted the NATO summit pledge to keep the Lance missiles and other forces 'up to date where necessary' as requiring only that they be kept in good repair[28] (the West German view all along), in contrast to Prime Minister Thatcher's position that a modernised replacement missile was needed – a decision that the summit postponed.

The debates over NATO's military down-scaling, residual force deployments, strategy adjustments and arms control positions formed but part of the larger issue of the Alliance's role in Europe's future in the 1990s. Despite the sharp diminution of NATO's *raison d'être* as a defensive coalition, and partly because of it, attention focused on the political role of the Alliance as a stabilising factor in the new environment. Not surprisingly, the sheer novelty and unpredictability of the situation, which had challenged assumptions, attitudes and behavioural patterns nurtured by decades of cold war confrontation, encouraged an instinctive caution in charting the future as well as a 'back to basics' reappraisal of fundamental national and Alliance interests. In an important sense, of course, these interests remained constant: prevention of war in Europe and the preservation of democratic values and institutions that were now spreading eastward. What had changed was the rapid disappearance of a palpable threat to those interests – posing questions as to the continued relevance of an alliance whose principal purpose, function and public identity had always been associated mainly with military deterrence and defence.

For the United States, the ending of the cold war posed the prospect of declining American influence in Europe, to the extent that influence had derived from Western Europe's security dependence on the US through NATO. As discussed in previous chapters, the East–West confrontation, particularly its military dimension, had been the central and preponderantly defining context for Atlantic unity, and the ultimate source of American leverage *vis-à-vis* Western Europe on both Alliance and non-Alliance issues. The sudden disintegration of the cold war environment, if not yet of its structures, thus posed the question of redefining the American role in a post-cold war Europe.

Secretary of State Baker's speech in Berlin on 12 December 1989[29] outlined the rudiments of the Bush administration's approach in the new circumstances, beginning with the premise that 'the United States is and will remain a European power', and that the architecture for the new Europe should reflect that America's political, military and economic security would continue to be linked to it. Those links, as Baker clarified, should be elaborated through existing Atlantic and European structures regarded as central to the management of change and to the consolidation of a new Atlantic and European political, security and economic order: NATO, the Conference on Security and Cooperation in Europe (CSCE) and the European Community.

In suggesting new missions for NATO, Baker emphasised the importance first of achieving conventional force reductions through a CFE accord, after which non-military aspects of European security were expected to grow as NATO's role assumed a more expressly political character. With arms-control agreements, confidence-building measures, and other pan-European links becoming more important, 'NATO will become the forum where Western nations cooperate to negotiate, implement, verify, and extend agreements between East and West'. Alluding to dangers arising from the proliferation of missiles and nuclear, chemical and biological weapons, Baker proposed intensified NATO consultations to seek common Western approaches to regional conflicts.

Moreover, Baker advocated a NATO role in considering further Western initiatives through the 35-nation CSCE to build economic and political ties with the East and to promote respect for human rights and the consolidation of democratic institutions. The CSCE process, bringing together all European states except Albania plus the US and Canada, was based on the Final Act of the Conference adopted by all participants at Helsinki in 1975. While not a legally binding document, it nevertheless represented a political commitment to observe basic principles of international conduct including respect for sovereignty, independence and borders, non-interference in the internal affairs of other European states, and the non-use or threat of force. Signatories had also subscribed to the observance of basic principles of human rights, agreed to facilitate and expand economic and commercial ties, and adopted a voluntary regime of military confidence-building measures which was later strengthened and made obligatory through a CSCE-sponsored accord reached at Stockholm in 1986. Since 1975 the Helsinki Final Act had served as a rallying point for East European dissident groups demanding change in their own countries and, through periodic CSCE review conferences, had provided a basis for Western pressure to encourage liberalisation in Eastern Europe. Yet the CSCE was an unwieldy body – more a process than an institution – and the requirement for unanimity among its 35 participants and the absence of provisions for enforcement or for high-level political decision-making posed problems with respect to expanding its functions and responsibility.

The European Community, as the third element of Baker's architectural triptych, was the only one which did not include US membership and hence was least susceptible to direct US influence, a situation reinforced by declining American leverage in NATO as the reduced importance of defence issues diminished the significance of West European dependency. Less beholden to Washington on matters of security, the EC could be expected to seek expanded manoeuvring room in areas of foreign policy traditionally more strongly subject to considerations of Alliance solidarity. Thus, while reaffirming US support for the EC, Baker stressed the importance of transatlantic cooperation 'keeping pace' with progress in European integration. In particular, Baker proposed 'a significantly strengthened set of institutional and consultative links', in treaty or some other form, between the United States and the European Community, embracing economics, foreign policy and other fields. To promote balanced progress in European and Atlantic development, Baker suggested that discussions toward closer Atlantic ties proceed in parallel with the EC's 1992 internal market programme 'so that plans for US–EC interaction would evolve with changes in the Community'. Interestingly, the

Baker initiative resembled in some respects the Nixon administration's call for closer US–EC consultations in 1973/74 (see Chapter 6). In both cases, the EC's apparent movement toward stronger internal cohesion and an expanded range of activity prompted the US to seek closer consultative access to the Community (a seat at the EC table, as some put it) to assure a full hearing for American interests.

The purpose of the Baker speech was to assert American initiative and leadership in the flourishing debate over Europe's future and to position the United States to be a major player in the shaping of that future. On one level, the idea of a continued role for NATO provoked little controversy. Paradoxically, indeed, it seemed likely that the Alliance would acquire a more widely accepted political role in Europe just at the time when its defence role was being questioned and increasingly stressed by debates over nuclear weapons and military impaction in light of actual and prospective Soviet withdrawals. The appeal of NATO on both sides of the Atlantic derived from a combination of traditional and new considerations. From an American perspective, use of the Alliance as a major forum for coordinating and aligning Western responses carried the obvious advantage of assuring the United States a central role in the process. Furthermore, despite NATO's shift to more of a political role with a pan-European outreach, its essential character as a Western defensive coalition remained important as insurance against the possibility that current trends could be reversed. Relatedly, it was the obvious mechanism to coordinate Western military down-scaling, as the defence debate shifted from burden-sharing to burden-shedding, and the Alliance searched for a residual force posture and strategy attuned to the new circumstances. Moreover, in a transitional period during which Soviet conventional and nuclear capabilities in Europe remained formidable, the Alliance's defence role continued to constitute a necessary basis for Western security. Finally, there was little support in Western Europe for devising a European alternative to NATO in the area of defence policy. Any such idea was clearly out of tune with the new ambience and dynamics of pan-European reconciliation, while it would once again risk setting in motion a further reduction of the American security role in Europe beyond that already projected as a result of East–West military de-escalation. Hence, the new activity of WEU in such areas as exploring means of arms control verification and the idea of multinational brigades (which would increase the level of existing Alliance military integration) closely paralleled that of NATO.

Furthermore, the sheer enormity of the European geopolitical transformations underway focused attention on the Alliance as a stabilising factor, at least for a transitional period of uncertain duration. In this sense, as we have seen, Western support for German unification was linked to the assumption that a united Germany would remain in NATO, reinforcing the similar linkage between unification and strengthening the EC – views also shared by Czechoslovakia, Hungary and Poland. In short, close German bonding to the EC *and* NATO were prerequisites for establishing confidence that a unified Germany would remain anchored in a wider European and Atlantic political and institutional framework. This also comported with the prevailing West German attitude. In rejecting neutrality and reaffirming its NATO and EC attachments, the Kohl government recognised the need to reassure its allies that unification would not portend a weakening of its Western commitments. Nor could Bonn afford the risk of isolation or only begrudging support from its Western partners in its pursuit of unification and thereafter. Likewise, a firm German mooring in the EC and NATO offered welcome reassurance to Eastern Europe. Moreover, and somewhat paradoxically, a united Germany could expect to acquire expanded manoeuvring room in foreign policy precisely to the extent that concerns about any German temptations toward unilateralism could be assuaged by its close ties to the West.

Finally, the profound domestic transformations in Eastern Europe and the Soviet Union since the late 1980s were a stunning reminder of the rapidity with which the character of national regimes can change. However unlikely, Western governments could not responsibly ignore the possibility of Soviet reversion to more aggressive policies if Gorbachev were to be replaced, or as an assertive response to domestic instabilities, or as a reaction to the steep decline in the Soviet Union's external position. Indeed, whatever the character of its government, even after implementation of expected arms control agreements, the Soviet Union (or even only the Russian Republic) would remain by far the most formidable conventional and nuclear power on the Continent. Nor could the potential power projection capabilities of a united Germany, in circumstances not foreseeable in 1990, be overlooked as part of the new European security situation.

Initial Soviet opposition to the idea of a unified Germany in NATO was part of the larger question of the role of the Soviet Union in Europe's post-cold war security arrangements. Faced with the loss of East Germany, the disintegration of the Warsaw Pact, the westward leaning of its former satellites, and fissiparous momentum within its own borders, the Soviet Union confronted a weakening of its European position unparalleled since the eighteenth century. Despite Western assurances that at least for a transitional period NATO's role would not be extended to the eastern part of a united Germany, which could only partly assuage Soviet concerns, Soviet officials alternatingly advanced a bewildering parade of ideas designed to mitigate or mask their strategic setback: a unified neutral Germany, a unified Germany remaining attached to both alliances for a transitional period, postponement of definitive arrangements for Germany's security orientation until some time after unification, continued Four Power responsibilities with regard to Germany for a period after unification, and the eventual dissolution of both alliances in favour of a new pan-European security system. While the Western powers rejected all such proposals, they were nonetheless attentive to the need to devise an approach that would address Soviet security concerns arising from a unified Germany's membership in NATO. Indeed, herein lay the payoff of the new US–West German partnership.

As suggested by the foregoing considerations, increasingly during 1990 NATO deliberations came to be driven by the closely connected issues of German unification and Soviet security concerns in Europe, and the need to adapt the Alliance to both. Thus in May 1990, NATO foreign ministers endorsed a somewhat belated decision by the Bush administration to cancel plans to develop a modernised replacement missile for the Lance as well as new nuclear-tipped artillery shells. In a further shift away from the May 1989 summit position, it was agreed that negotiations with the Soviet Union on reducing short-range nuclear forces could begin once an agreement on cuts in conventional forces had been reached, yet before its implementation had begun.

Moving in the same trajectory, the July 1990 NATO summit in London took further steps, some mainly symbolic, designed to facilitate Soviet acceptance of a united Germany in NATO and to articulate to Western publics the rationale for the Alliance in the new circumstances.[30] Particular measures included a proposed non-aggression declaration with Warsaw Pact states and other CSCE members, and an invitation to President Gorbachev and East European leaders to visit NATO headquarters and for their governments to establish regular diplomatic liaison with NATO. On the arms control side, a second CFE negotiation was endorsed which would seek wider and deeper European force reductions. As a new incentive for Moscow, Alliance leaders accepted a West German proposal that, upon conclusion of the first CFE agreement, a commitment would be made on the military manpower levels of a unified Germany, thus addressing a key Soviet concern that otherwise would have been deferred to the second CFE negotiation. With respect to nuclear weapons, it was agreed that upon commencement of negotiations to reduce short-range nuclear forces, the Alliance would propose the elimination of all its nuclear artillery shells from Europe linked to reciprocal action by the Soviet Union. More broadly, it was anticipated that the military strategy of forward defence would be modified by reducing front-line forces and relying increasingly on mobile units configured in multinational corps. Overall, it was expected that NATO would field fewer active forces and rely more on increased warning time and mobilisation capability to respond to any military contingency.

With regard to NATO's strategy of flexible response (see Chapter 2), the London communiqué further obfuscated a doctrine already deliberately ambiguous concerning the point at which nuclear weapons might be used in a European war. Proclaiming that NATO nuclear forces would become 'truly weapons of last resort' (upon the withdrawal of Soviet forces and implementation of a CFE accord), it was not clear what was really being changed, since it had always been assumed that NATO would consider nuclear escalation only as a 'last resort' to prevent defeat by a large-scale conventional offensive. Nevertheless, many believed that the formal relegation of nuclear weapons to last resort status would weaken an important element of traditional NATO deterrence strategy, namely that a potential aggressor would risk provoking a nuclear retaliation at some intermediate point in his attack. To meet this objection, advanced particularly by Britain and France, the communiqué affirmed that 'there are no circumstances in which nuclear retaliation in response to military action might be discounted', a provision that was in sharp variance with the concept of last resort. The manifestly contradictory nature of the two versions in the same document would have been unimaginable in an earlier era. Yet with the virtual disappearance of any Warsaw Pact conventional forces threat to Europe, disagreement over the fine points of deterrence doctrine seemed less important compared to the political need to adjust the Alliance's military image in light of the new circumstances.

At a summit devoted to accenting the Alliance's unity and adaptiveness to change, the nettlesome question of NATO's future nuclear deployments was avoided. The issue was whether the Alliance would move toward eventual deployment of a tactical air-to-surface missile

(TASM), as had been advocated by the US and Britain, though resisted by West Germany. The London summit declaration, while noting requirements for 'far fewer nuclear weapons' and a diminished need for short-range nuclear forces, nonetheless reaffirmed that for the foreseeable future the Alliance must maintain an appropriate mix of conventional and nuclear forces based in Europe and kept up to date where necessary. The generous elasticity of the language closely resembled previous NATO formulations and amounted to a restatement of basic principles with ample tolerance for their later implementation or even abandonment altogether: 'foreseeable future' could be a very short period of time; 'appropriate mix' could accommodate an essentially symbolic nuclear presence; 'based in Europe' left open the question of where; and 'up to date where necessary' could embrace either maintenance/adaptation of existing systems or modernised replacements. But the traditional language acquired a sharper meaning in the context of the prospective withdrawal of all NATO nuclear artillery shells and the decision not to modernise the Lance missile, which portended the eventual steep reduction or elimination of all of NATO's ground-based nuclear forces except for aircraft delivered gravity bombs. Thus the TASM system under development offered a means for maintaining a high confidence short-range nuclear capability that could be widely dispersed, thus reducing the extent of German singularisation (more accurately, concentration) in existing deployments, and that because of its range would not be closely identified with possible targets in the emerging democracies of Eastern Europe. Moreover, an air-launched deterrent might provide a politically more acceptable way for Germany to share both the risks and benefits of the Alliance, while reducing the possibility that some future German government might determine that Germany needed its own nuclear force.

On the other hand, TASM posed a host of formidable political problems. Obviously, the idea of NATO moving toward adoption of a major new nuclear weapons system was almost grotesquely incongruous with the mood and progress toward East–West *rapprochement* and cooperative security, the Alliance's own conciliatory moves toward the East, and the NATO proposal for a joint declaration with Warsaw Pact states that 'we are no longer adversaries'. In such an atmosphere it was difficult, to say the least, to make a persuasive case for a new nuclear system to address some future hypothetical contingency. Moreover, deferral of the TASM question was a key aspect of the Western effort to secure Soviet acceptance of German membership in NATO. Also, any effort by the Bush administration to push the issue within the Alliance would have risked a major rupture of the new US–West German partnership. Indeed, Bonn's resistance to deploying any new nuclear systems on its territory was clear after the May 1989 NATO summit, and by November it had become, in the words of a West German official, 'a question that makes us laugh'.[31] However, if TASM were eventually deployed in parts of Europe other than Germany, it would pose the problem of German singularisation in reverse, that is, a special status for Germany with respect to Alliance obligations and a further step down the road toward its de-nuclearisation. Arguably, on the other hand, this might well be the price for German membership in NATO in the long run, particularly in view of uncertainties as to whether a united Germany moving to the forefront of European leadership would continue to accept a significant foreign military presence on its territory. Thus a decision on TASM, which in any case was not urgent, would have prematurely forced to the surface controversial subjects that might prove more soluble further down the road of East–West arms control negotiations.

As indicated above, the broad objectives of the London summit were to articulate a new direction for the Alliance in the post-cold war circumstances and, relatedly, to make the case for its continued support by Western publics. More situationally, however, the German and Soviet questions were the driving factors behind the agreements reached. At least in the short term, the summit appeared to be a resounding success. Within two weeks Gorbachev announced the withdrawal of Soviet objections to a united Germany's membership in NATO, citing 'a very important impulse'[32] from the London conference as a major factor in the decision. Gorbachev had probably surmised that the London summit was the Alliance's 'bottom line' on the twinned issues of NATO adjustments and German membership and, fortified by his strengthened position at the 28th Party Congress in July, concluded that the time was ripe to remove the last remaining obstacle to unification.

Nevertheless, the manner and timing of the announcement (which took Western governments by surprise), in the context of an exceptionally cordial visit by Kohl to the Soviet leader, raised some unsettling questions. On the one hand, the symbolism of Gorbachev making his key concession directly to Kohl (rather than, for example, in the setting of the Two plus Four talks) seemed intended, or in any case had the effect, of pointing toward a new Soviet–German partnership potentially spanning a wide range of their bilateral relations. On the agreement itself, a British diplomat sniffed: 'It's not enormously elegant for just the two of them to announce this'.[33] Furthermore, to seal up the Soviet concession, Kohl appears to have moved beyond the London understanding by pledging a 370 000 limit on a united Germany's armed forces well before the conclusion of the CFE accord. Indeed, Kohl's declaration on this point was indicative of the shift of gravity in Germany's position toward the east driven by the momentum for unification. Previous West German commitments to maximum military manpower levels had been made to the Western powers through the Paris agreements in connection with the Federal Republic's entry into NATO in 1955 (see Chapter 1). In 1990, though the London summit had endorsed a pledge on German manpower levels to be made upon signature of a CFE accord, Kohl unilaterally advanced the timetable and, moreover, announced the numerical commitment in the setting of a Soviet–German negotiation about which the Western powers were later informed. Thus, the later confirmation of understandings on German military personnel levels recorded in the final settlement treaty ending the Two plus Four talks essentially registered a *fait accompli*. In addition, the West German position that no nuclear weapons or foreign troops should be based on the territory of eastern Germany[34] (after unification) differed from the US view that NATO forces would not be extended to eastern Germany for a transitional period following unification. To be sure, Kohl stated publicly in his joint news conference with Gorbachev only that NATO structures would not be extended to eastern Germany during the three to four year period after unification while Soviet forces were being withdrawn. Nevertheless, Gorbachev directly attributed to Kohl the view that even after this period foreign forces would not 'appear' in eastern Germany.[35] The final settlement treaty, stipulating that foreign armed forces and nuclear weapons/carriers will not be stationed or deployed in eastern Germany following the withdrawal of Soviet forces, left to Germany the application of the term 'deployment', hence allowing the possibility of some NATO presence in the east as a symbol of Germany's membership in the Alliance. Whatever the ambiguities, the Kohl–Gorbachev agreement revived concerns in the West about German unilateralism and questions about the implications of the Soviet–German understanding for future German ties with the West.

The London declaration was a logical and effective response to the short-term need of removing Soviet objections to a united Germany's membership in NATO. Moreover, the agreed adjustments to

NATO's strategy and forces were a cogent adaptation to the diminished military threat in Europe while leaving intact the essentials of the Alliance as a defensive coalition. Yet the combination of West German policy and public attitudes, the dynamics of unification, the new Soviet–German relationship, the CFE negotiations, and the US and Alliance diplomacy, pointed toward a continued de-nuclearisation in Germany after unification and the strong possibility that allied forces would be expected to leave to reciprocate Soviet withdrawals from eastern Germany and Eastern Europe. Indeed, the London summit made clear what was becoming increasingly apparent before, that German interests were the driving force in shaping NATO policy and that, at least implicitly, Alliance adaptations were the price not only of Soviet acceptance of German membership in NATO but of continued German participation after unification. Yet if over time the German role in NATO were to become essentially nominal, creating an imbalance in German costs and benefits of membership, the political cohesion of the Alliance, and perhaps the Alliance itself, could be critically undermined. On the other hand, having gained Soviet assent to a united Germany's membership in NATO, and particularly after the withdrawal of Soviet forces, German incentives for accommodating Moscow on security questions should diminish.

Nevertheless, it would be a curious result indeed if the process of NATO–German–Soviet mutual accommodation were to lead toward the *de facto* neutralisation of Germany, notwithstanding its formal membership in the Alliance. Like the childhood story of the contest between the sun and the wind to see which could motivate the man to remove his coat, the combination of Soviet weakness and concessions had prompted German inching in a direction that Soviet policies during the cold war period had been unable to accomplish. In fact the declining significance of alliances, and hence of neutralisation itself, was at least implicit within the notion of common East–West security structures in Europe which formed part of the foundation of the new German–Soviet relationship. Yet if future Soviet policies toward Europe were to become more assertive, an Alliance weakened by qualified German participation would be in a poor position to respond. More plausible, perhaps, was the possibility of a prolonged albeit subtly conducted struggle between the Soviet Union and the West for a Germany closely identified with both, enhancing German leverage in both directions as long as remnants of the East–West division remained and even thereafter.

Regardless of NATO's renovations, it was obvious that the Atlantic Alliance would constitute but one element of the emerging European architecture for the 1990s. As with the EC, NATO's Western membership configuration, whatever the new outreach impulse toward the East, limited its utility and relevance in the new politics of East–West reconciliation. In a continent searching for inclusiveness, for many NATO remained a symbol of division.

Even within the West, differences quickly surfaced as to the role NATO should play. France, while supporting the Alliance as a framework for anchoring Germany in the West and avoiding a strategic vacuum in Central Europe, nonetheless resisted the view expressed by Baker that 'NATO will become the forum' for Western cooperation in the negotiation, implementation, verification and extension of agreements between East and West.[36] Nor was France sympathetic to the idea of intensified NATO consultations to seek common Western approaches to regional conflicts, which could limit France's freedom of action in areas still largely subject to unilateral policy determinations and discourage distinctively European approaches such as through the WEU. Much of the Mitterrand government's attitude was shaped by traditional French aversion to the use of NATO as a body for concerting Western positions which, in the French view, perpetuated American dominance in the transatlantic relationship. Similarly, France resisted 'bloc to bloc' approaches toward East–West negotiations because this, too, reinforced superpower primacy within the respective alliances while limiting the role of the European members. In this sense, Mitterrand's policy remained closely attuned to classic Gaullist 'manoeuvre' diplomacy: the pursuit of French interests through a network of bilateral ties and multilateral groupings while resisting associations and processes wherein French leadership could not be assured and, in particular, where American (or Soviet) influence would likely predominate. This also partly explained the French tolerance for strengthening the EC, even accepting some limits on national manoeuvre, while opposing such moves in NATO. Reinforced by the Franco-German tie at the core of the Community, and because of Germany's special need for both to achieve European legitimation and stability in the drive for unification and thereafter, France could be assured a continued prominent role in the EC of the 1990s. Moreover, though the Community role in security policy remained limited, it was a natural vehicle for seeking broader consensus for French ideas; failing that, independent French initiatives would not be precluded. Nevertheless, whatever the value of the EC and the

Alliance in the French scheme of things, neither was sufficient in itself, nor were the two together, to address the new politics of pan-European *rapprochement*.

The outbreak of the Persian Gulf crisis in August 1990 immediately revived the issue of the role of the Alliance with respect to out-of-area conflicts. The Bush administration, in line with the pattern of US diplomacy discussed in Chapter 10 (and Baker's Berlin speech), sought a prominent role for NATO in orchestrating Western responses to the crisis, a move that was widely resisted in Europe. Indeed the WEU ministerial statement of 21 August, which repeatedly cited UN Security Council resolutions as the basis for European action without mentioning the Atlantic Alliance, signalled a preference for a European rather than a NATO umbrella for the coordination of military deployments, albeit in cooperation with other forces in the region including those of the United States. Thus, given the out-of-area status of the Gulf crisis, the Alliance was used essentially for consultations, mobilisation of consensus for military deployments to support the embargo and deter possible further Iraqi actions, and endorsement of measures taken by individual members. However, with the notable exception of Britain (and later, France), there was a general European reluctance to endorse blockade measures to enforce the trade embargo, as announced by the United States, pending approval of such action by the UN Security Council which occurred later in the month. On 10 August, NATO foreign ministers backed US, British and French military measures already undertaken and agreed that Alliance members 'will contribute each in its own way' to stopping further Iraqi military aggression – a consensus that fell short of the Bush administration's hopes for a stronger statement of Alliance solidarity in responding to the crisis. Typifying the traditional European reluctance to directly associate the Alliance as such with out-of-area actions, only the Secretary General's summary of conclusions reached at the meeting was issued, rather than a ministerial statement.

While military and economic support measures by other Alliance members soon followed, some mainly symbolic, the huge imbalance between US commitments and those of its NATO allies, despite Europe's more than three times greater dependence on Persian Gulf oil, quickly revived the burden-sharing issue and prompted the Bush administration to press its allies in Europe and elsewhere for stronger support. Nevertheless, the expansion of British and French military forces in the Gulf region, small contingents sent by most other

NATO countries, and hefty financial contributions from Germany and Japan (both constitutionally restricted from military deployments), plus close US–European political alignment on UN Security Council measures against Iraq, soon moderated the burden-sharing issue. In any case, European unwillingness to deal with the Gulf crisis as a NATO issue was in fact compatible with US efforts to build a global coalition against Iraq, a strategy that would have been undermined by undue emphasis on an exclusively Western alliance. Hence, as US policy concentrated on building solidarity against Iraq in the UN Security Council, complemented by bilateral coalition-building elsewhere, in particular with states in the Middle East, the role of the Atlantic Alliance became relegated to the background.

ARCHITECTURE FOR THE NEW EUROPE: THE CONFERENCE ON SECURITY AND COOPERATION IN EUROPE

Early in 1990, the Conference on Security and Cooperation in Europe (CSCE) emerged as the leading candidate to assume a larger role in the search for a post-cold war all-European security order. As the only grouping that embraced Eastern and Western Europe plus the Soviet Union, the United States and Canada, the CSCE possessed the requisite inclusiveness for a pan-European security framework. Moreover, the CSCE process of periodic review conferences, guided by the principles of the Helsinki Final Act, had gained status and respect by facilitating improved protection of human rights in Eastern Europe in the 1980s, while providing external support for the reform movements in individual countries. CSCE-sponsored activity in furthering East–West economic cooperation and in promoting coordinated approaches to environmental problems represented other areas of potential progress. The security principles of the Helsinki Final Act provided a basis for considering a broader CSCE role in monitoring and facilitating their observance. In particular, the successful implementation of the CSCE-sponsored Stockholm accord on obligatory confidence and security-building measures – including advance notification of military activities, invited observation of military manoeuvres, and limited rights of short-notice inspection on demand – had established a CSCE role in pan-European security arrangements. Hence, CSCE's substantive involvement already addressed much of the expected Europe-wide agenda of the 1990s.

The CSCE also seemed well suited to the trend toward de-bipolarisation in Europe, the declining prominence of the superpowers (however different in scope and degree), and the emergence of a more fluid and multipolar pan-European field of play, albeit one internally structured in the West by European and Atlantic groupings and to a much lesser extent in the East. By including alliance members as well as neutral and non-aligned countries, the CSCE embraced the diversity of European security policy orientations, while its consensual method of operation theoretically equalised the influence of all states which had particular appeal to the smaller countries.

In France, CSCE resonated with the Gaullist vision of a European association from the Atlantic to the Urals. Moreover, France had long supported an all-European approach to arms control issues which partly accounted for French abstention from the geographically more restricted NATO–Warsaw Pact Mutual and Balanced Force Reduction (MBFR) negotiations in the 1970s and 1980s, a forum also rejected by Paris because of its bloc to bloc configuration. In 1978, French President Giscard d'Estaing proposed convening a Conference on Disarmament in Europe (CDE) to be held in the framework of the CSCE, an idea that François Mitterrand had advanced publicly the previous year[37]. Giscard's initiative envisaged strengthening and making mandatory the voluntary military confidence-building measures already in place under the Helsinki Final Act, after which conventional forces throughout Europe capable of supporting offensive military operations would be reduced. The French proposal was warmly welcomed by other EC governments, though its only lukewarm endorsement by NATO ministers reflected US apprehensions that a new European arms control initiative could undermine prospects for progress in the MBFR talks. Nevertheless, the French proposals furnished much of the impetus that later culminated in the 1986 CDE accord at Stockholm on confidence and security-building measures, as well as the launching of East–West conventional force reduction negotiations (CFE) in 1989. With regard to the latter, even though the negotiations were conducted by the members of the two alliances whose forces were to be reduced, France insisted upon a CSCE-wide umbrella role for the talks, thus emphasising at least symbolically the multilateral and pan-European nature of the negotiations and of the resulting security regime. Thus France's support for a stronger CSCE role in the new circumstances represented a logical and timely extension of French policy over the previous decade, while broadly comporting with Mitterrand's vision of a European confederation.

For West Germany, the CSCE framework offered obvious advantages for Bonn's effort to promote confidence in its commitment to a European Germany through 'the process of embedding German unification in the European structure'.[38] Indeed, it was recognised that this was necessary not only to smooth the path to unification, but also to establish conditions that would enable a united Germany to exercise influence, commensurate with its new power, without arousing undue anxieties elsewhere. Thus an expanded role for the CSCE held some promise as a pan-European complement to the EC and NATO, with the three groupings together comprising the main elements of the German compact with Europe, while at the same time providing added safeguards that a united Germany would not pose a future danger to European stability. Moreover, the principles of the Helsinki Final Act, though conceived in entirely different circumstances, served to legitimise key elements of West Germany's position. The acknowledged right of self-determination, together with the principle of the 'inviolability' of European state frontiers (a term insisted upon by Bonn), had left the door open to a future peaceful change of borders and unification. Furthermore, the Helsinki accord had affirmed the right of participating states to membership in alliances, thus bolstering Bonn's position that a unified Germany would remain in NATO.

In addition, as the only European-wide security body, the CSCE had strong appeal as the chief exemplar of the new politics of East–West *rapprochement* and constructive engagement. Its main areas of activity – human rights, economic and environmental cooperation, and confidence and security-building measures – fit nicely with the emerging all-European agenda. Moreover, the CSCE offered a means of associating the East European states on an equal basis in a wider European security structure, while helping to assuage concerns about a united Germany and the Soviet Union. Finally, and of central importance, the CSCE offered a framework for clarifying and institutionalising the place of the Soviet Union in the new security order, given the demise of the Warsaw Pact, while helping Moscow to come to terms with a united Germany's membership in NATO.

The Soviet Union's advocacy of an all-European security order – an element of Gorbachev's notion of a common European home – was in fact not new. Gorbachev's apparently only half-facetious remark to Bush at the June 1990 Washington summit, that the Soviet Union perhaps should consider joining NATO, resonated with a similar suggestion advanced by Soviet leader Nikita Khrushchev in 1954. In both cases, the idea was closely linked to a parallel Soviet promotion of a Europe-wide security arrangement that would eventually replace the existing alliances. The idea held particular appeal for the Soviet Union in 1990 in view of the disintegration of the Warsaw Pact as a military alliance, in contrast to NATO's relative cohesion and adaptiveness to the new situation. Relatedly, movement toward a stronger pan-European security order could both mask and offset the Soviet retreat from Eastern Europe, mitigate the political effects of the grossly asymmetrical positions of the two alliances, and initiate a dynamic that could culminate in the eventual dissolution of both groups. While Soviet statements seemed to accept the premise of a continued US defence role in Europe, this role (and that of the Soviet Union) would presumably come to be defined increasingly in terms of a pan-European security system rather than through the existing alliances

Strong European support for an enhanced CSCE role quickly sur-faced in 1990. Mitterrand endorsed Gorbachev's November 1989 proposal for convening a CSCE summit conference to endorse the expected agreement on reduction of conventional forces, and to consider ways of strengthening CSCE involvement in constructing new pan-European security arrangements. EC-wide endorsement of the conference idea in January was followed by adoption at the Dublin summit in April of guidelines for expanding the CSCE pro-cess as 'a framework for reform and stability . . . [which] should be developed in new directions'.[39] EC leaders looked toward a balanced development of the CSCE encompassing the consolidation of pluralist democracy and the rule of law, advances in respect for human rights and the protection of minorities, cooperation in the areas of security, economics and the environment, and expanded institutional and con-sultative provisions.

The Bush administration reacted to the CSCE's new lustre in Europe with measured support and caution. Secretary of State Baker's speech in Berlin had sought to steer CSCE's evolution away from a poss-ible role as an all-European collective security body which event-ually might assume defence functions. Instead, Baker called for the strengthening of confidence-building measures, already being nego-tiated by the CSCE states in Vienna, and for measures to facilitate pan-European economic and commercial interchange in conjunc-tion with the East European reform process. In the area of human rights, Baker proposed the institutionalisation of the right to regular, free, open, multiparty elections – not yet fully guaranteed under the Helsinki Final Act.

The idea of an all-European collective security body in the framework of the CSCE posed some obvious problems. NATO's success in this role had been largely attributable to a substantial consensus among its members as to the domestic values the Alliance was maintained to protect – an interest that remained despite the sharp drop in the external threat. Yet such a consensus on a pan-European level was in a stage of fragile incipiency at best, particularly with respect to the Soviet Union, whose military power, both conventional and nuclear, continued to constitute the main potential European threat to Western security. If the CSCE process were to be extended to encompass collective security functions in the realm of defence, the role of the Atlantic Alliance would inevitably decline, thus weakening a major element of the Euro-Atlantic 'housing' for a united Germany. Moreover, movement toward such a pan-European security order would tend toward the equalisation of the roles of the United States and the Soviet Union in European security at the very time of a precipitous decline in the Soviet position and the relative stabilisation of the American role facilitated by NATO's adaptive measures. Finally, the consensual nature of the CSCE decision-making procedure, if utilised in implementing collective security undertakings, would weaken any such body as a reliable instrument for deterrence and defence.

Thus a key issue that emerged in 1990 was the roles to be played by the alliances and by the CSCE process in Europe's future security architecture, an issue that inevitably intertwined with the process of German unification and the position of a united Germany in the new Europe. While the Soviet Union was unable to block the internal dynamics of unification, the continued presence of large Soviet forces in East Germany underscored Moscow's leverage with respect to the external aspects of a unified Germany's position. Much of this leverage was latent and unexploitable, however, since the Soviet Union did not wish to be portrayed as a spoiler on unification and risk jeopardising the broader Soviet interest in improving ties with the West. The Western insistence that the internal and external aspects of unification be resolved essentially simultaneously, rejecting Moscow's proposal that the latter be deferred, thus put pressure on all the parties to come to an agreement. It was apparent of course, as in the case of the CFE negotiations, that much of the Western haste for an understanding was motivated by the uncertainties of the Soviet domestic situation, and thus by the desire to bank advantageous agreements as a hedge against the possibility of abrupt change in the leadership and policies of the Soviet Union. It was clear, nonetheless, regardless of the timetable, that a stable solution to the German question could only be achieved with the consent of the Soviet Union.

In this context, as we have seen, much of West German (and US) policy was driven toward building incentives for the Soviet Union to accept a unified Germany in NATO and to persuade Moscow's leadership that such an outcome would not threaten, in fact or in appearance, the Soviet position in Europe. Hence, Bonn took a leading role in promoting a shift in Alliance strategy on the use of nuclear weapons and in pushing for short-range nuclear de-escalation measures and East–West military dialogue; gained Western acceptance that at least for a transitional period NATO activity would not be extended to the eastern part of a united Germany; agreed to the permanence of existing borders and to reaffirm the German commitment not to produce or possess nuclear, biological or chemical weapons; strongly backed an eventual CFE II negotiation which would seek deeper reductions of armed forces throughout Europe including Germany; accepted a ceiling of 370 000 on the armed forces of a united Germany to help clinch Soviet acceptance of German membership in NATO; extended and advocated wider direct financial aid to the Soviet Union to help prop up Gorbachev's sagging reform programme; and in general fostered the concept of common security in Europe, of which an expanded role for CSCE was a major component, to assure the Soviet Union that its interests would be adequately preserved.

Most of these elements of West German policy, with the notable exception of direct financial aid to the Soviet Union, generally corresponded with the Bush administration's nine-point position presented to Gorbachev at the Washington summit in June,[40] intended to encourage Soviet acquiescence to a united Germany's membership in NATO. But the Bush administration was openly wary about the future security role of CSCE and was privately critical of some West German formulations of it. West German Foreign Minister Genscher, an avid proponent of CSCE, had called for East–West cooperative security structures 'in which the alliances could later be absorbed',[41] and on another occasion called on both alliances to define their roles increasingly as political ones 'and in the long term to merge into an instrument'[42] that would promote cooperative stability in Europe. Social Democrats in East and West professed support for a new European security organisation that would render the existing alliances 'superfluous'.[43] The clear suggestion that NATO itself should be viewed as a transitional body that would eventually blend into some future pan-European security structure only increased the Bush administration's coolness toward significantly expanding CSCE's role in this area. Remarks by administration officials that the Atlantic Alliance had always been the basis for American public understanding and acceptance of the US defence presence in Europe were intended to emphasise that that support would be undermined if the Alliance's security role were to be put into question. Chancellor Kohl, no doubt seeking to assuage US concerns on this point, assured an American audience so as to 'avoid any misunderstanding: It is not a case of the CSCE replacing the North Atlantic defense alliance, but of suitably supplementing it'.[44] Moreover, thinking in the EC Commission was generally opposed to major CSCE involvement in security matters, seeing in such an evolution a barrier to the EC itself eventually acquiring a role in defence.[45] Even France had reservations about the CSCE acquiring a collective security role, given French concerns about an emerging 'strategic vacuum' in Central Europe and scepticism that the CSCE, with its unwieldy size and consensual approach to decision-making (like the League of Nations in the 1920s and 1930s), could provide a satisfactory basis for European security.[46]

The July 1990 NATO summit declaration, while noting that the Conference on Security and Cooperation in Europe 'should become more prominent in Europe's future', nonetheless carefully steered the pan-European body away from any collective security role that might overlap with the Alliance. Indeed, Gorbachev's announcement of Soviet acceptance of German membership in NATO, made shortly after the Alliance summit, reduced the Western need to consider more far-reaching measures to expand the CSCE role in European security arrangements. Moreover, the Soviet Union's interest in the CSCE cooled somewhat, prompted by concerns that it could become a forum for internationalising debate on the country's mounting domestic problems.

The Charter of Paris, adopted by CSCE leaders in November 1990, closely followed the NATO proposals endorsed at the July summit. Symbolically marking the end of the cold war, the Charter endorsed principles of human rights, democracy, and market economy, reaffirmed the Helsinki Final Act pledge to refrain from the threat or use of force against any state, and looked toward a more structured pan-European cooperation on security matters including new negotiations on disarmament and confidence and security-building measures to begin by 1992. Modest institutionalisation measures were accepted, including establishment of a small secretariat in Prague, annual sessions of the foreign ministers, and meetings every two years at the summit – the next scheduled for 1992 in Helsinki. It was agreed to create an office in Warsaw to monitor elections, and to establish a conflict prevention centre in Vienna to focus initially on information exchanges about military activities. While such measures provided an agenda and framework for advancing the pan-European dialogue, they stopped well short of movement toward a European-wide collective security body.

As discussed previously in this chapter, the radical changes during 1989/90 materially altered the context, dynamics and structure of US–European and East–West relations – though for the most part changes at the domestic level in East Germany, Eastern Europe and, in part, in the Soviet Union were more thoroughly renovating than those at the international level. The accomplished and probable adaptations of the EC, NATO, and the CSCE – the main multilateral components of the new architecture – were broadly consistent with their traditional functions. In all three cases, though in varying degrees, the dynamics and ramifications of German unification and the East European transition were major catalysts for change. In two of the cases (NATO and the CSCE), the accepted need to accommodate the Soviet Union to the new circumstances was a key contributing factor. Nevertheless, a central motivation spurring attention to the EC, NATO and the CSCE – the need for wider foundations to 'secure' a united Germany (to use a polite though somewhat ambiguous Bush administration term) – could not obscure the fact, particularly with respect to NATO, that German interests (and concerns about Germany) had been the principal influence. Indeed, to the extent that such structures were conceived as a harnessing framework for a united Germany, it was fair to ask, who was harnessing whom? While arguably this formulation misapplies the metaphor, which could be expressed more comfortingly as Germany and the three structures moving in harness with each other, nonetheless German influence in shaping the character of the three was bound to become more important.

CONCLUSION AND PROSPECTS

As illustrated in earlier chapters and summarised in Chapter 10, much of the tension in US relations with the EC (acting through European Political Cooperation) in the 1970s and 1980s resulted from the fact that each entity viewed its interests and the situations at hand in different lights and each had an assertive disposition on issues involving the other, even though in most cases Europe was reacting to American initiatives and policies rather than vice versa. In these circumstances, American administrations often exhibited frustration and irritation when European positions differed significantly from those of the United States. Relatedly, the cold war context produced a dual and partly counteractive effect on US–European relations during this period. On the one hand, different assessments on dealing with the Soviet Union and handling East–West issues in general were a major source of transatlantic friction. Yet on the other, the cold war milieu and the formidable Soviet military position in Europe moderated US–European divergences in the name of preserving the political cohesion and defence preparedness of the Alliance.

The Euro-Atlantic situation in the early 1990s presented a sharply different picture. Of principal importance was the ending of the communist military and ideological threat and thus of the East–West confrontation that had furnished the defining context for post-war US foreign policy, and the main rationale for the global extension of American power and for efforts to rally allied support in the cause of containing communism. The events of 1989/90 accelerated the emergence of a more multipolar world, exemplified in Europe by the growing role of Germany and momentum toward strengthening the EC. The changes in Eastern and Central Europe shifted the gravitational points of East–West relations from the superpower periphery toward the centre, with the United States and the Soviet Union playing important but no longer dominant roles in the process and in the molding of the new order. In retrospect, it was apparent that the cold war to an extent had artificially augmented and sustained the positions of the US and the Soviet Union as superpowers, partly because of the inevitable preoccupation with the military aspects of the East–West confrontation and the hierarchical alliances as its foremost expression. By the early 1990s, the very term 'superpower' as applied to the Two on European issues had acquired a somewhat hollow ring, albeit in different degrees.

The ending of the cold war, and hence the lessened importance of the Alliance as a military coalition, altered the nature of the traditional West European security dependence on the United States. Yet a role for the Alliance as part of the structure for stabilising and steering Europe's post-cold war transition was widely supported, not least because of the latent if remote possibility of some future hegemonic ambitions by a united Germany or the Soviet Union.

Nevertheless, the general contextual shift in East–West relations from confrontation to cooperation, combined with momentum for deepening economic and political unity in Western Europe, created conducive circumstances for the strengthening of the European pillar around the core of the European Community/European Political Cooperation.

However, there are countervailing factors at work that will influence prospects for a further strengthening of EPC as an effective political arm of the EC. These factors may produce offsetting effects conducive to the preservation of essentially the existing symbiosis between European and national foreign policy levels with an only modest expansion of the functional scope and external role and visibility of EPC. On the positive side, the momentum of the EC's 1992 single market programme should exert spill-over pressures encouraging greater European foreign policy unity through EPC. While the functional and institutional linkage between EPC and the EC is only partial (though growing), nonetheless the success and self-confidence of the EC as an economic entity may be expected to increase support for a more cohesive and effective European political identity and influence as well. Moreover, as previously discussed, the blurring of the line between economic and political issues and the growing importance of economic instruments as expressions of EC foreign policies should draw EPC into closer association (and public identification) with the EC as the centrepiece of European integration. As we have seen, the changes in Eastern Europe occasioned the launching of combined EC-level economic and political responses that were virtually inseparable. Similarly, the Community's response to Iraq's invasion and annexation of Kuwait exemplified the growing coherence between the Twelve's actions through political cooperation and through the EC. Nevertheless, admittedly, a positive spill-over relationship between the EC and EPC would run counter to the historical experience of a largely independent progression of the two areas of activity.[47] Yet this historical lack of association may be of limited relevance to the recent buoyant phase of the EC's development and the new circumstances favourable to the economic and political strengthening of the Community.

In addition, as was already apparent in 1989/90, a unified Germany will increase the motivation for solidifying the EC as a political entity in order to anchor Germany more firmly in the ethos and institutional structure of a united West European community. However, the strength of this motivation will probably depend upon how skilfully Germany manages to balance its western and eastern interests and whether it displays worrisome unilateralist tendencies. Moreover, the prospect of a sharply reduced US military presence in Europe should encourage greater West European political cohesion and support for a clearer EC role in security matters, though this will partly be offset by the lessened importance of defence issues as long as a benign East–West political climate prevails. Nevertheless, the October 1990 EC Council statement on 'the objective of a common foreign and security policy . . . to go beyond the present limits in regard to security',[48] extended at the December summit to include consideration of a defence role, pointed to growing European coalescence in these areas, whatever specific agreements may emerge from the intergovernmental conference on political union. Other factors may be expected to enhance EPC's internal cohesion, while not necessarily generating a major shift toward a more centralised European foreign policy-making process. These include the growing acculturation of officials to the now routinised practice of consultation and coordination, the expansion of EPC working-group activity and coordination of positions in international organisations and foreign capitals, and the interest of other countries in establishing a political dialogue with the EC. Furthermore, the maturing sense of a collective European identity and efforts to achieve common positions will be reinforced by international expectations for a 'European' response on particular issues. Finally, the role of EPC as potentially leveraging the influence and visibility of individual countries (including the prestige of the rotating Council presidency), while affording flexibility for national variations, will continue to exert positive appeal.

On the other hand, a major factor inhibiting deeper political unity is the problem of achieving consensus among the Twelve as to the programmatic scope and institutional provisions of the political union that all, at least nominally, profess to support. Notwithstanding the growing Europeanisation of the foreign policy process, the current EPC system has been acceptable and attractive precisely because it keeps the reins of decision-making in the hands of member governments. Ambitious initiatives such as the Kohl–Mitterrand proposal for a common EC foreign and security policy may encounter difficulties similar to those of the Genscher–Colombo plan a decade earlier (see Chapter 9). Yet an ultimately state-centred locus for foreign policy decision-making will obviously enfeeble efforts to build an effective and respected political entity at the European level. One possible approach under consideration, which might be dubbed

Europeanisation 'by stealth', would entail enlarging and upgrading EPC's central staffing and merging it with the Secretariat of the Council of Ministers. This would retain the intergovernmental character of political cooperation while shifting the focus of decision-making from national foreign ministries (which could be expected to balk) to Community institutions in Brussels where the process of multilateral accommodation, as well as coordination with the EC, would be facilitated.

Another potentially inhibiting factor is the uncertain influence of the EC's 1992 programme which could have more negative than positive consequences for closer political unity. The very success of the EC in consolidating the internal market, coupled with the expanding role of EC processes and institutions in setting economic policy, could produce a backlash effect of discouraging further transfers of national sovereignty to a European level, especially in the traditionally sensitive and jealously guarded spheres of foreign and security policy. Moreover, given the recent period of radical change in Europe – including uncertainty about the future of the Soviet Union, the implications of a unified Germany, and prospects for a sharply reduced US military presence – EC governments may shy from significantly expanding EPC's security role out of concern that it could encourage US neo-isolationist sentiments and lead to an erosion of transatlantic security ties. During the cold war era of predominantly adversarial East–West (or at least US–Soviet) relations, concerns about decoupling focused largely on Western Europe's military vulnerability. In the emerging post-cold war period of declining military threats, though with potentially powerful Soviet and German states astride the Continent, European interests in avoiding decoupling are unlikely to diminish.

Moreover, the newly invigorated pan-European vision, growing East–West economic and political connections, the changing orientation of East European states toward the West, movement toward convergence on Western models of Eastern political, economic and social systems, and the shift from confrontational toward cooperative approaches to security, have altered the traditional context and, to a significant extent, even the meaning of European unity. While deepening the EC remains the Community's first priority, not to be retarded or impaired by developing ties with EFTA and Eastern Europe, nonetheless the new pan-European consciousness and openness may discourage the Twelve from further consolidating their political structure in a Western framework in the interest of facilitating flexible ties and associations with Eastern Europe and the Soviet Union.

In light of the preceding discussion, the outlook for US–EC political relations provides a basis for cautious optimism with several caveats. Whereas the initial attitude of the Bush administration toward the EC as a political entity bordered on indifference,[49] in May 1989 (well before the onset of the eastern upheavals later in the year) President Bush told an audience at Boston University: 'We are ready to develop, with the European Community and its member states, new mechanisms of consultation and cooperation on political and global issues, from strengthening the forces of democracy in the Third World, to managing regional tensions, to putting an end to the division of Europe'.[50] On one level, the Bush administration's interest in developing a closer political dialogue with the EC was in line with the Kennedy administration's promotion of the Atlantic partnership concept in the early 1960s (see Chapter 2). In both cases, US initiatives were prompted by a major growth phase in the EC and an expansion of its attributes as an independent collective actor. Yet the partnership concept was mostly visionary in the early 1960s, given the fledgeling nature of the EC as an economic body and the paralysis of efforts to create a political union.

By 1989, of course, the EC had acquired impressive status as a global economic power and member states were acting increasingly in concert on foreign policy matters as well. Indeed, growing European self-consciousness, confidence, institutional capacity and an expanding range of collective activity all pointed to a continued incremental consolidation of the European pillar around the EC – a pillar that could expect increased margin for manoeuvre in a world no longer dominated by the East–West issues of the cold war era that had virtually ordained a US–Soviet duopoly of influence. Thus, in contrast to the largely hypothetical nature of the Kennedy initiative, the Bush administration's proposal (reaffirmed and strengthened in Baker's Berlin speech in December) signalled a US accommodation to the reality of the EC as a formidable economic entity and a developing political power as well. Moreover, in view of the lessened role of the Atlantic Alliance as an instrument of US influence in Europe, it represented an effort to adjust the alignment of America's European diplomacy more toward the EC. In addition, the Eurocentric and non-military nature of many of the emerging issues, together with US fiscal constraints, argued for a larger European role in the new circumstances. Reinforcing the new perspective, the EC's second banking directive (enacting less restrictive rules for foreign financial institutions in the Community, partly in response to US complaints) helped to ease initial American concerns about a 'fortress Europe' emerging from the 1992 programme.

Nevertheless, it appeared that the EC's readiness for a closer dialogue with Washington fell short of the Bush administration's seemingly more ambitious suggestion for strengthened institutional and consultative links 'whether in treaty or some other form'. There was suspicion that the United States sought consultative status as the '13th member of the EC', reminiscent of the Nixon administration's approach in 1973/74 (see Chapter 6). In the same vein, there was scant European interest in the Bush administration's idea that the forging of closer US–EC ties should proceed in parallel and 'keep pace' with progress in European integration. The US–EC agreement in February 1990 to hold twice-yearly summits and meetings between the secretary of state and EC foreign ministers built upon existing consultation practices, while not altering the essentials of the Gymnich formula adopted in 1974.

A Transatlantic Declaration between the United States and the European Community was adopted in November which, though little noted at the time, represented a formal response to the earlier US initiative. Proclaiming a wide range of common goals, the declaration pledged that the EC and its member states (reflecting the distinctive nature of EPC) and the US 'will inform and consult each other on important matters of common interest, both political and economic, with a view to bringing their positions as close as possible without prejudice to their respective independence'.[51] However, this fell short of the US preference, according to one formulation, that consultations should 'enhance the practice and expectation of joint action'.[52] The provisions for consultation reiterated the February agreement and, by repeated references to 'the EC–US partnership' and to the US 'on one side' and the EC and its member states 'on the other', underscored the distinctiveness and independence of the two entities. While the declaration noted the commitment of the US and EC member states concerned to the Atlantic Alliance (though without mentioning NATO as such), France resisted a reported American proposal that transatlantic coordination precede that among the Twelve on the ground that this would constitute US interference in EC affairs.[53] Germany had promoted the declaration, partly as an Atlantic counterweight to its eastern reorientation in the context of unification. Nevertheless, the declaration added little new to the transatlantic relationship, either substantively or procedurally, though it did mark a further symbolic step toward a twin pillar conceptualisation and institutionalisation of US–West European relations.

As we have seen, most of the instances of US–West European divergence in the 1970s and 1980s were linked, directly or indirectly, to differing attitudes and approaches toward the Soviet Union and communism in general. With the rapid disappearance of the traditional cold war issues, and significant US–West European convergence on many of the new ones, the outlook for greater transatlantic comity may be more promising. In the new circumstances, issues will be addressed more on their own merits rather than as instances of a wider East–West confrontational pattern about which Washington and European capitals had often disagreed. This could create propitious circumstances for closer transatlantic alignment (or a narrowed range of differences) in cases where underlying Western values and interests are deemed to be at stake. Such an emerging pattern was suggested in 1989/90 by the broadly similar US–EC/EPC responses to China's June 1989 Tiananmen Square crackdown against its pro-democracy movement (limited sanctions), government sponsored violence against protesters in Romania in 1990 (threatened sanctions), Iraq's invasion of Kuwait in August 1990 (US, EC and UN Security Council economic sanctions, with European participation in or cooperation with US military measures); and similar US and Franco-German approaches to Lithuanian independence demands (suggesting suspension of the implementation of its Declaration to facilitate negotiations with the Soviet Union). Most EC governments opposed a UN General Assembly resolution that deplored the US intervention in Panama in 1989, while only Spain supported the measure and Greece and Ireland abstained. Britain and France joined the US in vetoing a similar resolution in the Security Council. In Central America, US–European differences in the 1980s (see Chapter 8) contrasted with the Bush administration's open solicitation of European support for its Enterprise for the Americas Initiative to focus on the region's trade, investment and debt problems.

Whereas US–West European differences on the Middle East persisted, a return to the confrontational atmosphere of the early 1980s (see Chapter 8) seemed unlikely. The June 1989 EC Council meeting in Madrid called for PLO 'participation' in the peace process, thus going beyond the 'association' language of the Venice Declaration. EC governments continued to be more sharply critical of Israeli settlement policies in occupied lands, and of Israeli measures in dealing with the Palestinian uprising, than was the United States. In 1990, the EC Twelve reiterated their call for an international peace conference under UN auspices to provide a framework for a comprehensive Middle East peace. The United States, while not opposing such an approach in principle, continued to believe that the establishment of a positive Israeli–Palestinian dialogue was a precondition for such a conference to be successful, and to avoid possible pressures for an externally imposed settlement. However, despite such differences, EC governments supported US efforts to encourage Israeli–Palestinian dialogue, and an EPC *troika* mission to Israel in July 1990 to make known European views was coordinated in advance with the Bush administration. Yet for reasons previously discussed, European influence on the peace process (in any case interrupted by the Gulf crisis) was likely to remain negligible.

On the other hand, the factors conducive to the EC's economic and political consolidation could prove troublesome to the future of transatlantic relations. The very existence of an independent European policy-making entity, combined with reduced European Alliance dependency and a more diffused range of post-cold war global issues and actors, will provide expanded opportunities for the forging of distinctive European positions. Nevertheless, as long as the dual-level West European foreign policy system persists, differences at the national level will limit the EC's ability to speak and act with one voice on international issues. As in the past, this will allow continued scope for US bilateral relations with individual EC governments which will provide the most accessible American opportunities for influencing European positions. The role and significance of US–EC/EPC consultations in this process remains to be seen. In January 1990, the Bush administration was openly annoyed when EC foreign ministers informally endorsed the Soviet proposal to convene a CSCE summit by the end of the year to address the changes in Europe without prior consultation with the United States. The Bush administration had expected that such a summit would be confined largely to endorsing a conventional arms treaty and had resisted a broader mandate for the conference unless certain conditions were met. Although the issue was resolved, clearing the way for the November summit, it illustrated differing US and European perspectives on the role of the CSCE in the process of change and the occasional European disposition toward unilateral action on matters also involving the United States. Moreover, possible European movement toward a common security policy, particularly if it were to include defence, could be expected to provoke

US–European tensions unless it became part of a new transatlantic understanding for a devolution of major security responsibilities to Europe in a reconstituted Alliance. President Bush's remark, in the speech cited above, that we 'applaud' growing defence cooperation in the Western European Union signalled the continued US preference that such activity occur within an explicit Alliance context rather than in the EC.

However US–West European relations may evolve in the 1990s, it is clear that the earlier conditions of America's transatlantic hegemony – a dominating paradigm of East–West confrontation and an only adolescent European pillar within it – had been substantially transformed by the beginning of the decade. As attention continues to focus on 'Europe 1992', and despite the changed agenda, transatlantic relations are evolving closer toward the 'partnership of equals' that President Kennedy dramatised 30 years before.

Notes

FOREWORD

1. Josef Joffe is foreign editor and columnist of the *Süddeutsche Zeitung* in Munich and Visiting Beton Michael Kaneb Professor of National Security Affairs at Harvard University. He is the author of *The Limited Partnership: Europe, the United States and the Burdens of Alliance*, (Cambridge, MA.: Ballinger, 1987).

1 THE FORMATIVE PERIOD OF ATLANTIC RELATIONS AND THE EUROPEAN PILLAR, 1948–55

1. *Department of State Bulletin* (hereafter *DOSB*), 18 January 1948, p. 80.
2. Harry B. Pryce, *The Marshall Plan and Its Meaning* (Ithaca, New York: Cornell University Press, 1955) pp. 63–4.
3. Alan S. Milward, *The Reconstruction of Western Europe, 1945–1951* (Berkeley: University of California Press, 1984). See especially chapter 5.
4. *Foreign Relations of the United States* (hereafter *FRUS*), 1951, vol. IV, part 1 (Washington: US Government Printing Office, 1985) p. 121.
5. Hearings before the Committee on Foreign Relations, US Senate, 4–5 June 1953 (Washington: US Government Printing Office, 1953), pp. 2,4.
6. Escott Reid, *Time of Fear and Hope, The Making of the North Atlantic Treaty, 1947–1949* (Toronto: McClelland & Stewart, 1977) ch. 10.
7. *DOSB*, 17 September 1950, p. 458.
8. *Assignment of Ground Forces of the United States to Duty in the European Area*. Hearings before the Committee on Foreign Relations and the Committee on Armed Services, US Senate, February 1951 (Washington: US Government Printing Office, 1951) p. 19.
9. *FRUS*, 1951, vol. III, part 1 (Washington: US Government Printing Office, 1985) p. 802.
10. Ibid., p. 829.
11. Ibid., p. 830.
12. *FRUS*, 1952–54, vol. V, part 1 (Washington: US Government Printing Office, 1983) p. 451.
13. *FRUS*, 1951, vol. III, part 1, p. 835.
14. Ibid., p. 850.
15. Ibid., p. 761.
16. *DOSB*, 10 March 1952, p. 364.
17. *DOSB*, 27 October 1952, p. 651 (emphasis in original).
18. *FRUS*, 1952–54, vol. V, part 1, pp. 247–8.

19. *Mutual Security Act of 1952*, 82nd Congress, 2nd Session.
20. Edward Fursdon, *The European Defense Community: A History* (New York: St. Martin's Press, 1980) p. 215; Basil Karp, 'The Draft Constitution for a European Political Community', *International Organization*, vol. III (May 1954) no. 2, pp. 181–202.
21. *FRUS*, 1952–54, vol. V, part 1, 1983, pp. 248–9.
22. Fursdon, *The European Defense Community*, p. 210.
23. *FRUS*, 1952–54, vol. V, part 2, p. 1623.
24. Stanley R. Sloan, *NATO's Future* (Washington: National Defense University Press, 1985) p. 23.
25. *New York Times*, 15 December 1953; *DOSB*, 4 January 1954, p. 7.
26. *FRUS*, 1952–54, vol.V, part 1, p. 656.
27. Ibid., p. 1170 (emphasis in original).

2 WHAT KIND OF EUROPEAN PILLAR?

1.   The European Communities, often referred to collectively as the European Community, include the European Coal and Steel Community established in 1952 and the European Economic Community and European Atomic Energy Community established in 1958.
2.   Elliot R. Goodman, *The Fate of the Atlantic Community* (New York: Praeger, 1975), pp. 148–9.
3.   *DOSB*, 23 July 1962, p. 132.
4.   *DOSB*, 24 February 1964, p. 290.
5,   *DOSB*, 23 April 1962, pp. 666–73.
6.   Arthur M. Schlesinger, Jr, *A Thousand Days* (New York: Fawcett Crest, 1967) p. 771.
7.   William W. Kaufmann, *The McNamara Strategy* (New York: Harper & Row, 1964) p. 117.
8.   Letter to Raymond Aron, 24 May 1962. *Papers of President Kennedy*, National Security Files, Box 71A, John F. Kennedy Library.
9.   Theodore C. Sorensen, *KKennedy* (New York: Bantam, 1966) p. 645.
10. *DOSB*, 14 January 1963, p. 44.
11. *Major Addresses, Statements and Press Conferences of General Charles de Gaulle*, 19 May 1958–31 January 1964. (New York: French Embassy, Press and Information Division) p. 214.
12. Kaufmann, *The McNamara Strategy*, p. 107.
13. Sorensen, *Kennedy*, p. 639.
14. *DOSB*, 22 October 1962, pp. 604–5.
15. McGeorge Bundy, 'Friends and Allies', *Foreign Affairs*, vol. XXXXI (October 1962) no. 1, pp. 21–2.
16. Memorandum for Ambassador Bohlen, 16 October 1962. *Papers of President Kennedy*.
17. *DOSB*, 31 December 1962, p. 995.
18. Press Conference on 5 September 1960. *Major Addresses*, op. cit., p. 93.
19. Josef Joffe, *The Limited Partnership*, p. 186.
20. Elliot R. Goodman, 'De Gaulle's NATO Policy in Perspective', *Orbis*,

vol. X (Fall 1966) no. 3, pp. 702–3.
21. Wilfrid L. Kohl, *French Nuclear Diplomacy* (Princeton University Press, 1971) pp. 134–5.
22. David Schoenbrun, *The Three Lives of Charles de Gaulle* (New York: Atheneum, 1968) pp. 306–7, 316.
23. Charles de Gaulle, *Memoirs of Hope: Renewal and Endeavor*, Terence Kilmartin (trs.) (New York: Simon & Schuster, 1971) p. 203.
24. Press Conference on 11 April 1961, *Major Addresses*, op. cit., p. 124.
25. European Parliament, *Towards Political Union* (General Directorate of Parliamentary Documentation and Information, January 1964) p. 10.
26. Ibid., pp. 11–14.
27. Edward A. Kolodziej, *French International Policy Under De Gaulle and Pompidou* (Ithaca, NY: Cornell University Press, 1974) p. 296.
28. Telegram no. 1705, 15 March 1962; telegram no. 1993, 20 April 1962; and telegram no. 2047, 28 April 1962 from the US Embassy in Belgium to the Secretary of State. Obtained from the Department of State through the Freedom of Information Act.
29. *DOSB*, 25 December 1961, pp. 1042, 1045.
30. Telegram no. 1993, 20 April 1962 from the US Embassy in Belgium to the Secretary of State. Department of State, op. cit.
31. *DOSB*, 29 January 1962, p. 162.
32. *DOSB*, 5 March 1962, p. 366.
33. *DOSB*, 4 June 1962, p. 907.
34. Telegram no. 5425, 16 May 1962 from the US Embassy in France to the Secretary of State. *Papers of President Kennedy*, op. cit.
35. Message from President Kennedy to Ambassador Gavin via State Department telegram no. 6203, 18 May 1962. *Papers of President Kennedy*, op. cit.
36. *DOSB*, 23 July 1962, p. 132.
37. F. Roy Willis, *France, Germany and the New Europe, 1945–1967* (New York: Oxford University Press, 1968) pp. 312–14.
38. European Parliament, *Towards Political Union*, p. 51.
39. Frank Costigliola, 'The Pursuit of Atlantic Community: Nuclear Arms, Dollars, and Berlin', in Thomas G. Paterson (ed.), *Kennedy's Quest for Victory* (New York: Oxford University Press, 1989) pp. 50–51.
40. Ibid.
41. J. Robert Schaetzel, 'The Nuclear Problem and Atlantic Interdependence', *Atlantic Community Quarterly*, vol. I (Winter 1963/64) no. 4, p. 567.
42. Address in Brussels, 8 November 1963. *DOSB*, 2 December 1963, pp. 853–4.
43. News conference, 24 January 1963. Brussels, US Information Service.
44. Sorensen, *Kennedy*, p. 640.
45. Ibid., p. 641; Schlesinger, *A Thousand Days*, p. 799.
46. Schlesinger, *A Thousand Days*, p. 797.

3   THE EUROPEAN IMPULSE REVIVED: EUROPEAN DEFENCE COOPERATION AND THE UNITED STATES, 1968–73

1. Portions of this chapter have been adapted from William C. Cromwell, *The Eurogroup and NATO* (Philadelphia: Foreign Policy Research Institute, 1974).
2. Address in New York, 2 December 1967. *DOSB*, 25 December 1967, p. 858.
3. Address in Chicago, 13 January 1968. *DOSB*, 5 February 1968, pp. 170–71.
4. Address in New York, 4 January 1968. *DOSB*, 19 February 1968, p. 237 (emphasis added).
5. Reported in the *Washington Post*, 18 May 1968.
6. *New York Herald Tribune*, 5 September 1966.
7. Henry Kissinger, *White House Years* (Boston: Little, Brown, 1979) p. 385.
8. Ibid., p. 386.
9. *New York Times*, 20 October 1969.
10. Ibid., 21 October 1969.
11. Reported by Chalmers Roberts in the *Washington Post*, 7 December 1969.
12. Ibid.
13. *Washington Post*, 8 March 1970.
14. Cromwell, *The Eurogroup and NATO*, pp. 3–4.
15. *The American Commitment to NATO*. Report of the Special Sub-committee on North Atlantic Treaty Organization Commitments of the Committee on Armed Services, House of Representatives, 17 August 1972 (Washington: US Government Printing Office, 1972), pp. 14974–5.
16. John Newhouse, with Melvin Croan, Edward R. Fried and Timothy W. Stanley, *US Troops in Europe* (Washington: Brookings Institution, 1971) p. 17.
17. *The Eurogroup* (Brussels: NATO Information Service, 1972) p. 9.
18. Reported in the *New York Times*, 21 October 1969.
19. Helmut Schmidt, 'Germany in the Era of Negotiations', *Foreign Affairs*, vol. IL, (October 1970) no. 1, p. 43.
20. *Washington Post*, 20 May 1971.
21. *New York Times*, 27 September 1973.
22. *The Congressional Record – Senate*, 25 September 1973, S17621.
23. Communiqué of the Defence Planning Committee, 7 December 1973.
24. Kissinger, *White House Years*, p. 385.

4   THE EUROPEAN IMPULSE REVIVED: THE BIRTH OF EUROPEAN POLITICAL COOPERATION, 1969–73

1. Kissinger, *White House Years*, pp. 87–8; Edward A. Kolodziej, *French International Policy*, pp. 401–2.
2. Kolodziej, *French International Policy*, pp. 392–3.

3. Kissinger, *White House Years*, p. 422.
4. Ibid.
5. Helen Wallace, William Wallace, and Carol Webb (eds), *Policy-Making in the European Community*, 2nd edn (New York: Wiley, 1983) p. 376.
6. Pierre Lellouche, 'Does NATO Have a Future?' in Robert W. Tucker and Linda Wrigley (eds), *The Atlantic Alliance and its Critics* (New York: Praeger, 1983) p. 144.
7. Timothy W. Stanley and Darnell M. Whitt, *Detente Diplomacy: United States and European Security in the 1970s* (New York: Dunellen, 1970) p. 116.
8. Panayiotis Ifestos, *European Political Cooperation: Towards a Framework of Supranational Diplomacy?* (Brookfield, VT: Avebury/Gower, 1987) p. 150.
9. *European Political Co-operation* (*EPC*), 4th edn (Bonn: Press and Information Office of the Federal Republic of Germany, 1982) pp. 25–8.
10. *European Political Co-operation* (*EPC*) 5th edn (Bonn: Press and Information Office of the Federal Republic of Germany, 1988) pp. 24–31.
11. Wallace, Wallace and Webb (eds), *Policy-Making in the European Community*, 2nd edn, p. 379.
12. *Report on the Conference on Security and Cooperation in Europe*, Working Documents, 1974–75. European Parliament, document 485/74, 21 February 1975, p. 21.
13. *EPC*, 5th edn, p. 32.
14. William Wallace and David Allen, 'Political Cooperation: Procedure as Substitute for Policy', in Wallace, Wallace and Webb (eds), *Policy-Making in the European Communities*, 1st edn (New York: Wiley, 1977) p. 236.
15. Ifestos, *European Political Cooperation*, p. 167.
16. *EPC*, 5th edn, p. 35.
17. Ifestos, *European Political Cooperation*, p. 171.

5 THE NIXON ADMINISTRATION AND EUROPE, 1969–73

1. Portions of this chapter and Chapter 6 have been adapted from William C. Cromwell, 'Europe and the "Structure of Peace"', *Orbis*, vol. XXII (Spring) no. 1, 1978.
2. J. Robert Schaetzel, *The Unhinged Alliance, America and the European Community* (New York: Harper & Row, 1975) p. 43.
3. Press conference on 4 March 1969, *DOSB*, 24 March 1969, p. 246.
4. Chalmers Roberts in *The Washington Post*, 6 March 1969.
5. *Time*, 3 January 1972.
6. *New York Times*, 19 February 1970.
7. Henry Kissinger, *White House Years*, p. 418.
8. *DOSB*, 13 March 1972, p. 333.

9. Henry Kissinger, *The Troubled Partnership* (New York: McGraw-Hill, 1965) p. 244. Also see Kissinger's statement in *United States Policy Toward Europe*, Hearings before the Senate Committee on Foreign Relations, June–July 1966 (Washington: US Government Printing Office, 1966) p. 175.
10. Kissinger, *The Troubled Partnership*, p. 40.
11. *United States Policy Toward Europe*, p. 175.
12. Kissinger, *White House Years*, p. 86.
13. *The Eurogroup – An Experiment in European Defence Co-operation*, a report by the Military Committee, North Atlantic Assembly, November 1972, pp. 13–14.
14. Schaetzel, *The Unhinged Alliance*, p. 49.
15. Ibid., p. 51.
16. Ibid.
17. Kissinger, *White House Years*, p. 403.
18. Raymond L. Garthoff, *Detente and Confrontation, American–Soviet Relations from Nixon to Reagan* (Washington: Brookings, 1985) p. 312.
19. Andrew J. Pierre, 'Can Europe's Security Be "Decoupled" From America?', *Foreign Affairs*, vol. LI (July 1973) no. 4, p. 764.
20. *The Washington Summit*, Department of State publication 8733 (Washington: US Government Printing Office, 1973) p. 30.
21. Henry Kissinger, *Years of Upheaval* (Boston: Little, Brown, 1982) pp. 285–6.
22. Garthoff, *Detente and Confrontation*, p. 338.
23. Ibid., p. 340.
24. Robert Kleiman, *New York Times*, 11 December 1973.
25. Kissinger, *The Troubled Partnership*, p. 26.

6 A MOMENT OF TRUTH: THE 'YEAR OF EUROPE' AND THE ATLANTIC CRISIS OF 1973/74

1. Kissinger, *Years of Upheaval*, p. 171.
2. *International Herald Tribune*, 15 December 1972.
3. Kissinger, *Years of Upheaval*, p. 132.
4. Press conference, 28 March 1974, *DOSB*, April 22, 1974, p. 422.
5. Kissinger, *Years of Upheaval*, pp. 142–3.
6. Ibid., p. 157.
7. Wilfrid L. Kohl, 'The Nixon–Kissinger Foreign Policy System and US–European Relations: Patterns of Policy Making', *World Politics*, vol. XXVIII (October 1975) no. 1, p. 16.
8. Address by Henry Kissinger in New York, 23 April 1973, *DOSB*, 14 May 1973, p. 595 (emphasis added).
9. News conference, 3 January 1974, *DOSB*, 28 January 1974, p. 84.
10. Kissinger, *Years of Upheaval*, p. 191.
11. Text in the *New York Times*, 24 September 1973.
12. Kissinger, *Years of Upheaval*, p. 716.

13. *New York Times*, 31 October 1973.
14. Robert L. Pfaltzgraff, Jr, 'The Middle East Crisis: Implications for the European–American Relationship', a paper prepared for the Annual Meeting of the American Political Science Association, Chicago, 20 August–2 September 1974, p. 6.
15. *Washington Post*, 31 October 1973.
16. *New York Times*, 13 November 1973.
17. Ibid., 31 October 1973.
18. Kissinger, *Years of Upheaval*, pp. 715–16.
19. *EPC*, 4th edn, p. 56.
20. *New York Times*, 15 December 1973.
21. Ibid., 6 February 1974.
22. Ibid., 15 February 1974.
23. Nationally televised remarks in Chicago, 15 March 1974; *New York Times*, 16 March 1974.
24. For the text of the European Community's proposal for the joint declaration, together with proposed US emendations, see the *New York Times*, 9 November 1973.
25. *New York Times*, 13 December 1973.
26. *Washington Post*, 12 March 1974.
27. Kissinger, *Years of Upheaval*, pp. 931–2.
28. Quoted by Leslie Gelb in the *New York Times*, 9 April 1974.
29. *Washington Post*, 20 March 1974.
30. Baard B. Knudsen, *Europe versus America: Foreign Policy in the 1980's*. The Atlantic Papers no. 56 (Paris: The Atlantic Institute for International Affairs, 1984) p. 23.
31. *Washington Post*, 11 June 1974.
32. Ifestos, *European Political Cooperation*, p. 183.
33. Text of declaration in the *New York Times*, 20 June 1974.
34. Statement by Assistant Secretary of State Arthur A. Hartman, *DOSB*, 18 March 1974, p. 279.
35. George W. Ball, *Diplomacy For a Crowded World* (Boston: Little, Brown, 1976) p. 159.
36. News conference, 21 November 1973, *DOSB*, 10 December 1973, p. 710.
37. Department of State summary of Secretary Kissinger's remarks at a meeting of US ambassadors in London, December 1975. *New York Times*, 7 April 1976.
38. Press conference, 21 May 1975. (French Embassy, Press and Information Service, 75/78).
39. Schaetzel, *The Unhinged Alliance*, p. 78.

7 THE UNITED STATES AND THE EUROPEAN PILLAR IN THE LATE 1970S AND THE 1980S

1. *DOSB*, 21 June 1976, p. 790, and 26 July 1976, p. 107.
2. *DOSB*, July 1985, p. 19.
3. *New York Times*, 29 October and 15 December 1987.

4.   *New York Times*, 27 May 1989.
5.   *DOSB*, 22 March 1976, p. 374 (emphasis added).
6.   Thomas O. Enders, 'Issues in US–European Community Relations', January 1981, p. 19. Text provided by the Department of State.
7.   *DOSB*, April 1983, p. 66.
8.   *Washington Post*, 27 October 1984.
9.   David Owen (British Foreign Secretary during the Carter administration), 'Disarmament, Detente and Deterrence', *European Affairs* (Summer 1987) no. 2, p. 12; *Financial Times*, 2 April 1985.
10. Stephen J. Ledogar, *European Defense Cooperation Outside the NATO Context: A US View*, The Alliance Papers no. 11 (Washington: The Atlantic Council of the US, n.d.) p. 6 (emphasis in original).
11. Kissinger, *The Troubled Partnership*, pp. 40, 244, 175.
12. *New York Times*, 7 May 1986.
13. Private correspondence between the Department of State and the *Washington Post*; *Washington Post*, 5 December 1979.
14. *Wall Street Journal*, 10 December 1979; see also Cyrus Vance, *Hard Choices* (New York: Simon & Schuster, 1983) p. 381.
15. Jimmy Carter, *Keeping Faith* (New York: Bantam Books, 1982) p. 466.
16. *Guardian*, 19 December 1979.
17. *The Economist*, 19 April 1980, p. 47.
18. Vance, *Hard Choices*, p. 400.
19. *Washington Post*, 9–10 February 1980.
20. Carter, *Keeping Faith*, p. 506.
21. *New York Times*, 11 April 1980.
22. *Washington Post*, 13 April 1980.
23. Wallace, Wallace and Webb, (eds) *Policy-Making in the European Community*, 2nd edn, p. 393.
24. *New York Times*, 14 April 1980.
25. *The Economist*, 7 June 1980, p. 77.
26. Christopher Hill, 'Changing Gear in Political Cooperation', *The Political Quarterly*, vol. LIII (January/March 1982) no. 1, p. 48.
27. Cited in *An Assessment of the Afghanistan Sanctions: Implications for Trade and Diplomacy in the 1980s*, Committee on Foreign Affairs, US House of Representatives, April 1981 (Washington: US Government Printing Office, 1981) p. 101.
28. Remarks to members of Congress, 8 January 1980. Cited in Garthoff, *Detente and Confrontation*, p. 972.
29. *Washington Post*, 4 February 1980.
30. *New York Times*, 6 February 1980.
31. Cited in *NATO After Afghanistan*, Committee on Foreign Affairs, US House of Representatives, 27 October 1980 (Washington: US Government Printing Office, 1980) p. 9.
32. *Washington Post*, 9 February 1980.
33. *EPC*, 5th edn, pp. 125–6.
34. Garthoff, *Detente and Confrontation*, p. 977.
35. *Washington Post*, 19 February 1982; *The Economist*, 27 February 1982, p. 50.

36. Statement on 10 February 1980, *The Week in Germany*, vol. XI (14 February 1980) no. 7 (New York: German Information Center).
37. *Washington Post*, 13 March 1980.
38. Ibid., 24 December 1981.
39. *New York Times*, 24 December 1981.
40. *Washington Post*, 30 December 1981.
41. *EPC*, 5th edn, p. 148.
42. *Declaration on Events in Poland*, 11 January 1982 (Brussels: NATO Press Service).
43. *New York Times*, 16 March 1982.
44. *The Economist*, 30 January 1982, p. 32.
45. *New York Times*, 12 March 1982; Peter Marsh, 'The European Community and East–West Economic Relations', *Journal of Common Market Studies*, vol. XXIII (September 1984) no. 1, p. 8.
46. *New York Times*, 19 June 1982. See also the excellent analysis of this and related issues in Antony J. Blinken, *Ally Versus Ally, America, Europe, and the Siberian Pipeline Crisis* (New York: Praeger, 1987).
47. *New York Times*, 19 June 1982.
48. *European Community News*, no. 20/1982 (Washington: EC Information Service).
49. *New York Times*, 23 July 1982; Blinken, *Ally Versus Ally*, p. 3.
50. Delegation of the Commission of the EC, Press and Information, July 1982.
51. *Comments of the European Community on the Amendments of 22 June 1982 to the US Export Administration Regulations*, 12 August 1982 (EC Information Service).
52. *New York Times*, 14 November 1982.
53. Cited in Blinken, *Ally Versus Ally*, p. 108.
54. *New York Times*, 11 December 1981.
55. Tim Zimmerman, 'The American Bombing of Libya', *Survival*, vol. XXIX (May/June, 1987) no. 3, p. 198.
56. *Current Policy*, no. 780, US Department of State, Bureau of Public Affairs, 1986.
57. *Washington Post*, 28 January 1986.
58. *New York Times*, 28 January 1986.
59. Edward Schumacher, 'The US and Libya', *Foreign Affairs*, vol. LXV (Winter 1986/87) no. 2, p. 335.
60. Zimmerman, 'The American Bombing of Libya', p. 204.
61. *Washington Post*, 15 April 1986.
62. *New York Times*, 16 April 1986; *Developments in Europe, May 1986*, Committee on Foreign Affairs, US House of Representatives (Washington: US Government Printing Office, 1986) p. 47.
63. Robert Oakley, 'International Terrorism', *Foreign Affairs, America and the World*, vol. LXV (1986) no. 3, p. 618; *The Economist*, 26 April 1986, p. 45.
64. *New York Times*, 16 April 1986.
65. *Washington Post*, 16 April 1986.
66. Ibid., 22 April 1986.
67. Oakley, 'International Terrorism', p. 620.

68.   *Washington Post*, 14 February 1988.
69.   Ibid., 5 February 1987.
70.   *New York Times*, 6 February 1987.

8   OTHER REGIONAL ISSUES

1.   Michael Harrison, 'Central America's Impact on the International Security Order', in Joseph Cirincione (ed.), *Central America and the Western Alliance* (New York: Holmes & Meier, 1985) p. 143.
2.   Sloan, *NATO's Future*, p. 105.
3.   Cirincione (ed.), *Central America and the Western Alliance*, p. 3.
4.   Andrew J. Pierre (ed.), *Third World Instability – Central America as a European-American Issue* (New York: Council on Foreign Relations, 1985) pp. 27–28, 117–20.
5.   Wolf Grabendorff, 'The Central American Crisis: Is There a Role for Western Europe?' in Cirincione, *Central America and the Western Alliance*, p. 133.
6.   Ibid.
7.   *New York Times*, 25 November 1981.
8.   Marc Bentinck, *NATO's Out-of-Area Problem*. Adelphi Papers no. 211 (London: International Institute for Strategic Studies, 1986) p. 77; Cirincione, *Central America and the Western Alliance*, p. 120.
9.   *Washington Post*, 19 February and 20 March 1981.
10.   Ibid., 20 March 1981.
11.   Ibid., 3 April 1982.
12.   Ibid., 10 August 1983.
13.   *European Community News*, 11/83, 20 June 1983; *Washington Post*, 10 August 1983.
14.   Michel Tatu, 'Europe, the United States and Central America: A Nest of Misunderstandings', in Cirincione, *Central America and the Western Alliance*, pp. 117–18.
15.   *EPC*, 5th edn, p. 183.
16.   Alfred Pijpers, Elfriede Regelsberger and Wolfgang Wessels (eds), *European Political Cooperation in the 1980s* (Dordrecht, The Netherlands: Nijhoff, 1988) p. 31.
17.   *Washington Post*, 29 September 1984.
18.   *European Community News*, no. 37/1985, 19 November 1985.
19.   *Washington Post*, 1 June 1985.
20.   Fernando Morán, 'Europe's Role in Central America: A Spanish Socialist View', in Pierre, *Third World Instability*, pp. 30–31.
21.   Roy H. Ginsberg, *Foreign Policy Actions of the European Community* (Boulder, CO: Lynne Rienner, 1989) p. 166.
22.   *EPC*, 4th edn, p. 107.
23.   Statement on the Middle East, *New York Times*, 28 June 1977.
24.   Ibid.
25.   *International Herald Tribune*, 21 November 1977.
26.   *EPC*, 4th edn, p. 121.
27.   Roger Tomkys, 'European Political Cooperation and the Middle East:

A Personal Perspective', *International Affairs* (London) vol. LXIII, (Summer 1987) no. 3, pp. 427, 432.
28. *EPC*, 4th edn, p. 129.
29. Ibid., p. 136.
30. *Washington Post*, 25 March 1979.
31. *EPC*, 4th edn, p. 163.
32. *Baltimore Sun*, 2 October 1979; *The Economist*, 15 September 1979, p. 54.
33. *Washington Star*, 10 February 1980.
34. Ibid., 11 March 1980.
35. Ifestos, *European Political Cooperation*, p. 456; *Washington Post*, 1 June 1980.
36. *DOSB*, July, 1980, p. 2.
37. Ibid., p. 4.
38. *Europe* Political Day, 13 June 1980.
39. Statements on 13 and 14 June 1980, cited in Ifestos, *European Political Cooperation*, p. 457.
40. *EPC*, 4th edn, p. 205.
41. *New York Times*, 14 June 1980.
42. Tomkys, 'European Political Cooperation and the Middle East', p. 431.
43. *Washington Post*, 30 July 1980.
44. Ifestos, *European Political Cooperation*, pp. 474–5.
45. *International Herald Tribune*, 2 March 1981.
46. Ifestos, *European Political Cooperation*, pp. 479–80.
47. *New York Times*, 6 and 10 November 1981.
48. *The Times*, 11 November 1981.
49. *EPC*, 4th edn, p. 294.
50. *Washington Post*, 24 November 1981.
51. Ifestos, *European Political Cooperation*, pp. 488–9.
52. *Washington Post*, 9 December 1981; *The Economist*, 12 December 1981, p. 35.
53. Ilan Greilsammer and Joseph Weiler, *Europe's Middle East Dilemma: The Quest for a Unified Stance* (Boulder, CO: Westview Press, 1987) p. 65.
54. *New York Times*, 4 December 1981.
55. Ibid., 1 February 1982.
56. Ifestos, *European Political Cooperation*, p. 489.
57. David Allen and Alfred Pijpers (eds), *European Foreign Policy-Making and the Arab–Israeli Conflict* (The Hague: Nijhoff, 1984) p. 222.
58. *EPC*, 5th edn, p. 306.

9 EUROPEAN PILLARS IN THE 1980S

1. Pijpers, Regelsberger and Wessels (eds), *European Political Cooperation in the 1980s*, p. 196.
2. *EPC*, 5th edn, p. 69.
3. *Bulletin of the European Communities*, no. 1, 1981, pp. 87–90.

4. Wallace, Wallace and Webb (eds), *Policy-Making in the European Community*, 2nd edn, p. 399.
5. Pijpers, Regelsberger and Wessels (eds), *European Political Cooperation in the 1980s*, p. 8.
6. Ifestos, *European Political Cooperation*, p. 289.
7. Phillip Taylor, *When Europe Speaks With One Voice* (Westport, CT: Greenwood Press, 1979) pp. 27–30.
8. *EPC*, 5th edn, 70–78.
9. Guy de Bassompierre, *Changing the Guard in Brussels, An Insider's View of the EC Presidency*. The Washington Papers/135, The Center for Strategic and International Studies (New York: Praeger, 1988) p. 78.
10. Ifestos, *European Political Cooperation*, pp. 305, 360–61.
11. de Bassompierre, *Changing the Guard in Brussels*, p. 78.
12. *EPC*, 5th edn, p. 73; de Bassompierre, *Changing the Guard in Brussels*, p. 79.
13. *Single European Act* (Brussels: Council of the European Communities, 1986) p. 37.
14. Ifestos, *European Political Cooperation*, p. 354.
15. See Ginsberg, *Foreign Policy Actions of the European Community*.
16. Wallace and Allen, 'Political Cooperation', in Wallace, Wallace and Webb (eds), *Policy-Making in the European Communities*, 1st edn, pp. 227–47.
17. de Bassompierre, *Changing the Guard in Brussels*, pp. 52–3.
18. Christopher Tugendhat, *Making Sense of Europe* (New York: Columbia University Press, 1988) p. 67.
19. Ibid., p. 66.
20. Jean De Ruyt, *European Political Cooperation: Toward a Unified European Foreign Policy* (Washington: The Atlantic Council of the US, 1989) p. 14; de Bassompierre, *Changing the Guard in Brussels*, pp. 72–3.
21. De Ruyt, *European Political Cooperation*, p. 36.
22. Helmut Sonnenfeldt, 'The European Pillar: The American View', *The Changing Strategic Landscape*, Part I, Adelphi Papers no. 235 (London: Brassey's/International Institute for Strategic Studies, 1989) pp. 95–6.
23. David Garnham, *The Politics of European Defense Cooperation* (Cambridge, MA.: Ballinger, 1988) p. 126.
24. Ian Gambles, *Prospects for West European Security Cooperation*, Adelphi Papers no. 244 (London: Brassey's/ International Institute for Strategic Studies, 1989) p. 33.
25. *Washington Post*, 27 December 1983.
26. Cited in Peter Schmidt, 'The Franco-German Defence and Security Council', *Aussenpolitik* (English edition) vol. XL (April 1989) p. 363.
27. *Wall Street Journal*, 27 January 1988.
28. *New York Times*, 26 September 1987.
29. *Christian Science Monitor*, 21 December 1987.
30. Schmidt, 'The Franco-German Defence and Security Council', pp. 367–8.

31. *New York Times*, 23 January 1988; *Washington Post*, 23 January 1988.
32. *Christian Science Monitor*, 25 January 1988.
33. *Washington Post*, 30 January 1988.
34. *New York Times*, 30 January 1988.
35. de Bassompierre, *Changing the Guard in Brussels*, p. 73; see also, William Wallace, 'European Defence Co-operation: The Reopening Debate', *Survival*, vol. XXVI (November/December 1984) no. 6, p. 260.
36. Garnham, *The Politics of European Defense Cooperation*, p. 117; *Washington Post*, 13 July 1984.
37. *Washington Post*, 21 June 1984.
38. *Statements and Speeches*, vol. VII, (20 November 1984) no. 21 (New York: German Information Center).
39. See Chapter 7, note 9.
40. *New York Times*, 24 April 1985.
41. *Washington Post*, 24 April 1985.
42. Ibid., 5 April 1985.
43. Ibid., 7 June 1985.
44. Ivo H. Daalder, *The SDI Challenge to Europe* (Cambridge, MA.: Ballinger, 1987).
45. *Wall Street Journal*, 27 January 1988.
46. British Information Services, Policy Statements, 8/87, 18 March 1987.
47. *Platform on European Security Interests*, Western European Union, The Hague, 27 October 1987.
48. *Washington Post*, 28 October 1987; *Christian Science Monitor*, 12 November 1987.
49. Geoffrey Howe, 'The WEU: The Way Ahead', *NATO Review* (June 1989) no. 3, p. 13.
50. Gambles, *Prospects for West European Security Cooperation*, p. 32.
51. Ibid.
52. *Washington Post*, 20 September 1987.
53. *New York Times*, 9 October 1987.
54. Gambles, *Prospects for West European Security Cooperation*, p. 40.
55. Ibid., pp. 31, 40.
56. *Washington Post*, 24 and 26 January 1988.

10 THE UNITED STATES AND THE EUROPEAN PILLAR IN THE 1970S AND 1980S: CONCLUDING ASSESSMENT

1. Allen and Pijpers (eds), *European Foreign Policy-Making and the Arab–Israeli Conflict*, p. 189.
2. Gregory F. Treverton, *Making the Alliance Work* (Ithaca, NY: Cornell University Press, 1985) p. 23.
3. Michael Welsh, 'Collective Security: The European Community and the Preservation of Peace', in Alfred Cahen, *The Western European Union and NATO* (London: Brassey's, 1989) p. 103.

11   THE UNITED STATES AND THE NEW EUROPE IN THE 1990S

1.   Statement by Soviet Foreign Minister Eduard A. Shevardnadze, *Washington Post*, 4 July 1990.
2.   John D. Steinbruner, 'Revolution in Foreign Policy', in Henry J. Aaron (ed.), *Setting National Priorities: Policy for the Nineties* (Washington: Brookings, 1990) pp. 93–4.
3.   Eduard N. Luttwak, 'Soviet Military Concerns and Prospects in Eastern Europe', in Aurel Braun (ed.), *The Soviet–East European Relationship in the Gorbachev Era: The Prospects for Adaptation* (Boulder, CO: Westview, 1990) p. 59.
4.   *New York Times*, 2 April 1989.
5.   Jim Hoagland, 'Europe's Destiny', *Foreign Affairs*, vol. LXIX (1990) no. 1, p. 38; *New York Times*, 7 July 1989.
6.   John Palmer, *1992 and Beyond* (Luxembourg: Commission of the European Communities, 1989) p. 27; Leigh Bruce, 'Europe's Locomotive', *Foreign Policy* (Spring 1990) no. 78, p. 75.
7.   *New York Times*, 15 November 1989.
8.   Ibid., 30 May 1990.
9.   *Washington Post*, 10 December 1989.
10. Ibid., 5 December 1989.
11. Ibid., 20 April 1990.
12. *European Community News*, no. 20/90, 30 April 1990 (Washington: EC Information Service).
13. *New York Times*, 29 April 1990.
14. Ibid., 26 June 1990; *Washington Post*, 27 June 1990.
15. *European Community News*, no. 26/90, 27 June 1990 (Washington: EC Information Service).
16. *The Economist*, 3 February 1990, p. 50.
17. *European Marketing Data and Statistics – 1990* (London: Euromonitor, 1990) pp. 143, 174–5.
18. *European Community News*, no. 41/89, 11 December 1989 (Washington: EC Information Service).
19. Jacques Delors, address to the European Parliament, 17 January 1990.
20. *Financial Times*, 15 June 1990.
21. Council of Europe – Information Department, vol. I (17 January 1990) no. 2.
22. *Foreign Broadcast Information Service* – Western Europe, 90–091-A, 10 May 1990, p. 1.
23. Edward A. Kolodziej, *French International Policy*, p. 347.
24. New Years's Eve Broadcast, 31 December 1989 (London: French Embassy).
25. Dr Lutz G. Stavenhagen, Minister of State, West German Foreign Ministry, *Statements and Speeches*, vol. IX (7 March 1986) no. 3 (New York: German Information Center).
26. *New York Times*, 8 June 1990.
27. *Washington Post*, 4 June 1989.
28. *New York Times*, 2 June 1989.

29. *Current Policy*, no. 1233, US Department of State, Bureau of Public Affairs.
30. *New York Times*, 7 July 1990.
31. *Washington Post*, 21 November 1989.
32. *New York Times*, 17 July 1990.
33. *Washington Post*, 17 July 1990.
34. *New York Times*, 17 July 1990.
35. Ibid.
36. *Washington Post*, 16 December 1989.
37. Jonathan Dean, *Watershed in Europe* (Lexington, MA.: Lexington Books, 1987) p. 187.
38. West German Foreign Minister Hans-Dietrich Genscher, address at the Tutzing Protestant Academy on 31 January 1990, *Statements and Speeches*, vol. XIII, no. 2 (New York: German Information Center).
39. *European Community News*, no. 20/90, 30 April 1990 (Washington: EC Information Service).
40. *Washington Post*, 3 June 1990.
41. Genscher, address at the Tutzing Protestant Academy, 31 January 1990.
42. Genscher, address at a meeting of the Western European Union, 23 March 1990, *Statements and Speeches*, vol. XIII, no. 8 (New York: German Information Center).
43. Malcolm Chalmers, 'Beyond the Alliance System', *World Policy Journal*, vol. VII (Spring 1990) no. 2, p. 226.
44. West German Chancellor Helmut Kohl, address at Harvard University, 7 June 1990, *Statements and Speeches*, vol. XIII, no. 16 (New York: German Information Center).
45. *The Economist*, 7 July 1990, p. 34.
46. David S. Yost, 'France in the New Europe', *Foreign Affairs*, vol. LXIX (Winter 1990/91) no. 5, pp. 113–17.
47. Alfred E. Pijpers, 'European Political Cooperation and the Realist Paradigm', paper presented at the Inaugural Conference of the European Community Studies Association, George Mason University, 24–25 May 1989, pp. 25–6.
48. European Council, *Conclusions of the Presidency*, Rome, 27–8 October 1990, SN 304/2/90 (Washington: EC Office of Press and Public Affairs, 1990).
49. Unattributed interview by the author with a European official close to the EPC process, March 1989; *Washington Post*, 3 March 1990.
50. *Department of State Bulletin*, July 1989, p. 18.
51. *European Community News*, no. 41/90, 27 November 1990 (Washington: EC Office of Press and Public Affairs).
52. Address by the Department of State Counselor Robert B. Zoellick, 21 September 1990, *Current Policy*, no. 1300, US Department of State, Bureau of Public Affairs.
53. *Le Monde*, 22 November 1990.

Select Bibliography

Alford, Jonathan, and Kenneth Hunt (eds), *Europe in the Western Alliance* (London: Macmillan, 1988).

Allen, David, Reinhardt Rummel, and Wolfgang Wessels, *European Political Cooperation: Towards a Foreign Policy for Western Europe* (Boston: Butterworth Scientific, 1982).

Allen, David, and Alfred Pijpers (eds), *European Foreign Policy Making and the Arab–Israeli Conflict* (The Hague: Nijhoff, 1984).

Beloff, Max, *The United States and the Unity of Europe* (Washington, DC: Brookings Institution, 1963).

Blinken, Antony J., *Ally Versus Ally: America, Europe, and the Siberian Pipeline Crisis* (New York: Praeger, 1987).

Cahen, Alfred, *The Western European Union and NATO* (London: Pergamon-Brassey's, 1989).

Calleo, David P., *The Atlantic Fantasy* (Baltimore, MD: Johns Hopkins University Press, 1970).

Carpenter, Ted G. (ed.), *NATO at 40* (Lexington, MA.: Lexington Books, 1990).

Chace, J., and E. Ravenal, *Atlantis Lost: US–European Relations After the Cold War* (New York University Press, 1976).

Cirincione, Joseph (ed.), *Central America and the Western Alliance* (New York: Holmes & Meier, 1985).

Cleveland, Harold van B., *The Atlantic Idea and Its European Rivals* (New York: McGraw-Hill, 1966).

Coffey, Joseph I., and Gianni Bonvicini, *The Atlantic Alliance and the Middle East* (University of Pittsburgh Press, 1989).

Cook, Paul, *Toward a 'European Pillar?' Enhanced European Security Cooperation and Implications for US Policy* (Washington: Center for Strategic and International Studies, 1988).

Czempiel, Ernst-Otto, and Dankwart A. Rustow, *The Euro-American System: Economic and Political Relations Between North America and Western Europe* (Boulder, CO: Westview, 1976).

de Bassompierre, Guy, *Changing the Guard in Brussels, An Insider's View of the EC Presidency*, The Washington Papers no. 135, The Center for Strategic and International Studies (New York: Praeger, 1988).

Deporte, A. W., *Europe Between the Superpowers: The Enduring Balance* 2nd edn (New Haven, CT: Yale University Press, 1986).

De Ruyt, Jean, *European Political Cooperation: Toward a Unified European Foreign Policy* (Washington: The Atlantic Council of the US, 1989).

De Vree, J. K., P. Coffey and R.H. Lauwaars (eds), *Towards a European Foreign Policy* (Boston: Martinus Nijoff, 1987).

Douglass, Gordon, *The New Interdependence: The European Community and the United States* (Lexington, MA.: Lexington, 1979).

Everts, Philip (ed.), *The European Community in the World* (Rotterdam

University Press, 1972).

Feld, Werner J. (ed.), *Western Europe's Global Reach* (New York: Pergamon, 1979).

Feld, Werner J., and Robert S. Jordan, *Europe in the Balance: The Changing Context of European International Politics* (London: Faber & Faber, 1986).

Fursdon, Edward, *The European Defense Community: A History* (New York: St. Martin's, 1980).

Galtung, Johan, *The European Community: A Superpower in the Making* (New York: Praeger, 1980).

Garfinkle, Adam M., *Western Europe's Middle East Diplomacy and the United States* (Philadelphia, PA: Foreign Policy Research Institute, 1983).

Garnham, David, *The Politics of European Defense Cooperation* (Cambridge, MA.: Ballinger, 1988).

Ginsberg, Roy, *Foreign Policy Actions of the European Community* (Boulder, CO: Lynne Rienner, 1989).

Godson, Joseph (ed.), *Transatlantic Crisis: Europe and America in the 1970s* (London: Alcove, 1974).

Goldsborough, James O., *Rebel Europe: How America Can Live With a Changing Continent* (London: Collier-Macmillan, 1982).

Goodman, Elliot R., *The Fate of the Atlantic Community* (New York: Praeger, 1975).

Greilsammer, Ilan, and Joseph Weiler, *Europe's Middle East Dilemma: The Quest for a Unified Stance* (Boulder, CO: Westview, 1987).

Grosser, Alfred, *The Western Alliance* (New York: Vintage, 1982).

Hager, Wolfgang, and Max Kohnstamm (eds), *A Nation Writ Large* (London: Macmillan, 1973).

Hill, Christopher (ed.), *National Foreign Policies and European Political Cooperation* (London: Allen & Unwin, 1983).

Ifestos, Panayiotis, *European Political Cooperation: Towards A Framework of Supranational Diplomacy?* (Brookfield, VT: Avebury/Gower, 1987).

Joffe, Josef, *The Limited Partnership: Europe, the United States, and the Burdens of Alliance* (Cambridge, MA.: Ballinger, 1987).

Kissinger, Henry, *The Troubled Partnership* (New York: McGraw-Hill, 1965).

Kohl, Wilfrid L., *French Nuclear Diplomacy* (Princeton University Press, 1971).

Kraft, Joseph, *The Grand Design: From Common Market to Atlantic Partnership* (New York: Harper, 1972).

Langer, Peter H, *Trans-Atlantic Discord and NATO's Crisis of Cohesion* (Washington, DC: Pergamon, 1986).

Mally, Gerhard, *The New Europe and the United States* (London: Lexington, 1974).

Morgan, Roger, *High Politics, Low Politics: Toward a Foreign Policy for Western Europe* (London: Sage, 1973).

Palmer, John, *Europe Without America? The Crisis in Atlantic Relations* (Oxford University Press, 1987).

266   *The United States and the European Pillar*

Pierre, Andrew J. (ed.), *Third World Instability – Central America as a European–American Issue* (New York: Council on Foreign Relations, 1985).
Pijpers, Alfred, Elfriede Regelsberger and Wolfgang Wessels (eds), *European Political Cooperation in the 1980s* (Dordrecht, The Netherlands: Nijhoff, 1988).
Reid, Escott, *Time of Fear and Hope, The Making of the North Atlantic Treaty, 1947–1949* (Toronto: McClelland & Stewart, 1977).
Rollo, J. M. C., *The New Eastern Europe: Western Responses* (New York: Council on Foreign Relations Press for the Royal Institute of International Affairs, 1990).
Rudney, Robert, and Luc Reychler (eds), *European Security Beyond the Year 2000* (New York: Praeger, 1988).
Rummel, Reinhardt, *European Political Cooperation: Towards a Foreign Policy for Western Europe* (London: Butterworths, 1982).
Rummel, Reinhardt (ed.), *The Evolution of an International Actor: Western Europe's New Assertiveness* (Boulder, CO: Westview, 1990).
Schaetzel, J. Robert, *The Unhinged Alliance: America and the European Community* (New York: Harper & Row, 1975).
Sloan, Stanley R. (ed.), *NATO in the 1990s* (London: Pergamon-Brassey's, 1989).
Stevens, Christopher (ed.), *EEC and the Third World: The Atlantic Rift* (London: Hodder & Stoughton, 1983).
Stuart, Douglas, and William Tow, *The Limits of Alliance: NATO Out-of-Area Problems Since 1949* (Baltimore, MD: Johns Hopkins University Press, 1990).
Taylor, Phillip, *When Europe Speaks With One Voice* (Westport, CT: Greenwood, 1979).
Treverton, Gregory F., *Making the Alliance Work* (Ithaca, NY: Cornell University Press, 1985).
Treverton, Gregory F. (ed.), *The Atlantic Alliance in the Year 2000* (New York: Council on Foreign Relations Press, 1989).
Tucker, Robert W., and Linda Wrigley (eds), *The Atlantic Alliance and Its Critics* (New York: Praeger, 1983).
Tugendhat, Christopher, *Making Sense of Europe* (London: Viking, 1986).
van der Beugel, Ernst H., *From Marshall Aid to Atlantic Partnership: European Integration as a Concern of American Foreign Policy* (London: Elsevier, 1966).
Wallace, Helen, William Wallace, and Carol Webb (eds), *Policy-Making in the European Community*, 2nd edn (New York: Wiley, 1983).
Wallace, William, *The Transformation of Western Europe* (New York: Council on Foreign Relations Press for the Royal Institute of International Affairs, 1990).

Index

Mitterrand, François 122, 133, 136,
152, 156, 167–8, 174, 204, 208, 210,
214–15, 230, 233, 235
Monnet, Jean 3
Montebello decision (1983) 194
Morán, Fernando 138, 258
Multinational Force and Observers
(MFO) *see* Middle East
Muskie, Edmund 147
Mutual and Balanced Force Reduction
(MBFR) negotiations 51–4, 74,
99, 233

Nassau conference 22–5, 36, 38
Netherlands 1, 14, 29–34, 61, 80,
89, 127–8, 133, 148–9, 151–3, 161,
172, 179
Newhouse, John 252
Nicaragua 134–9
Nixon, Richard 47, 51, 53, 58, 70–74,
76, 79, 81, 84–5, 88, 91–2, 97, 181
Nixon administration 50, 54, 67, 70,
74–6, 78–86, 188
Atlantic charter proposal
and 80–81, 189
European unity and 45, 55, 72–3,
91–5, 97, 99–100
Nixon Doctrine 70
North Atlantic Treaty Organisation
(NATO) *see* Atlantic Alliance
Norway 161, 212
Nunn, Sam 172

Oakley, Robert 257
Olympic boycott 112, 114–15
Organisation for Economic Cooperation
and Development (OECD) 204
Organisation for European Economic
Cooperation (OEEC) 1–2, 8, 14, 191
Ostpolitik 58–60, 76, 81, 99, 111, 116
out-of-area issues 87–8, 104, 132,
183–8, 196–7, 217, 220, 230–32, 246
Owen, David 256

Palestine *see* Middle East
Palestine Liberation Organisation
(PLO) *see* Middle East
Palmer, John 262
Panama 135, 246
Papandreou, Andreas 160
Paris agreements (1954/55) 12, 13,
172, 228
Persian Gulf 184, 231, 241
Persian Gulf crisis 216, 231–2, 246;
Atlantic relations and 231–2; EPC
and 216–17, 241

Pfaltzgraff, Robert L., Jr 255
Pierre, Andrew J. 254, 258
Pijpers, Alfred 154, 258, 259, 260,
261, 263
Platform on European Security Interests
(1987) *see* Western European Union
Pleven Plan 4–7
see also European Defence
Community
Poland 115, 118, 200–201, 203–5,
214, 223
Polish crisis 115–18, 181; EPC
and 115–17, 181
Polaris missile 22–3, 26, 38
Pompidou, Georges 58–61, 68, 76,
80–82, 98
Portugal 42, 87, 98, 128, 137–8, 162,
178
Pryce, Harry B. 249

Qaddafi, Muammar 122, 124–9
see also Libya

Reagan, Ronald 101, 115–16, 118,
121–3, 150, 166, 174, 177
Reagan administration 102–3, 115–19,
132–9, 150–51, 154, 159, 172–5,
181–2, 189, 191, 196, 218
Regelsberger, Elfriede 161, 258, 259,
260
Reid, Escott 249
Reykjavik summit (1986) 166, 175
Roberts, Chalmers 252, 253
Rogers, William 47, 82
Rome declaration (1984) *see* Western
European Union
Romania 200, 246
Rumsfeld, Donald 86
Rusk, Dean 25–6, 43, 74

Sadat, Anwar 88, 142, 152
SALT I and II Treaties 60, 76, 99, 111
sanctions,
EPC and 106–10, 113–14, 116–17,
120, 123, 125, 127–8, 216–17
US and 107–8, 111–15, 127–8, 136,
138, 231
see also name of individual countries
Sandinista government *see* Nicaragua
Saudi Arabia 151
Schaetzel, J. Robert 38, 70, 76, 99,
251, 253, 254, 255
Schlesinger, Arthur, Jr 17, 40, 250, 251
Schmidt, Helmut 50, 111–12, 116, 252
Schmidt, Peter 260
Schoenbrun, David 251